KT-379-988

Classic VEGETARIAN C·U·I·S·I·N·E

Edited by Rosemary Moon

TIGER BOOKS INTERNATIONAL
LONDON

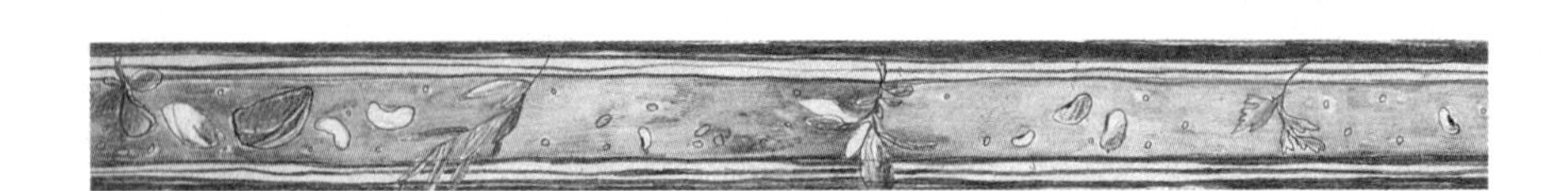

Illustrations by
Camilla Sopwith and Rod Ferring

CLB 4365
This edition published 1995 by
Tiger Books International PLC, Twickenham
© 1995 CLB Publishing, Godalming, Surrey
Typeset by SX Composing, Rayleigh, Essex
All rights reserved
Printed and bound in South Africa
ISBN 1-85501-618-4

Contents

INTRODUCTION

Every generation considers that it has invented, re-invented, or at least significantly improved, The Wheel! Surely no-one can ever have thought of doing this or that before! It is therefore easy to assume that vegetarianism really appeared in the latter half of the 20th-century, during a period when we have become more aware of our environment, the damage that we are inflicting on it, and have begun to question our omnipotence over the animals with which we share our planet.

What, exactly, is Vegetarianism

Vegetarianism may be defined as the belief in, and practice of, eating foods obtained exclusively from the vegetable kingdom, and hence the abstaining from meat and other animal foods. The strictest group of vegetarians eat nothing at all which is even derived from any animal source, so that they will not drink milk or eat eggs. However, the degree to which such rules are applied varies enormously between the different groups of vegetarians.

The Origins of Vegetarianism

This is definitely not a way of life established since the second world war – vegetarianism is an ancient custom and tradition. Many of the foods that we enjoy today have reached our cultures through the influence of the Greeks and Romans, having first been refined and experimented with by the cooks and farmers of those ancient civilisations. Many philosophers and writers of both those cultures advocated a meat-free diet, but the thought was not original even to them.

Vegetarianism also existed within the ancient religions of the East and certain sects of both the Hindu and Bhuddist faiths have long practised abstinence from a flesh-based diet as all animal life is considered by them to be sacred. As Christianity spread throughout the world so certain divisions of that faith adopted the practice; within the Roman Catholic church Trappist monks have been vegetarians since 1666. They were formed within the Cistercian order as strict observers of monastic practices under the direction of Abbot de Rancé of the Abbey Notre Dame de la Trappe. Adherence to his Strict Observances, including vegetarianism, led to the monks becoming known as Trappists.

The Seventh-Day Adventists more recently adopted vegetarianism within the Protestant Church, when their sect was established in the mid 19th-century in America. They also avoid the use of stimulants and drugs, especially narcotics, and place great emphasis on health. The vegetarian movement really arrived in England when members of the Bible Christian Church based near Manchester adopted vegetarianism in 1809.

Religion has had enormous effects on so many areas of our lives. Many foods and drinks have been developed and produced by religious orders for centuries and, in the spread of vegetarianism, the influence of people's faith can clearly be seen in the adoption of the dietary regime.

A World-Wide Way of Life

The modern vegetarian movement spread on from England,

across Europe and over to America in the mid 19th-century, then, in 1908, the International Vegetarian Union was founded. The Vegetarian Society, a member of the International Union, was already well-established in England, having been founded in 1847.

The Vegetarian Society promotes vegetarian food as the diet of the future – healthier, kinder and far less wasteful of the world's resources. The Society is a registered charity and works to promote vegetarianism by publicity campaigns at both national and local levels. Through the Cordon Vert Cookery School it is able to give informative cookery demonstrations and it also helps in dietary planning for thousands of people by the use of a unique 'V' symbol on food packaging, to show which processed foods contain no ingredients that might make them unsuitable for vegetarians.

Why Vegetarianism?

Although many people originally chose vegetarianism as a way of life for religious or ethical reasons, this is not now generally the prime reason for making the change in habit. As religion has less effect on people's day-to-day lives, so aesthetic and emotional reasons have greater influence. Many young people try vegetarianism for a while in their teens, inspired by peer pressure or the realisation that the animals that we all enjoy seeing running free in the fields may later be served up at the dining table. Perhaps it is not so bad if the animals actually have been running free in the sunshine for part of their lives. Modern farming methods, the intensive rearing of animals for cheap food for the masses, often degrade the animals and are so distressing that anyone with the slightest conscience would have to question whether the demands that are made on the food chain are justified.

Humanitarian vegetarians believe that the killing of animals is unnecessary or cruel and that the trades which such practices support, for example butchering, are actually degrading, not only to the animals but also to those humans employed within the profession.

Many vegetarians actually dislike handling meat. I have enormous admiration for people who are vegetarian themselves but still prepare animal proteins for their partners or families if they too have not made the decision to adopt the vegetarian way of life. Other people do not like the smell of meat during its preparation and cooking and there is little point, when kitchen activity is quite a major part of our lives, in labouring over a meal if the work is carried out in the absence of pleasure and commitment. I always feel that if you haven't enjoyed preparing a meal there is very little chance of it actually being at all memorable in any way; it merely becomes a way of refuelling the body.

Eating for Health

In my experience few people who embrace vegetarianism for health reasons do so because they are actually told that animal proteins are bad for them. It is more likely to be because they believe or feel that their own bodies are telling them that meat is harmful, and that a diet consisting of vegetable-based foods would be more beneficial.

I have more sympathy for those who opt for the regime for moral or aesthetic reasoned than for a conviction over the state of their health. Food allergies seem to be becoming more prevalent in our over-processed world, but these are usually concentrated on refined and coloured foods rather than animal proteins. An informed and reasoned approach will help to interest more and more people in vegetarian ways – gone are the days of jokes about long hair, sandals and 2CV's. If 2CV's are no longer in production then the image of the vegetarian has got to change!

A Vegan or a Vegetarian?

The one factor common to all groups of vegetarians is that they do not eat any animal flesh. The strictest group, vegans, do not eat any foods at all that are derived from animals, so they will not eat eggs, or take milk or any milk-based produce, including yogurt, butter and cheese. Some also refuse honey, believing that it should not be taken from the bees. A creative vegan diet is one of the severest tests of culinary flair that I have encountered!

Lacto-vegetarians will not eat any products that involve the slaughter of animals. They will therefore eat dairy products but still abstain from fish and eggs, whereas ovo-lacto-vegetarians will include eggs in their diet.

Many people who have recently converted to vegetarianism

are colloquially labelled 'demi-veg' – their conviction comes from the desire to forsake only red meats, so they will often eat fish and, in many cases, chicken. This is a half-way house in terms of true vegetarianism, but is one that many mothers are far happier to see their children and young people adopt.

The Need for Protein

Proteins are essential for health. Their main function is the growth and repair of the body's tissues, and it is therefore essential for all those practising a vegetarian way of life, but especially for children and young people, to supplement their diet with nuts, grains and vegetable protein substitutes so that their growth and physical development is not affected by protein deficiency. Proteins also supply energy and anyone who leads a particularly active and physical life must pay special attention to the protein intake in a vegetarian diet. A cousin of mine, a strict lacto vegetarian, went on a demanding expedition in South America and found that he was constantly exhausted until he relaxed his dietary regime and started eating fish. He felt better and stronger almost instantly and has kept fish in his diet ever since that telling experience.

Proteins have to be found in non-animal foods to ensure a healthy and balanced diet for vegetarians. Breads and cereals which are high in starches supply proteins in significant amounts due to the large quantities of these carbohydrates that are consumed. Pulse vegetables, including beans and lentils; grains such as rice, and nuts also provide proteins and are probably a richer source of this essential nutrient for the vegetarian than cereal foods. These are not complete proteins inasmuch as they do not contain all the essential amino acids, so they are best supplemented with other proteins such as cheese and milk, or for stricter vegetarians, vegetable-based proteins such as the micro-protein Quorn.

The Way We Use Our Resources

We are learning all the time about man's evolution here on earth. What we are certain of is that for most of human history, for about 98 per cent of the known existence of man on earth, we were hunters and gatherers of food, killing animals for meat and gleaning fruits and berries from bushes and trees. It is only comparatively recently, during the last 10,000 years, that man seized the initiative and became proactive to his environment, rather than simply responding to opportunities as they presented themselves.

Approximately 10,000 years ago man became a food producer and started to farm the first crops of wheat and barley. Animals were also domesticated and grazed and, as men settled in small groups, so life became more predictable and safer. The population started to expand in this more dependable environment so it became necessary to keep producing food to sustain the new way of life. This was the first move towards modern civilisation.

Opening Up New Worlds

The explorers who discovered the Americas and beyond not only contributed to our culinary knowledge by bringing back new ingredients such as potatoes, tomatoes and spices. They also created the opportunity significantly to increase the known world's food-producing ability by revealing vast new continents to be explored, cultivated and, some might say, exploited.

Some new animals were also domesticated and introduced to the food chain in the wider world. Travel between continents improved and it was possible to move crops from one part of the world to another. At this time, the increased ability to produce food was far greater than the increase in the world's population, but it was recognised that this would not always be the case.

The World Food Supply

The ability to supply the whole world with sufficient food has not yet been achieved and it is looking more and more doubtful that it ever will be, unless nations and governments make informed choices about our modern agricultural and ethical practices. We can all do our own little bit but the problems to be addressed need global action.

Tasks to be tackled include demand, availability and distribution of food, plus food loss and wastage. The availability of food for many under-developed countries of the world is influenced by the demands of the affluent, meat-eating West, which takes cereals to be fed to their intensively farmed animals, to produce cheap, mass-produced meat. These basic foodstuffs are needed by many for daily sustenance, not for luxury but simply to stay alive, but the food does not get through to them. About 60 per cent of the world's population is undernourished – many of the rest are overfed.

Vegetarianism Leads the Way

Every single one of us, of course, has the right to choose what he or she eats, but if carnivores limited their consumption of meat to one meal a day, the need for the intense, and often unethical, modern-day farming methods would start to disappear, leaving many more cereal crops available for people and not for animals.

There is absolutely no need for anyone to be starving or dying of malnutrition in the modern world. We currently produce enough food world-wide to provide the basic intake of calories required by every member of the world's population. The problem is that the food simply does not get distributed fairly and evenly. If this was redressed there would doubtless be an explosion in population in many hitherto undernourished cultures, just as there was when the first farmers settled to begin food production. However, modern methods could sustain the food supply, providing that we all faced the responsibility of re-thinking our attitude to the world's resources. Exploitation must give way to a recognition that things simply cannot go on as they are: the earth has a limited capacity and we must work with the system to make the best of it.

New Advances in Vegetable Proteins

Tofu is an ancient Chinese vegetable protein of great importance to vegetarians. It is soya bean curd and can be stir-fried or baked, proving to be especially valuable in the vegan diet. Many supermarkets now sell tofu, but it is usually in a long-life form. I actually prefer fresh tofu from health food shops, which I find has a more pleasant texture – the long-life varieties can be a bit slimy. Look out for smoked tofu – it has more flavour than plain varieties.

Science has also been employed to find alternative vegetable proteins. The first was Textured Vegetable Protein (TVP), which resembles minced beef and can be used in as many ways as its meaty counterpart. The trouble is that everything made with it then looks like meat!

A comparatively new product is Quorn, a solid protein made from a type of mushroom fungus mixed with egg whites. This is highly nutritive and also a joy to cook with, absorbing flavourings from marinades and producing very tasty stir-fries. It is also available minced but I find the diced Quorn far more versatile. I wanted to hate this new food when I first tried it, thinking it was far too hi-tech and scientific, but it is so adaptable that I am impressed. Quorn does benefit from being used with fresh ingredients and spices – if you add a prepared, bland sauce the Quorn will also be dull and bland. Spice it up and enjoy it!

Beware the Dietary Cranks!

Some years ago a highly successful chain of vegetarian restaurants and health food shops was opened under the name of 'Cranks'. Many vegetarians were attracted to these Meccas, where large bowls of salads filled the counters together with baskets of delicious baked goods. The name, however, kept many more potential customers away!

Anyone who becomes attracted to a dietary fashion easily becomes consumed by their own enthusiasm, turning the new way of life to a fad which, in turn, stands to become a way of life and sometimes almost as life governing as a religion. People take in into their heads that by eating in a certain way they are doing themselves a great deal of good, whereas in reality they are often doing a great deal of harm. We are used, in modern day Western society, to so-called slimming diseases. However, eating disorders are, like vegetarianism itself, nothing new and there are records from around AD 200 of two Greeks, having decided to live on fresh figs alone, refusing to change their diet even when they were ostracised at the public baths because of their rank, unpleasant smell. There is seldom any chance of reasoning with a food fanatic – a crank!

Dr Kellog, a Man with a Sound Idea

Dietary regimes have long been associated with religion, and vegetarianism has most recently been adopted by the Seventh-Day Adventists, a sect of the Protestant church centred in America. They embrace the vegetarian diet as part of their way of life.

In the late 19th-century Dr. J. H. Kellog, a prominent Seventh-Day Adventist, administered the Battle Creek Sanitarium in Michigan, a forerunner, it could be argued, of the modern health farm. No meat was served at Battle Creek and the whole daily routine was run in a strictly regimented style, down to the Grand March around the campus before bed.

Dr Kellogg did, however, realise the importance of varied and interesting combinations of foods within a satisfying diet and, to this end, he introduced some eighty or so foods to the Battle Creek kitchens. These included corn flakes for breakfast and peanut butter. Both were popular with residents and soon became equally popular with a wider public, forming, as they did, the firm foundations of the food company of his brother, W. K. Kellogg.

Don't Change Your Diet, Change Your Way of Life!

Anyone who has ever had to submit to the agonies of a weight-reducing diet will know that these are seldom undertaken with any degree of enthusiasm – all those favourite foods that you cannot have (the secret binges, the agonies of unassuaged hunger!) and the pressure to have slimmed before the next shopping trip, or the next visit to the doctor's surgery – ugh!

Changing your diet is awful, but changing your way of life is interesting and far more fulfilling, especially if you are undertaking the change for reasons that you believe in. So changing to a vegetarian diet, whether a lacto-vegetarian or a demi-veg way of life, can be beneficial to both health and hips as well as to the environment around you. Of course, becoming a vegetarian does not guarantee weight loss, but if you stop to think about your food, introducing more colour and variety in the vegetables and salads that you eat, then you will be well on the way to enjoying both your food and your lifestyle and will feel more comfortable and responsible in so many aspects of your life.

A Vegan Diet is Not for Me

I could never be a Vegan for one very simple reason – I adore cheese! For four years I ran a delicatessen, a specialist cheese shop, and (despite the obvious implications for the profitability of the business) it was one of my delights to trim the cheeses, keeping them fresh and in good condition for the customers. What did I do with the trimmings? Well, I wasn't going to throw them away!

Many cheeses are now sold under the label of *vegetarian cheese* or *suitable for vegetarians*. The term is usually applied to mass-produced cheeses, which are neatly (and helpfully) labelled up in the supermarket, but this doesn't tell the whole story. I am so passionate about cheese that I instinctively reject any hard cheese which says it is low fat, or reduced fat – I want the real thing – totally unadulterated!

We have a wealth of small cheese producers today making delicious hand-made products in the style of times gone by, yet marrying aesthetic and flavour demands to the requirements of today's health and hygiene regulations. Cheese makers begin their task by adding an enzyme starter culture to warm milk, to hasten the curdling of the milk by raising its acidity. Unpasteurised milk will curdle naturally, due to the enzymes present, but a starter culture must always be added to pasteurised milk and will also hasten the process in the unpasteurised liquid.

Once the milk has curdled, rennet needs to be deep stirred into the cheese vat to set the curds. This is where vegetarians need to be careful about their cheese. Traditional rennet is an extract from calves' stomachs containing the enzyme rennin, used to set milk. Vegetarian rennet may be used as a substitute and is a plant extract, creating exactly the same effect as traditional rennet. Many small cheese makers have forsaken the animal rennet totally, and their cheeses are therefore perfectly suitable for vegetarians. How do you find out about this? Well, any cheese seller worth buying from should know these sort of details but, if not, many of the small cheese makers are now listed in regional food guides. They always like to hear from customers and will be able to tell you how they make their cheese if you contact them.

To finish the cheese, the curds produced after the addition of rennet are cut and drained, then milled and packed into moulds for pressing. After wrapping in cloths or washing in brine or wine, the truckles are then stored for a number of months, being turned daily, until ready for sale. I never mind paying premium prices for hand-made cheeses – the makers work extremely hard.

An Enjoyable Eating Pattern

Although the very phrase a *healthy, balanced diet* sounds uninspiringly dull, it remains of utmost necessity to ensure that our intake of food looks good, tastes good and does us good. A diet that fulfils two of these criteria without the third is not good enough.

Why is a balanced eating regime so important? Well, we all have to equate what we actually need to eat to maintain a healthy and active life with what we do eat (if you do this honestly it has to include real meals and all the little extras that seem to force themselves upon us in moments of weakness!). This already explains why it is easier to change your eating habits than to go on a diet – there's interest involved and not guilt and longing!

To achieve a sound diet we need to understand the value of different foods and the nutrients that each food supplies. Foods are broken down into five groups: proteins, or building foods; carbohydrates, or energy foods; fats, which also supply energy; minerals, to regulate the body's activities; and vitamins, which also regulate the body's activities as well as ensuring that the proper use is made of other nutrients.

Vegetarians – a Special Needs Group?

The word *protein* comes from a Greek word meaning *first* – proteins are the first and most important of the food groups. They are usually derived from animals: meat, fish, eggs, milk and cheese. Because the vegetarian diet avoids some, if not all, of these foods it is vital that they are found from other sources.

Proteins are made up of amino acids, of which there are a great many, but eight are essential to the adult diet and ten to ensure healthy growth in children. Most animal proteins contain all these essential amino acids, but vegetables proteins frequently only contain one or two. It is possible, by using a wide variety of vegetable foods, to provide all the essential amino acids – this means a good mixture of dried beans and pulse vegetables, cereals (such as wheat, oats, barley and rye), nuts and fresh vegetables. Fresh vegetables do contain traces of protein but they are generally in such small amounts that they are seldom referred to as possible sources of the building nutrient.

Vegetarians who still eat eggs, milk, yogurt, cheese and other milk products should have very little trouble in including sufficient amounts of quality proteins in their diet. Vegans will find that very careful planning and a great variety of the foods listed above are needed for them to maintain a healthy lifestyle.

Carbohydrates supply the vast majority of energy to the body. Sportsmen are often reported to have eaten large quantities of pasta and beans in the run-up to competitions and big matches. Carbohydrates are divided into two main groups: sugars and starches. We are constantly being told of the need to eat fewer sugars because of problems such as tooth decay, but a little of these foods in the diet brings comfort and balance.

Starches are the most common group of foods in the vegetarian diet and include all cereal crops and the dried seeds of many vegetables, such as lentils and peas, that form the basis of so many delicious classic vegetarian dishes. These foods are also a vital source of protein within a meat-less diet.

Fats may be of both animal and vegetable origins, and include hard fats and oils. Proteins, such as cheese and cream should also be considered for their fat content. Some vegetarians may prefer to avoid animal fats, only using margarines and vegetable oils in cooking and at the table. My personal preference for hard fats is to use butter – in fact, if I can't have butter I would rather go without anything on bread, teabreads, scones or the vegetables such as asparagus and sweetcorn which are never the same with just a knob of sunflower spread!

Olive Oil – a Source of Pleasure to All

One of the greatest culinary changes in recent years has been the emergence of olive oil as a cooking ingredient for all occasions. When I was a child it was such a luxury that my mother kept a tiny bottle in the cupboard – and used it to put in our ears when we had earache! What a waste!

Olive oil is not new; the Romans certainly used it in their cooking and started to introduce it throughout Europe as their

Empire spread. As we have travelled and become progressively more international in our tastes so a demand has been created and all specialist shops and health food shops now stock a good variety of oils. I have been to several olive oil tastings, conducted in the same way as wine tastings, and they make a fascinating evening. OK, this oil is still a fat, but it is one of the healthiest of all the fats – indeed, it is proven to be beneficial in the breakdown of cholesterol absorbed into the system from other foods.

Care must be taken with the intake of fat in all types of diet. They are highly concentrated sources of energy and also providers of warmth. Their biggest drawback is that the body can only use so much of them but it has the unfortunate ability to store any excess....

It is very difficult to find anything new or entertaining to say about *vitamins* and *minerals*. Nevertheless, they are of prime importance and must not be dismissed or discounted when menu-planning. It is much better to get these essential nutrients from a balanced diet rather than by relying on a processed supplement in the form of a pill.

Minerals perform vital functions – it might sound dull but a good supply of mineral elements is essential to health. Minerals form the main fabric of bones and teeth; they are contained in the body cells which make up muscles, blood corpuscles and vital organs; and they maintain the correct composition of all body fluids including blood, lymph and perspiration. A restricted supply of minerals, especial calcium and phosphorous, can severely affect the development of children and the continuing health of children and adults alike.

The importance of *vitamins* in the diet was not fully recognised until the 20th century, although the connection between the lack of fresh vegetables and the occurrence of scurvy was made by Elizabethan sailors, whose health suffered once their fresh supplies were exhausted. It was not until much later that this was confirmed as being due to a lack of vitamin C. The word *vitamin* is actually derived from the Latin word meaning *Life*, which emphasises the importance of the role that they play in the diet.

As most vitamins are found in abundant quantities in fresh fruit and vegetables it is safe to assume that a balanced vegetarian diet will provide more than adequate quantities of these essential nutrients. Vegans should take care to obtain sufficient supplies of vitamin D. This is mainly found in fatty foods so less strict vegetarians will find plentiful supplies in butter, eggs and milk.

Any examples that I have given of sources rich in particular nutrients have been limited purely to foods, but drinks also have a nutritive value. Unless of a medicinal nature (for example, beef tea), the limited nutritive value of drinks, including such excellent brews as wines and beer, is (unfortunately) limited to carbohydrate. Some people might therefore say that drink is bad for you, with the exception of life sustaining water. Well, that's as maybe, but I'm definitely with the school of thought that says a glass (or two) of red wine a day is good for you!

Down With Stodge!

The most common complaint about vegetarian cuisine is that it is dull in both appearance and flavour, and that it is glorified stodge. If this is true it certainly doesn't have to be and, indeed, there is absolutely no excuse for such a description being applicable to good vegetarian cooking. Meal planning does, however, have to be a little more carefully executed for a vegetarian diet than for any other.

Variety is well-known to be the spice of life! Such things do not change simply because you have decided to forsake meat! Some of the most exciting flavours and ingredients to become widely available in the last few years are just as suitable for vegetarians as they are for others: sherry vinegar, balsamic vinegar, sun-dried tomatoes, fresh root ginger, limes and leaf coriander. All these things make my taste buds tingle just by thinking about them! The secret of a successful vegetarian diet is the same as for any other: choose a wide variety of ingredients, take care over your shopping and have a pride in your cooking and you will be producing truly memorable, classic vegetarian meals.

The recipes that follow have been collected over a number of years and reflect all the changes in vegetarian foods that I have talked about in this introduction. Try them and experiment with them, adding your own spices and seasonings if you prefer – I know that you will enjoy them.

SOUPS

Soup is so often considered to be unadventurous – a safe choice of starter or supper dish when you don't know your guests or haven't the time to prepare anything more exciting. Of course, this is not how soup needs to, or should, be! It is one of the most versatile and satisfying of foods; a cold soup for a light meal on a hot, summer day; a thick, creamy one with bread for lunch in the autumn; or a meal-in-a-bowl, full of beans or pulses and vegetables, for a satisfying meal to be eaten in a hurry.

Soup in History

The word 'soup' is actually derived from 'sop', a thin liquor or broth poured over bread before serving. This tradition goes back thousands of years, certainly to Biblical times. In many cases soup was, and still is, a meal in itself, a basic form of sustenance. Tradition dictates that soup is eaten with bread – in many countries, even today, this would be considered a luxury.

When cooking techniques were still governed by the fact that foods were prepared in one pot, hanging on a hook over an open fire, soups were certainly the standard fare for most families; filling, warming and restorative of health and strength after the rigours of the day. To be able to create varied and interesting soups required a great deal of culinary skill: indeed, the first eating establishment ever to be known as a 'restaurant' was in Paris and run by a soup maker, M. Boulanger, who served nothing but soups or 'restoratives'! Incidentally, the word *restaurant* comes from a Latin phrase which M. Boulanger had above the door of his soup kitchen: *Venite ad me, omnes qui stomacho laboratis et ego restaurabo vos* – 'Come to me, you whose stomachs labour and I will restore you'.

In the affluent West we are now privileged to be able to prepare soups from quality ingredients and to serve them with the traditional accompaniment of bread. We might choose to serve a soup for a dinner party with tiny rolls, or crispy croutons of fried bread added just before serving. Thinner soups, especially clear soups with vegetable or pasta garnishes, may be served with slices or chunks of fresh, crusty bread, or spooned over slices of bread, sometimes toasted, in the bottom of a deep soup bowl, very much in the way of the original *sops*.

The Basis of a Good Soup

The secret of a good soup is the same as that of a fine sauce or casserole – an excellent basic stock. For vegetarian cookery this is especially important as you will have no falsely meaty flavourings to add depth to the savouriness of your soup. Stock should be made from a variety of vegetables, for example, onions, celery, carrots, celeriac and leeks, with plenty of fresh herbs, sea salt and peppercorns. Remember to reduce the stock to concentrate its flavour before use. I leave the skins on vegetables for a general purpose stock as the natural pigments in the skin will add extra colour and flavour. If you are making a stock specifically for a lightly coloured or flavoured dish, then peel the vegetables before cooking. If you prefer to use a commercial stock preparation, take the trouble to go to a health food shop and find a really good example which is not overly spiced with salt to increase flavours.

Soup and the Vegetarian Diet

Soups may almost be considered to have regained their original importance in the vegetarian diet. As many meatless main courses are less substantial than their counterparts for carnivores it follows that other courses within a meal might be more filling. A starch-based soup, one made from sweet potatoes, chestnuts or lentils, will provide a satisfying start to a meal and will also negate the necessity for the main course to provide all the protein for the meal. Conversely, a main course of grains, nuts or pulse vegetables could comfortably be preceded by a puréed or creamed vegetable soup, to fulfil the original role of a starter, that is to stimulate and not to over-feed the appetite.

Don't be afraid to experiment with soups – there are many novel recipe ideas in the following chapter, including some for the more unusual cold soups. One of my favourites is the Spinach & Apple Soup on page 30: this is such an unusual combination of flavours that it is bound to invite compliments from both family and friends.

SWEET POTATO SOUP

Sweet potatoes have a deep nutty flavour and make excellent soup. They are more commonly used in curries, African and Caribbean dishes.

Serves 4-6

Ingredients
60g/2oz butter or margarine
1 large onion, finely chopped
460g/1lb sweet potato, peeled and diced
225g/8oz carrots, peeled and diced
1 tbsp freshly chopped coriander
1 lemon, zest and juice
850ml/1½ pints stock
Freshly ground black pepper
Coriander leaves to garnish

Melt the butter or margarine and cook the onion until transparent. Add the sweet potato and carrots and allow to 'sweat' over a very low heat for 10-15 minutes, stirring occasionally. Stir in the coriander, lemon zest, juice of half the lemon, stock and pepper; cover and simmer for 30-40 minutes. Pour into a liquidiser or food processor and blend until almost smooth, leaving some texture for the soup. Return the soup to the pan and reheat until piping hot. Garnish with coriander leaves and serve immediately.

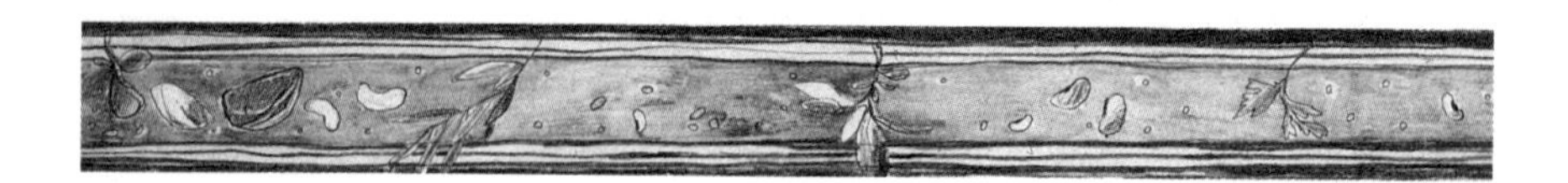

GAZPACHO

There are hundreds of recipes for gazpacho, all slightly different. The lime juice in this one adds sharpness and accentuates the flavours of the vegetables.

Serves 4

INGREDIENTS
460g/1lb ripe tomatoes
1 small onion
1 small green pepper
1 clove garlic, crushed
¼ medium cucumber
1 tbsp red wine vinegar
1 tbsp olive oil
400g/14oz can tomato juice
1-2 tbsps lime juice
Salt and freshly ground black pepper

Plunge the tomatoes into boiling water, leave for 2 minutes, then remove the skins and seeds. Chop the onion and pepper and place in a liquidiser or food processor with the tomatoes, garlic, cucumber, vinegar, oil and tomato juice, and blend until smooth. Add the lime juice and seasoning to taste. Pour the soup into a glass dish and chill until required. Extra chopped vegetables may be served with the soup as a garnish.

EASY LENTIL SOUP

Add a slightly different seasoning to this soup occasionally by using grated orange rind and a little chopped coriander leaf.

Serves 4-6

INGREDIENTS
225g/8oz split red lentils
30g/1oz butter or margarine
1 medium onion, finely chopped
2 stalks celery, finely chopped
2 carrots, scrubbed and finely diced
Grated rind of 1 lemon
1.14 litres/2 pints light vegetable stock
Salt and freshly ground black pepper

Pick over the lentils and remove any stones. Rinse well. Heat the butter or margarine in a pan and cook the onion for 2-3 minutes. Add the diced celery and carrots and let the vegetables sweat for 5-10 minutes. Stir in the lentils, add the lemon rind, stock and salt and pepper to taste. Bring to the boil, reduce the heat and simmer for 15-20 minutes until the vegetables are tender.

Roughly blend the soup in a liquidiser or food processor, it should not be too smooth.

Return the soup to the pan, check the seasoning and reheat gently.

SPINACH & APPLE SOUP

An unusual combination of ingredients that makes a delicious soup. Fruit soups are usually served cold, as a dessert, but the apple in this recipe blends well with the spinach for a savoury starter. Season boldly with nutmeg.

Serves 4

INGREDIENTS

30g/1oz butter or margarine
1 small onion, chopped
30g/1oz wholemeal flour
570ml/1 pint vegetable stock
460g/1lb spinach, shredded
225g/8oz apple purée
Salt and freshly ground black pepper
Pinch of nutmeg
Lemon juice
Natural yogurt
A little finely chopped parsley

Melt the butter in a large saucepan and fry the onion until soft. Add the flour and cook to a roux, then gradually add the stock, stir well and simmer for 10 minutes. Add the spinach and cook until tender, then allow to cool slightly and mix in the apple purée.

Place all the ingredients in a liquidiser or food processor and blend until smooth. Return the soup to the pan and reheat slowly together with the milk. Add the salt, pepper, nutmeg and lemon juice to taste. Serve in individual bowls with the yogurt swirled on the top and garnished with chopped parsley.

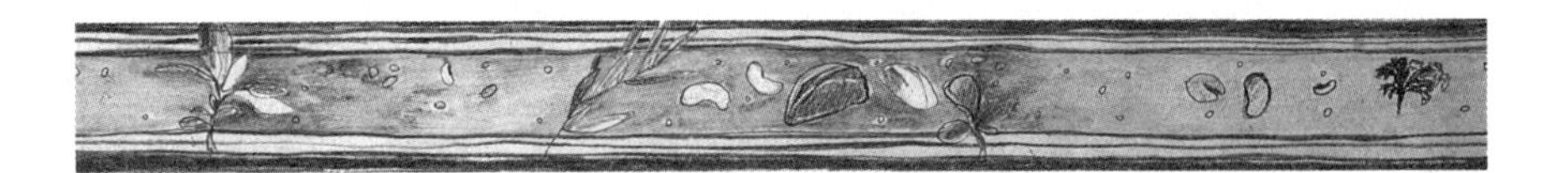

MISO SOUP

All the unusual ingredients for this soup are available in good healthfood shops and Japanese delicatessens.

Serves 2

INGREDIENTS
2 small onions, grated
2.5cm/1 inch fresh root ginger, peeled and finely chopped
1 clove garlic, crushed
1 tbsp sesame oil
1 carrot, peeled and finely sliced
¼ small cauliflower, divided into florets
1.14 litres/2 pints water
1 tbsp arame (Japanese seaweed)
30g/1oz peas (fresh or frozen)
2 tbsps shoyu (Japanese soy sauce)
1 tbsp miso (red bean paste)
Freshly ground black pepper to taste
2 spring onions, finely chopped

Cook the onion, ginger and garlic in the sesame oil for a few minutes, then add the carrot and cauliflower and cook gently for 5 minutes. Stir in the water, arame, peas and shoyu. Cook for 15-20 minutes until the vegetables are soft. Blend the miso to a paste with a little of the soup liquid, add to the soup, heat but do not allow to boil. Season with freshly ground black pepper to taste. Serve garnished with chopped spring onions.

FENNEL & WALNUT SOUP

The inclusion of Pernod in this soup really accentuates the aniseed flavour of the fennel.

Serves 4

INGREDIENTS
1 bulb fennel, chopped
1 head celery,chopped
1 large onion, chopped
1 tbsp olive or sunflower oil
90g/3oz walnuts, crushed
1.14 litres/2 pints vegetable stock, bean stock or water
3 tbsps Pernod
150ml/¼ pint single cream
Salt and freshly ground black pepper
Parsley to garnish

Cook the fennel, celery and onion in the oil over a low heat. Add the walnuts and stock and simmer for 30 minutes. Blend the soup until smooth in a liquidiser or food processor. Return the soup to the pan, add the Pernod, single cream and salt and pepper. Reheat gently and serve garnished with parsley.

CHESTNUT SOUP

Chestnuts are an invaluable ingredient for vegetarian cookery; they are full of flavour and provide lots of protein. What is more, they are satisfying and filling. Cook 460g/1lb shelled chestnuts in 150ml/¼ pint boiling water until soft then purée in a liquidiser or food processor to make this soup if commercial purée is not available. Sprinkle with chopped parsley or celery leaves to add colour just before serving.

Serves 4

INGREDIENTS

- 30g/1oz vegetable margarine
- 2 sticks of celery, trimmed and finely chopped
- 2 large onions, chopped
- 225g/8oz unsweetened chestnut purée
- 850ml/1½ pints homemade vegetable stock
- Salt and freshly ground black pepper
- Wholemeal croutons, to garnish

Melt the margarine in a large saucepan, add the celery and onion and cook until just soft. Blend the chestnut purée with a little of the stock and add to the pan with the remaining stock. Season with salt and pepper.

Bring slowly to the boil then simmer gently for 35 minutes. Serve garnished with croutons.

GREEN PEA SOUP

Peas are used throughout the world both fresh and dried. There are few other flavours so exquisite as freshly picked garden peas – but you need an allotment full of plants to have sufficient to spare for soup! So this recipe uses frozen peas which provide good flavour and colour and allow you to make this creamy, classic soup all the year round.

Serves 4

INGREDIENTS

30g/1oz butter or vegetable margarine
1 shallot, finely chopped
30g/1oz plain flour
280ml/½ pint vegetable stock
420ml/¾ pint milk
460g/1lb frozen peas
1 tsp dried marjoram
1 tbsp freshly chopped parsley
Salt and freshly ground black pepper
1 small bunch fresh mint
150ml/¼ pint single cream

Melt the butter or margarine in a saucepan, add the shallot and cook until soft. Stir in the flour and cook gently for about 1 minute. Remove from the heat and gradually add the stock and milk.

Reserve about 90g/3oz of the peas and add the rest to the pan, along with the marjoram, parsley and seasoning. Return to the heat and cook until slightly thickened, stirring continually. Pour the soup into a liquidiser or food processor and blend until smooth. Rinse the pan and pour the soup back into it. Chop the mint very finely and add it to the pan with the cream. Stir in the reserved peas and reheat gently before serving.

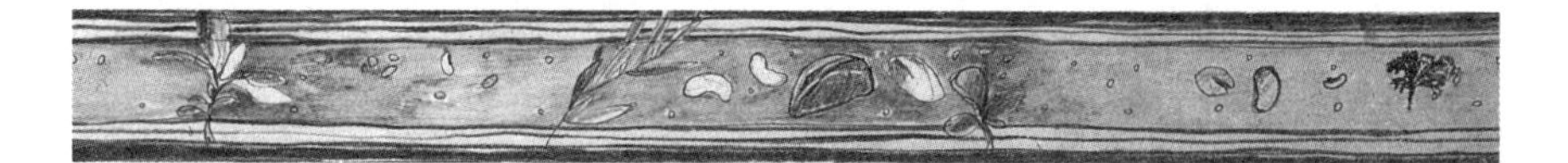

TOMATO & DILL BISQUE

I always think of a bisque as a summer soup and this recipe produces a sophisticated soup of intense flavour if you use homegrown tomatoes, late in the summer, which have ripened naturally in the sun. Dill is an elegant partner for the tomatoes – I use basil occasionally for a more robust flavour.

Serves 4

INGREDIENTS
900g/2lbs fresh tomatoes
1 tbsp vegetable oil
1 onion, chopped
2 large sprigs fresh dill
2 tbsps tomato purée
Salt and freshly ground black pepper
850ml/1½ pints vegetable stock
150ml/¼ pint double cream
2 tsps freshly chopped dill
4 tbsps natural yogurt
4 slices fresh tomato
4 small sprigs fresh dill

Cut the tomatoes in half over a bowl, discard the seeds but reserve any juice that is produced.

Heat the oil in a saucepan and cook the onion until softened. Add the tomato flesh, tomato juice, dill sprigs, tomato purée, salt, pepper and stock. Bring slowly to the boil and simmer for 10 minutes. Remove the sprigs of dill and blend the bisque in a liquidiser or food processor until smooth.

Strain the soup back into the pan through a sieve to remove the skins. Stir in the double cream and chopped dill. Reheat gently, stirring constantly – do not allow to boil. Garnish each serving with a spoonful of the yogurt, a tomato slice and a sprig of dill.

CREAM OF CUCUMBER WITH MINT

I took a few years to get used to the concept of chilled soups but this is one of my favourites. It is so easy to make – and very economical when cucumbers are plentiful. If the weather changes and chilled soup seems inappropriate, don't worry. Reheat the soup very gently – serve it warm rather than hot to let the flavour of the cucumbers shine through. Add the mint and yogurt just before serving.

Serves 4

INGREDIENTS

3 large cucumbers
1 litre/1¾ pints vegetable stock
salt and freshly ground black pepper
2-3 sprigs fresh mint
280ml/½ pint single cream
4tbsps natural yogurt, to garnish

Peel half a cucumber and chop it into small dice. Set to one side. Peel the remaining cucumbers and roughly chop into small pieces. Place in a large saucepan with the stock and seasoning. Remove the mint leaves from the sprig and add the stalks only to the pan. Bring slowly to the boil, then reduce the heat and simmer gently for 25 minutes or until the cucumber is tender.

Remove the mint stalk from the soup and blend in a liquidiser or food processor until smooth. Return to the rinsed out pan, stir in the single cream and reserved diced cucumber. Reheat gently for 5 minutes. Cool, then chill for about 2 hours. To serve, finely chop the mint leaves and add to the soup. Stir a spoonful of yogurt into each bowl before serving.

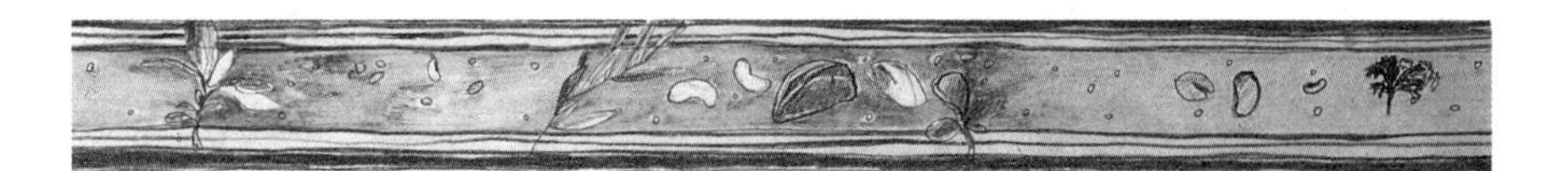

SWEETCORN & RED PEPPER SOUP

Sweetcorn is a starchy vegetable and I always find it very filling! Made into a thick soup with sweet red pepper you have a satisfying starter for a cold day – with a touch of spiciness from the chilli. Wash your hands after preparing the chilli and don't rub your eyes – the juices can be very fierce!

Serves 4

INGREDIENTS
- 4 medium potatoes, scrubbed and cut into even-sized pieces
- 1 bay leaf
- 570ml/1 pint vegetable stock
- 15g/½oz butter or vegetable margarine
- 1 onion, chopped
- 1 large red pepper, deseeded and chopped
- 1 red chilli, deseeded and chopped
- 225g/8oz sweetcorn kernels
- 570ml/1 pint milk
- Salt and freshly ground black pepper
- Freshly chopped parsley, to garnish

Place the potatoes in a saucepan with the bay leaf and cover with stock. Bring to the boil and simmer gently for 15 minutes until tender. Pour the potatoes and stock into a liquidiser or food processor and blend until smooth.

Melt the butter or margarine in another pan and add the onion, red pepper and chilli. Cook gently for 5 to 10 minutes until soft. Add the puréed potatoes with the sweetcorn and milk, stirring to blend thoroughly. Reheat gently and season to taste. Serve garnished with chopped parsley.

PURÉE OF ASPARAGUS SOUP

Asparagus is a real treat and one of my favourite heralds of summer. Towards the end of the season, when it is plentiful and slightly cheaper, asparagus makes a delicately flavoured soup and is enlivened with a little ground mace. Use frozen asparagus if you have no local growers.

Serves 4

INGREDIENTS
1.4kg/3lbs asparagus, fresh or frozen, thawed
1.14 litres/2 pints vegetable stock
1 tsp ground mace
Salt and freshly ground black pepper
280ml/ ½ pint single cream
150ml/ ¼ pint double cream, whipped
Sprinkling of ground mace

Trim the thick ends from the asparagus and cut away any tough outer skin. Chop the spears into 2.5cm/1 inch pieces. Boil the stock in a large pan, add the asparagus, mace and seasoning, and cook for about 10 minutes until the asparagus is just tender.

Blend the asparagus with the cooking liquid in a liquidiser or food processor until smooth. Return to the rinsed out pan and stir in the single cream. Reheat gently but do not allow to boil or the cream will curdle. Garnish each serving with a spoonful of the whipped cream and a dusting of the ground mace.

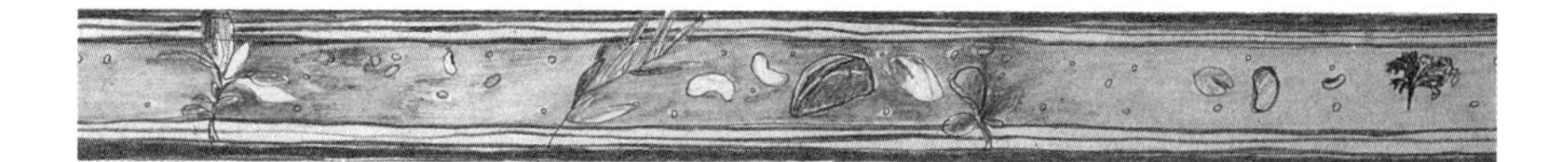

BEETROOT & SOUR CREAM SOUP WITH HORSERADISH

This recipe is based on the classic Russian beetroot soup called Borsch. It is actually made widely throughout Eastern Europe, each country adding its own variation to the classic Russian recipe. I like this version best, with the heat of the horseradish and freshness of the chives. For a touch of real authenticity serve with iced vodka!

Serves 4

INGREDIENTS
460g/1lb fresh beetroot
225g/8oz turnips, peeled and cut into even-sized pieces
1.14 litres/2 pints vegetable stock
1 bay leaf
Salt and freshly ground black pepper
280ml/½ pint sour cream
1 tbsp grated fresh or bottled horseradish
Snipped chives, to garnish

Boil the beetroot in salted water for about 30 to 40 minutes or until beetroots are soft. (Large, older beetroot may take longer.) Remove from the pan and leave until cold enough to handle. Carefully remove the skins from the cooked beetroots, using a small knife to cut away roots or rough skin. Cut the cooked beetroot into small pieces and place in a large saucepan with the turnips, stock, bay leaf, salt and pepper. Bring to the boil, then reduce the heat and simmer gently for 20 minutes or until the turnip is tender. Remove and discard the bay leaf.

Using a liquidiser or food processor, blend the soup until smooth then return it to the rinsed out pan. Reserve 4 tbsps of the sour cream and stir the remainder into the soup with the horseradish. Reheat gently for a few minutes but do not allow the soup to boil. Serve the soup topped with the reserved cream and a sprinkling of snipped chives.

MUSHROOM & SHERRY CREAM SOUP

Mushrooms and sherry are a perfect blend of flavours. I like to use a dry sherry for cooking but you may use a sweeter type if you prefer – Amontillado or pale cream are fine. Use a variety of mushrooms for extra flavour and serve with fresh crusty bread.

Serves 4

INGREDIENTS

900g/2lbs mushrooms, trimmed and chopped
5-6 slices stale bread, crusts removed
700ml/1¼ pints vegetable stock
1 sprig of fresh thyme
1 bay leaf
1 clove garlic, crushed
Salt and freshly ground black pepper
420ml/¾ pint single cream
60ml/2fl oz sherry
150ml/¼ pint double cream, whipped
Grated nutmeg, to garnish

Place the mushrooms in a large pan and break the bread into small pieces over them. Add the stock, thyme, bay leaf, garlic, salt and pepper. Bring to the boil, then reduce the heat and simmer gently for 20 minutes or until the mushrooms are soft, stirring occasionally. Remove the bay leaf and thyme. Blend the soup until smooth in a liquidiser or food processor. Return it to the rinsed out pan and whisk in the single cream and sherry. Reheat gently but do not allow to boil. Garnish each serving of soup with a spoonful of the whipped cream and a sprinkling of nutmeg.

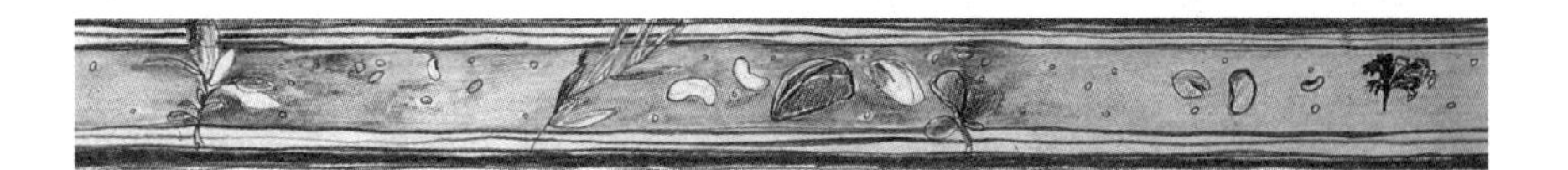

TOMATO & LEEK SOUP

This soup combines two of my favourite ingredients: tomatoes and leeks. It is quick and easy to make – use canned tomato juice if you haven't enough tomatoes to make fresh. Worcestershire Sauce may be used in place of Tabasco or soy. A perfect light lunch with bread and cheese.

Serves 4-6

INGREDIENTS
2 large leeks, washed, trimmed and finely sliced
570ml/1 pint fresh tomato juice
Dash Tabasco or soy sauce
1 tsp celery seasoning
Shake of garlic powder
Salt and freshly ground black pepper
4 fresh tomatoes, skinned and sliced

Cook the leeks in about 280ml/½ pint of boiling water for 15 minutes or until tender. Remove about half the leeks from the cooking liquid and set aside. Blend the remaining leeks with the cooking liquid in a liquidiser or food processor. Return to the rinsed out pan and add another 280ml/½ pint water, the tomato juice, Tabasco or soy sauce, celery seasoning and garlic powder. Heat gently to simmering point then add the reserved leeks and tomato slices. Season with salt and pepper and cook gently for 3 to 4 minutes. Serve hot.

PARSNIP & CARROT SOUP

I like to use small, young vegetables for this soup – both parsnips and carrots have a sweetness which blends perfectly with nutmeg and chives. When chives are out of season add the grated rind of an orange to the soup just before serving.

Serves 4

Ingredients

225g/8oz parsnips, peeled and sliced
225g/8oz carrots, peeled and sliced
280ml/½ pint vegetable stock
570ml/1 pint milk
Salt and freshly ground black pepper
Pinch ground nutmeg
1 small bunch chives, snipped
4 tbsps single cream

Cook the parsnips and carrots in the stock until tender – about 15 minutes. Blend until smooth in a liquidiser or food processor, then return to the rinsed out pan. Add the milk and season with salt, pepper and nutmeg, then stir in the chives. Reheat gently until simmering. Stir in the cream just before serving.

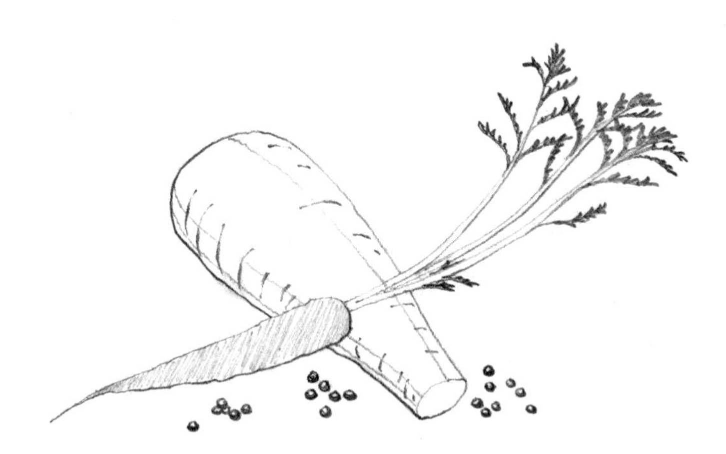

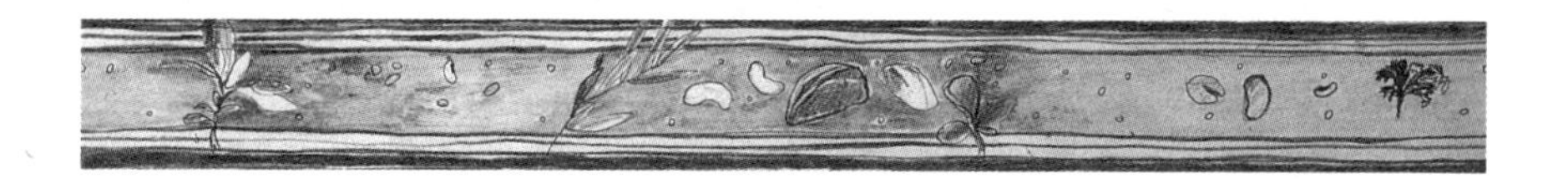

CHEDDAR CHEESE SOUP

I find this to be an excellent way of using up odd pieces of cheese left in the refrigerator! Cheddar Cheese Soup makes a good starter to serve before a main course of rice or grains. Try it – it's delicious!

Serves 4

INGREDIENTS

- 225g/8oz vegetarian Cheddar cheese or a mixture of different types of hard vegetarian cheeses
- 30g/1oz butter or vegetable margarine
- 1 carrot, peeled and diced
- 2 sticks celery, trimmed and chopped
- 30g/1oz plain flour
- 420ml/¾ pint vegetable stock
- 570ml/1 pint milk
- 1 bay leaf
- 1 tsp dried thyme
- Freshly chopped parsley, to garnish

Grate the cheese finely and, if using more than one type, mix together.

Melt the butter or margarine in a pan and cook the carrot and celery until just soft. Stir in the flour and cook for about 30 seconds. Remove from the heat and gradually add the stock and milk. Add the bay leaf and thyme. Return to the heat and cook gently until thickened slightly, stirring all the time. Gradually add the cheese, stirring until melted before adding a little more. Remove the bay leaf and serve the soup sprinkled with chopped parsley to garnish.

STARTERS

The purpose of a starter within a meal is to titillate and stimulate the appetite, to get the meal off to a good beginning and to generate some excitement in those around your table for what is to come. For this reason a starter should be interesting and appetising but not too much; there is nothing worse than feeling that you're never going to make it through to the end of the first plateful, let alone the main course and however many sweets and desserts there are to follow.

Creating a Good Impression

There are some very definite tricks of the trade in the selection and preparation of starters. I always prefer to serve a hot or a warm dish if I'm out to impress; the very fact that one has gone to the trouble of preparing such a starter indicates to the assembled diners that you have thought about and planned the meal.

This course provides the opportunity to indulge in small amounts of absolute luxury; expensive ingredients that would be prohibitive in cost for a main course. Asparagus in season and globe artichokes are two examples of special vegetables which spring to mind: their flavour shines through so much more clearly when they are cooked and served simply, rather than to accompany a main dish. There is a heavenly recipe here for asparagus with an orange dressing: try it, the combination of flavours is truly mouthwatering.

Always take care to balance your starter and main course; if the starter is to be rich and covered in sauce then the main course should be plainer and lighter, perhaps with more emphasis on grains or nuts.

Stimulate the Palate

It is more important for a starter to be visually (as well as tastefully) appetising and attractive than it is for any other course in a meal. This is where you create your first, and most lasting, impression so take a little extra care and trouble with this part of the meal. The size of the portion is also important and this can often go hand in hand with the choice and quality of the main ingredient: it is better to have a small and delectable quantity of something fine and in season than absolute mountains of an inferior quality ingredient.

Although I admitted earlier than a hot or warm starter makes a better impression with me, that is not to say that cold starters should never be served! On balmy, summer days there can be nothing better than a cold dish which refreshes a jaded, overheated palate. Light summer pâtés, such as that made with mushrooms and watercress on page 48, stimulate and revive, but don't fall in to the trap of being too generous and serve too much. I think this mistake is easier to make with a cold starter than hot, so be warned. Of course, if you have chosen to serve the Crudités and delicious dips on page 47 and your family and friends keep dipping and helping themselves, well that's their lookout!

Fashion or Fantasy?

Vegetable terrines, either set with agar-agar or baked in the oven, provide colourful starters. Sliced thinly and served with toast, bread or biscuits and a little salad garnish, these show considerable culinary skill and are also most fashionable. Also to be found in the top restaurants are warm salads, a mixture of salad leaves, cheese and other ingredients, bound together with a warm dressing and served immediately, before the salad wilts and becomes slimy. The blending of blue cheese, avocado, grapes and fresh wet walnuts with crisp salad leaves, served with a warm walnut oil dressing is one of my favourite recipes – it's on page 59. I sometimes add fresh garlic croutons when I'm feeling indulgent! I shall be eating this forever, whether it remains in fashion in the stylish restaurants of the world or not – it is one of my culinary fantasies!

A Final Word on Presentation

To return to warm or hot starters. Without doubt, these look better if contained in individual dishes, especially if dressed with a sauce or garnish. Serve in individual dishes, set on saucers with the smallest amount of garnish, and the food justifies the effort that you have put into it. A simple touch, like the grinding of fresh black pepper around the edge of a plate, also helps the presentation but don't use too much, otherwise your friends will be sneezing all through the meal!

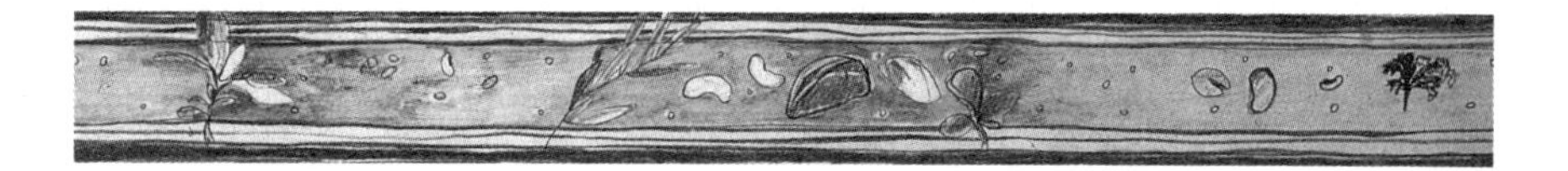

CRUDITÉS

Everyone loves dips and crudités – don't eat too much or your main course appetite will suffer; I know, from experience!

Serves 6-8

INGREDIENTS

Choose from the following vegetable selection:

Cauliflower, broccoli – divided into small florets
Carrots, celery, courgettes, cucumber – cut into matchsticks
Chicory – separate the blades
Mushrooms – sliced or quartered
Peppers, kohlrabi, fennel – sliced
Radishes, spring onions, cherry tomatoes – leave whole

Tomato and Cheese Dip

1 tbsp butter or margarine
1 tbsp grated onion
225g/8oz tomatoes, skinned and diced
60g/2oz vegetarian Cheddar cheese, grated
60g/2oz breadcrumbs
1 free-range egg, beaten
½ tsp dried mustard
Salt and freshly grated black pepper
2-4 tbsps Greek yogurt

Creamed Curry Dip

1 tbsp mango chutney
6 tbsps home-made or good quality mayonnaise
1 tsp curry paste
2 tbsps double cream
Pinch ground cumin

Avocado Dip

2 ripe avocados
1 onion, diced
½ clove garlic, crushed
2 tbsps lemon juice
Salt and freshly ground black pepper

Tomato and Cheese Dip

Melt the butter and gently fry the onion for 2 or 3 minutes until soft. Add the tomatoes, cover and simmer for 10 minutes, then add the cheese, breadcrumbs and egg and cook for a further minute, stirring all the time, until thickened. Do not allow to boil. Add the mustard and seasoning and blend until smooth in a liquidiser or food processor. Mix in enough Greek yogurt to ensure a smooth 'dipping' consistency and store in the refrigerator until required.

Creamed Curry Dip

Chop the pieces of mango in the chutney with a sharp knife then place in a bowl with all the other ingredients and mix well. Refrigerate until required.

Avocado Dip

Peel the avocados, remove the stones and chop the flesh roughly. Blend in a liquidiser or food processor with the onion, garlic and lemon juice until smooth. Season to taste and refrigerate until required.

WATERCRESS & MUSHROOM PÂTÉ

Serve this creamy pâté on slices of hot brown toast.

Serves 4

INGREDIENTS
30g/1oz butter
1 medium onion, finely chopped
90g/3oz dark, flat mushrooms, finely chopped
1 bunch watercress, finely chopped
120g/4oz low fat curd cheese
Few drops shoyu sauce (Japanese soy sauce)
½ tsp caraway seeds
Freshly ground black pepper

Melt the butter over a low heat, add the onion and cook until soft but not coloured. Raise the heat, add the mushrooms and cook quickly for 2 minutes. Add the chopped watercress and stir for about 30 seconds until it becomes limp. Place the contents of the pan in a liquidiser or food processor together with the cheese and shoyu sauce, and blend until smooth. Stir in the caraway seeds and pepper to taste. Pile into individual ramekin dishes or one large serving dish and chill for at least 2 hours until firm.

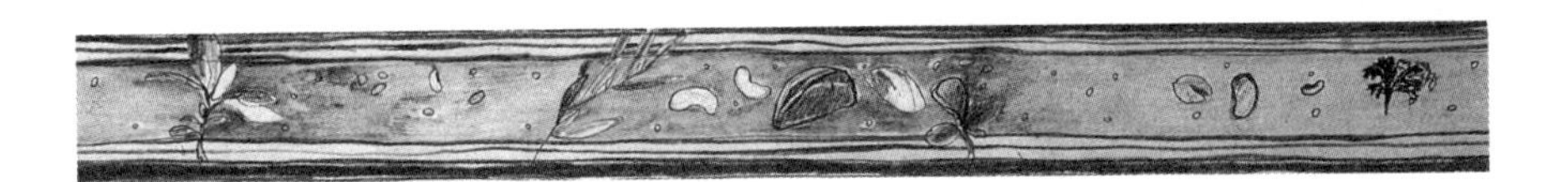

IMAM BAYILDI

This apparently means 'the priest has fainted' – from sheer delight over such a tasty starter! Always choose smooth, shining aubergines when shopping – older vegetables will be bitter in taste.

Serves 4

INGREDIENTS
2 large aubergines
Salt
150ml/¼ pint olive oil
2 onions, finely chopped
2 cloves garlic, crushed
250g/9oz tomatoes, skinned and chopped
½ tsp mixed spice
Juice of ½ lemon
1 tsp brown sugar
1 tbsp freshly chopped parsley
1 tbsp pine nuts
Salt and freshly ground black pepper

Halve the aubergines lengthways and scoop out the flesh with a sharp knife, leaving a substantial shell so that they will not disintegrate when cooked. Sprinkle the shells with a little salt and leave upside down on a plate for 30 minutes to drain away any bitter juices. Preheat the oven to 180°C/350°F/Gas Mark 4.

Meanwhile, heat half the oil in a saucepan and fry the onion and garlic until just softened. Add the scooped out aubergine flesh, tomatoes, mixed spice, lemon juice, sugar, parsley, pine nuts and a little seasoning. Simmer for about 20 minutes until the mixture has thickened. Wash and dry the aubergine shells and spoon the filling into the halves. Place side by side in a buttered ovenproof dish. Mix the remaining oil with 150ml/¼ pint of water and a little seasoning, and pour around the aubergines. Bake for 30-40 minutes or until completely tender.

MUSHROOMS & TOFU IN GARLIC BUTTER

Mushrooms in garlic butter are always popular – the addition of tofu adds protein and substance to the dish. Serve with crusty bread to mop up the butter.

Serves 4

Ingredients
225g/8oz button mushrooms
2.5cm/1 inch piece root ginger
225g/8oz smoked tofu
120g/4oz butter
4 small cloves garlic, crushed
2 tbsps freshly chopped parsley

Wipe the mushrooms with a damp cloth. Peel and grate the root ginger. Cut the smoked tofu into small 1.25cm/½ inch squares.

Melt the butter in a frying pan, add the crushed garlic and ginger and fry gently for two minutes, then add the mushrooms and cook gently for 4-5 minutes until softened. Finally, add the smoked tofu and warm through. Divide the mixture between 4 individual dishes, sprinkle with chopped parsley and serve at once.

DATE, APPLE & CELERY STARTER

I think the toasted coconut really makes this one!

Serves 4

INGREDIENTS
1 tbsp desiccated coconut
2 crisp eating apples
3-4 sticks celery
90g/3oz dates
2 tbsps natural yogurt
Salt and freshly ground pepper
Pinch of nutmeg

Toast the coconut in a dry frying pan over a low heat until it is golden brown, then put it to one side. Core and dice the apples and chop the celery finely. Plunge the dates into boiling water, drain and chop finely. Combine the apples, celery and dates in a mixing bowl, then add the yogurt, seasoning and nutmeg and mix thoroughly so that the salad is completely coated. Transfer to a serving bowl and garnish with the toasted coconut. Serve at once.

CARROT & SWEETCORN MEDLEY

It is most unusual to garnish with grated root ginger, but it really brings this starter to life.

Serves 6

INGREDIENTS
460g/1lb carrots
1 clove garlic, crushed
2-3 tbsps lemon juice
Salt and freshly ground black pepper
340g/12oz canned sweetcorn
Lettuce
1 small piece of fresh root ginger, peeled and grated
Few black olives, stones removed

Scrub and grate the carrots and place them in a mixing bowl. Combine the garlic, lemon juice, salt and pepper in a screw topped jar and shake well. Mix the dressing with the grated carrot and add the sweetcorn. Place a little finely shredded lettuce in the bottom of individual stem glasses and arrange the carrot and sweetcorn mixture over the top. Garnish with grated ginger and olives. Chill for 30 minutes before serving.

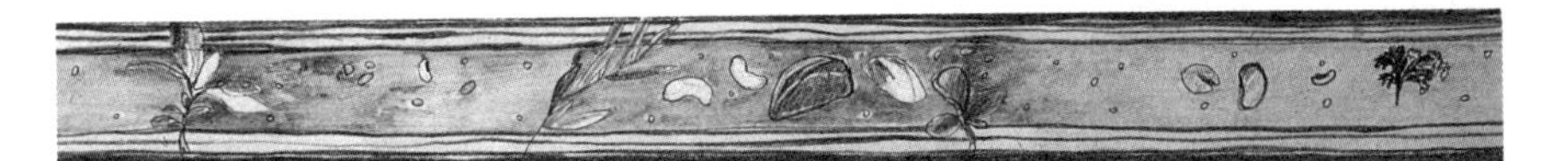

FENNEL & ORANGE CROUSTADE

I find the combination of the crispy bread casing with the vegetables delicious. Try using large tomatoes, sliced and drizzled with olive oil, in place of the fennel.

Serves 4

INGREDIENTS

4 2.5cm/1 inch thick slices wholemeal bread
Oil for deep-frying
2 fennel bulbs (reserve any fronds)
4 oranges
1 tbsp olive oil
Pinch salt
Freshly chopped mint for garnishing

Trim the crusts off the bread and discard. Cut into 7.5cm/3 inch squares, and hollow out the middles, leaving evenly shaped cases. Heat the oil and deep-fry the bread until golden brown, then drain well on absorbent kitchen paper, and leave to cool.

Trim the fennel bulbs, slice thinly, then place in a mixing bowl. Remove all the peel and pith from the oranges and cut them into segments – do this over the mixing bowl to catch the juice. Mix the orange segments with the fennel, add the olive oil and salt and mix together thoroughly. Just before serving, divide the fennel and orange mixture evenly between the bread cases and garnish with fresh mint and fennel fronds.

BULGAR BOATS

This salad may also be served on a bed of shredded lettuce – a chiffonade. Bulgar is sometimes called cracked wheat; it is a very versatile ingredient and makes wonderful salads.

Serves 6

INGREDIENTS
60g/2oz green lentils
120g/4 oz bulgar wheat
1 red pepper
1 green pepper
1 medium onion
60g/2oz pine nuts (dry roasted in a pan)
2 tsps dried salad herbs (tarragon, chives or parsley)
Juice and rind of 1 lemon
Salt and freshly ground black pepper
Cos lettuce to serve

Remove any grit or stones from the lentils and rinse well. Place in a pan, cover with plenty of water and boil for about 20 minutes – do not overcook. Place the bulgar wheat in a mixing bowl and cover with boiling water. Leave for about 10 minutes – the grain will then have swollen, softened and absorbed the water.

Dice the peppers and chop the onion finely. Drain the lentils and add to the bulgar, together with the peppers, onion, nuts, herbs, lemon juice and rind, salt and pepper. Using one large lettuce leaf per person, spoon the salad into the centre of the leaves and arrange on a large serving dish garnished with wedges of lemon.

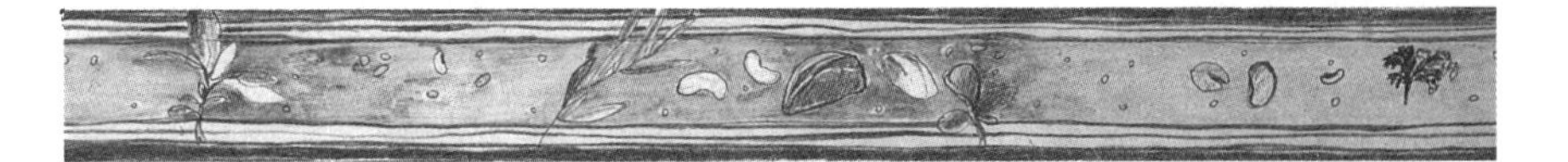

MIXED NUT BALLS

Mixed Nut Balls make an excellent starter or drinks party nibbles. Prepare them in advance and chill in the fridge until required, then pop them straight into the oven.

Serves 8

INGREDIENTS

75g/2½oz ground almonds
75g/2½oz ground hazelnuts
75g/2½oz ground pecan nuts
90g/3oz wholemeal breadcrumbs
120g/4oz vegetarian Cheddar cheese, grated
1 free-range egg, beaten
4-5 tbsps dry sherry or 2 tbsps milk and 3 tbsps dry sherry
1 small onion, finely chopped
1 tbsp grated fresh ginger
1 tbsp freshly chopped parsley
1 small red or green chilli, finely chopped
1 medium red pepper, diced
1 tsp sea salt
1 tsp freshly ground black pepper

Mix the almonds, hazelnuts and pecan nuts with the breadcrumbs and cheese. In a separate bowl, mix the beaten egg with the sherry, onion, ginger, parsley, chilli and red pepper. Combine with the nut mixture and add the salt and pepper – if the mixture is too dry, add a little more sherry or milk. Form into small balls, about 2.5cm/1 inch in diameter.

Do not preheat the oven. Arrange the balls on a well greased baking tray and bake from cold at 180°C/350°F/Gas Mark 4 for about 20-25 minutes, until golden brown.

PARSNIP FRITTERS

Serve with a crispy salad garnish.

Serves 4

INGREDIENTS
120g/4oz plain unbleached flour
2 tsps baking powder
1 tsp salt
½ tsp freshly ground black pepper
1 free-range egg
150ml/¼ pint milk
1 tbsp melted butter
680g/1½lbs cooked parsnips, finely diced
Oil or clarified butter for frying

Sift together the flour, baking powder, salt and pepper into a bowl. Beat the egg and mix with the milk and melted butter, then stir this mixture into the dry ingredients, followed by the cooked parsnips. Divide the mixture into 16 and shape into small fritters. Fry in oil or clarified butter until browned on both sides.

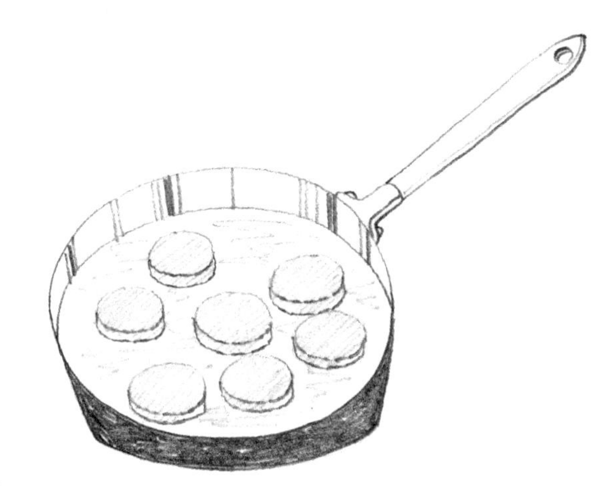

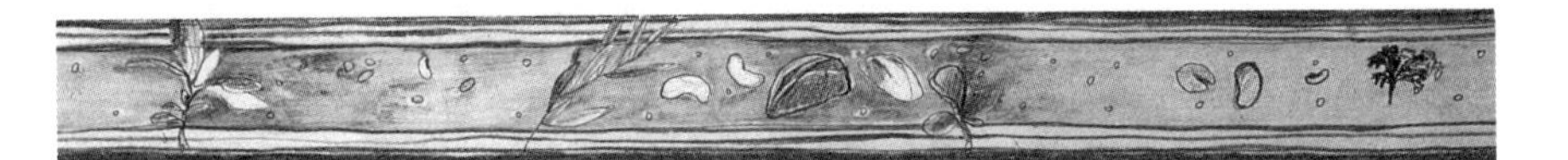

TABOULEH

This salad originates in the Middle East where many different variations exist. The essential ingredient is the bulgar wheat, the essential seasoning the mint.

Serves 6

Ingredients
175-200g/6-7oz bulgar wheat
1 tsp salt
340ml/12fl oz boiling water
460g/1lb tomatoes, chopped
½ cucumber, diced
3-4 spring onions, chopped

Dressing
60ml/2fl oz olive oil
60ml/2fl oz lemon juice
2 tbsps freshly chopped mint
4 tbsps freshly chopped parsley
2 cloves garlic, crushed

Mix the bulgar wheat with the salt, cover with the boiling water and leave for 15-20 minutes. All the water will then be absorbed. Mix the ingredients together for the dressing and pour over the soaked bulgar, then fold in lightly with a spoon. Leave for two hours or overnight in the fridge or a cool place. Add the tomatoes, cucumber and spring onions.

DANISH EGG SALAD

I usually serve Danish Egg Salad as a starter but it also makes a light lunch or supper dish for 2. Use mange touts or French beans in place of the peas for a change.

Serves 4

Ingredients
2 free-range eggs
1 tbsp single cream
Salt and freshly ground black pepper
Knob butter or vegetable margarine
225g/8oz fresh or frozen peas
280ml/½ pint soured cream
4 tbsps mayonnaise
2 tbsps freshly chopped dill
Pinch paprika
6 sticks celery, trimmed and diced
120g/4oz vegetarian cheese of your choice, diced
120g/4oz cucumber, diced
3 spring onions, chopped
½ head Chinese leaves, shredded

Beat together the eggs, cream and seasonings in a small bowl. Melt the butter in a frying pan and pour in the egg mixture, tilt the pan so that the egg coats the base in a thin layer. Cook gently for 1 to 2 minutes or until set. Carefully flip over and cook the other side. Remove from the pan and allow to cool.

Cook the peas and refresh them in cold water. Drain and set aside. Whisk together the soured cream, mayonnaise, dill, paprika and a little salt. Reserve a few tablespoons of the mixture. Mix the remaining dressing with the peas, celery, cheese, cucumber and spring onions. Arrange the Chinese leaves in a serving dish and pile the vegetable mixture into the centre. Shred the omelette with a sharp knife and use to garnish the salad. Finally, drizzle the reserved soured cream dressing over the salad.

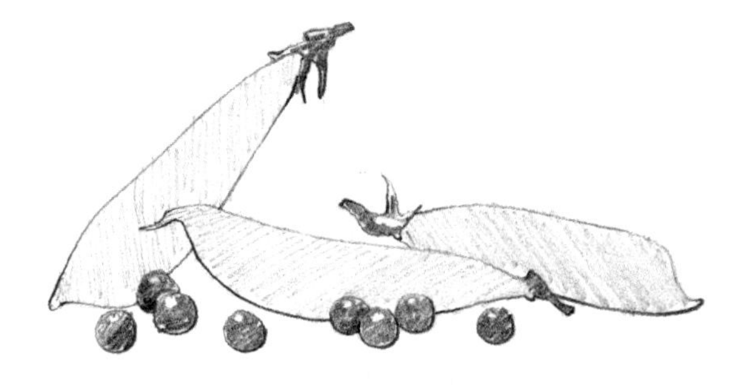

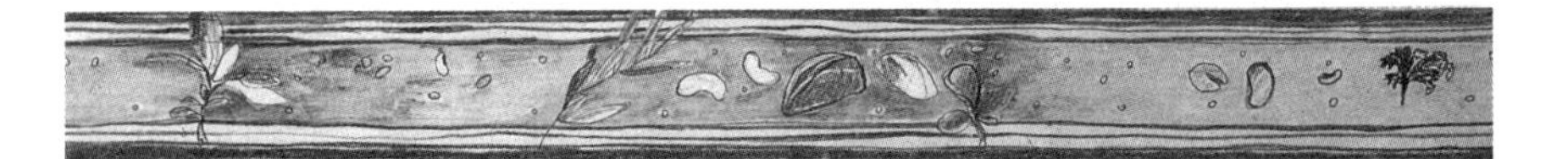

WARM SALAD WITH AVOCADO, GRAPES, BLUE CHEESE AND WALNUTS

Warm salads are very sophisticated but speed is of the essence. They must be served immediately to prevent the leafy ingredients from going limp! I like to make this salad with fresh walnuts when they are in season in the autumn but packeted nuts are fine to use all the year round.

Serves 4

INGREDIENTS

Mixed salad leaves, eg frisee, chicory, radicchio, lamb's lettuce, watercress or iceberg lettuce
2 avocados
175g/6oz black grapes
4 tbsps freshly chopped mixed herbs
120g/4oz walnut pieces
120g/4oz vegetarian blue cheese, diced or crumbled
3 tbsps walnut oil and grapeseed oil, mixed
2 tbsps lemon vinegar
Pinch unrefined sugar

Tear the salad leaves into small pieces and place in a large bowl. If using lamb's lettuce separate the leaves and leave whole. Remove any tough stalks from watercress. Peel the avocados and cut into neat slices, add to the salad leaves. Cut the grapes in half and remove pips, add to the salad with the chopped herbs, walnuts and cheese.

Put the oils, vinegar and sugar into a screw top jar and shake vigorously until the dressing is well blended. Pour into a large frying pan and heat until bubbling. Remove from heat, add to the prepared salad and toss, taking care not to break up the avocado pieces. Arrange on plates and serve immediately.

COURGETTE AND CARROT TERRINE

I always think that vegetable terrines look so elegant with their brightly coloured layers of varying textures. I never know whether to take the whole terrine to the table so that friends can be impressed when the layers are revealed, or whether to arrange the slices artistically in the sanctuary of the kitchen! Either way, serve with fresh wholemeal or melba toast.

Serves 6-8

INGREDIENTS
- 6-8 large green cabbage leaves
- 1-2 carrots, peeled and cut into thin sticks
- 1-2 courgettes, washed and cut into thin sticks
- 340g/12oz low fat vegetarian curd cheese
- 4 slices white bread, crust removed and made into crumbs
- 2 free-range eggs, beaten
- 150ml/¼ pint double cream lightly whipped
- 2 tbsps freshly chopped chives
- Salt and freshly ground black pepper
- 280ml/½ pint natural yogurt
- 175ml/¼ pint mayonnaise
- 2 tomatoes, skinned, seeded and diced
- 2 tbsps lemon juice or dry white wine
- Pinch unrefined sugar (optional)

Preheat the oven to 160°C/325°F/Gas Mark 3. Trim the thick spine away from the cabbage leaves by cutting a triangular section out of each one. Blanch the leaves in boiling water for 2 minutes, then refresh in cold water. Blanch the carrot sticks for 4 minutes and the courgette for 1 minute in boiling water, refresh in cold water. Drain the blanched vegetables well, and pat dry with absorbent kitchen paper. Combine the cheese, breadcrumbs, eggs, cream, chives and seasoning, mix well.

Leaving at least 5cm/2 inches of leaf hanging over the edges, carefully line a 900g/2lb loaf tin with the cabbage leaves. Overlap each leaf slightly to ensure that no gap appears when the terrine is turned out. Place one quarter of the cheese mixture in the lined tin and spread it evenly.

Add a layer of carrots and top with cheese then a layer of courgettes and top with more of the cheese mixture. Repeat until all the vegetable and cheese mixtures are used.

Fold the cabbage over the terrine completely to enclose the filling. Cover with a sheet of non-stick parchment then foil. Place in a roasting tin filled with hot water. Bake for 1¼-1½ hours or until the terrine feels firm to the touch. Cool the terrine completely and chill before turning out.

Combine the yogurt, mayonnaise, tomatoes, lemon juice or wine, sugar and a little more seasoning to make a sauce. Serve the terrine cut into slices with a little of the sauce spooned over.

SPINACH STUFFED ARTICHOKE HEARTS

Artichokes look complicated which, unfortunately, discourages people from buying them! Please don't be put off – they are a rare treat among vegetables. It is the base of the leaves and the 'fond' or heart that are edible. This recipe prepares the artichokes so that only the best parts are left. To enjoy the leaves, pull them away from the stalk then drag the base across your teeth to remove all the edible fleshy part – delicious!

Serves 4

INGREDIENTS

4 globe artichokes
15g/½oz butter or vegetable margarine
1 shallot, finely chopped
460g/1lb fresh spinach leaves, stalks removed, washed
60g/2oz breadcrumbs
1 free-range egg, beaten
150ml/¼ pint double cream
Pinch ground nutmeg
Pinch cayenne pepper
Salt
60g/2oz vegetarian Cheddar cheese, finely grated
4 tbsps double cream

Cut the leaves of each artichoke to about halfway down and trim the stalk end to allow the artichoke to sit upright. Trim away the outer tough, inedible leaves and cut out as much of the fluffy 'choke' as possible to form a firm shell. Cook in lightly salted boiling water for about 10 minutes or until the hearts are tender. Drain and cool. Trim any remaining 'choke' away.

Melt the butter or margarine in a large pan and cook the shallot until soft. Add the spinach with just the water that remains clinging to the leaves after washing. Cover and cook until the spinach wilts. Remove from the heat and add the breadcrumbs, egg, cream, nutmeg, cayenne and salt. Pile equal amounts into the centre of the artichokes and place in the top of a steamer. Cover and steam for 10 minutes or until the filling is just set.

Mix together the cheese and the remaining cream and use to top each of the filled artichokes. Steam for a further 1 minute. Sprinkle with a little ground nutmeg and serve.

AUBERGINE CAVIAR

Aubergines are so often served hot in spaghetti sauces or moussaka that it is easy to forget how delicious they are when served cold as a salad. I actually prefer them cold – it makes me think of Greek Islands and sunshine!

Serves 4

INGREDIENTS
1 large or 2 small aubergine
Salt
4 tbsps walnut oil
1 clove garlic, crushed
Juice of ½ lemon
Pinch cayenne pepper
2 hard boiled free-range eggs (optional)
1 small onion, finely chopped
4-8 slices French bread, toasted
2 tbsps freshly chopped parsley

Remove the stalk from the aubergine and cut in half lengthways. Using a small sharp knife, score and cut the flesh on each half of the aubergine, at about 1.25cm/½ inch intervals, diagonally, first in one direction, then the other. Sprinkle each cut surface with a little salt and leave to stand for 30 minutes, to draw out any bitterness and excess water. Rinse the aubergines thoroughly and pat dry with absorbent kitchen paper. Cut into chunks. Heat the oil in a frying pan and fry the aubergine and garlic until the aubergine is tender. This will take about 10 minutes.

Place the aubergine in a food processor with the lemon juice, cayenne and salt; process until finely chopped. Adjust the seasoning and chill thoroughly. Cut the eggs in half and separate the yolks from the whites; push the yolks through a nylon sieve and finely chop the egg whites. Pile the aubergine caviar on to the French bread and top with chopped onion, then the egg white and egg yolk. Sprinkle with chopped parsley and serve.

INDONESIAN-STYLE STUFFED PEPPERS

I only serve a tossed green salad with stuffed peppers – these need nothing more.

Serves 8 as a starter

INGREDIENTS

- 2 tbsps olive oil
- 1 medium onion, peeled and chopped
- 1 clove garlic, crushed
- 2 tsps turmeric
- 1 tsp coriander seeds, crushed
- 2 tbsps desiccated coconut
- 120g/4oz mushrooms, chopped
- 90g/3oz bulgar wheat
- 60g/2oz raisins
- 30g/1oz creamed coconut
- 280ml/½ pint stock or water
- 200g/7oz tomatoes, skinned and chopped
- 60g/2oz cashew nuts
- 4 small green peppers, de-seeded and cut in half lengthways
- 2 tsps lemon juice
- Extra stock for cooking

Preheat the oven to 180°C/350°F/Gas Mark 4. Heat the oil in a frying pan and fry the onion and garlic until lightly browned. Add the turmeric, coriander and dessicated coconut and cook gently for about 2 minutes. Add the mushrooms and bulgar wheat and cook for a further 2 minutes, then add the rest of the ingredients except the nuts, peppers, lemon juice, and extra stock. Simmer gently for 15-20 minutes until the bulgar wheat is cooked.

Toast the cashew nuts in a dry frying pan until golden brown. Blanch the peppers in boiling water for 3 minutes. Mix the nuts and lemon juice with the rest of the ingredients and fill the peppers with the mixture. Place the filled peppers in a large casserole dish and pour extra stock around the peppers. Cook for 20 minutes in the preheated oven. Drain the peppers and serve.

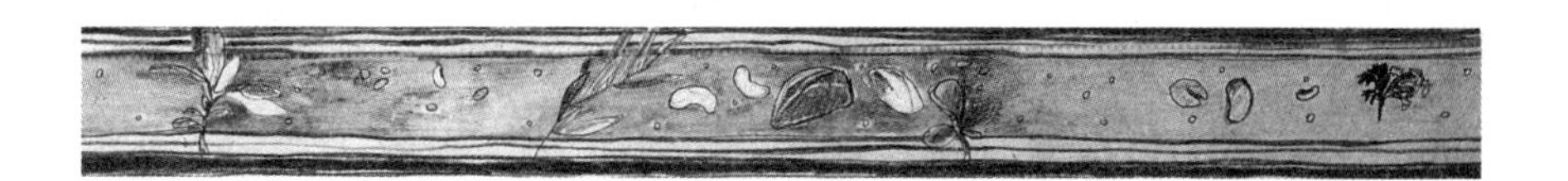

BRAZILIAN AVOCADOS

I find that the easiest way to scoop the flesh out of an avocado, without splitting the skin, is by working round the flesh with the handle of a teaspoon.

Serves 4

INGREDIENTS
2 large ripe avocados
A little lemon juice
Salt and freshly ground black pepper
60g/2oz Brazil nuts, finely chopped
60g/2oz vegetarian Cheddar cheese, grated
2 tbsps Parmesan cheese
2 tbsps freshly chopped parsley
2 firm ripe tomatoes, skinned and finely chopped
Wholemeal breadcrumbs
30g/1oz butter, melted
A little paprika

Preheat the oven to 200°C/400°F/Gas Mark 6. Halve the avocados and carefully remove the flesh from the skins. Brush the inside of the skins with a little of the lemon juice. Dice the avocado and place in a bowl with a sprinkling of lemon juice and the seasoning. Add the nuts, cheeses, parsley and tomato and mix carefully. Spoon the filling into the avocado shells, sprinkle with the breadcrumbs and drizzle the butter over the top.

Dust with the paprika and bake for 15 minutes. Serve immediately.

ASPARAGUS WITH ORANGE HOLLANDAISE

Asparagus has such a short season so I like to eat it prepared as simply as possible. However, I have found two delicious ways of accentuating the delicate flavour; one is by serving it with a light garlic butter, and the other is with this fruity butter sauce.

Serves 4

INGREDIENTS

900g/2lbs asparagus spears
Grated rind and juice of ½ orange
Juice of ½ lemon
1 bay leaf
Blade mace
60g/2oz butter
3 free-range egg yolks, beaten
Salt and freshly ground black pepper
Strips of blanched orange rind, to garnish (optional)

Trim away any thick, tough ends from the asparagus and rinse well. Bring a frying pan of lightly salted water to the boil. Move the pan so that it is half on and half off the direct heat (take care not to spill the water). Place the asparagus in the pan so that the tips are in the part of the pan off the heat. Cover the pan and bring back to the boil. Cook the asparagus for about 5 minutes or until just tender, drain and keep warm.

Meanwhile prepare the sauce. Heat the orange juice, lemon juice, bay leaf and mace in a small pan to almost boiling and allow to stand for a few moments. Melt the butter in the top of a double boiler or in a bowl placed over a pan of gently simmering water. Whisk the beaten egg yolks into the butter and add the orange rind. Strain the juice into the butter and egg mixture and whisk well. Cook gently until the sauce thickens, whisking constantly. Once the sauce has reached the desired consistency immediately remove it from the heat and stand in a bowl of cold water to prevent further cooking.

Arrange the asparagus on serving plates and pour equal amounts of sauce over each serving. Garnish with strips of orange rind if desired.

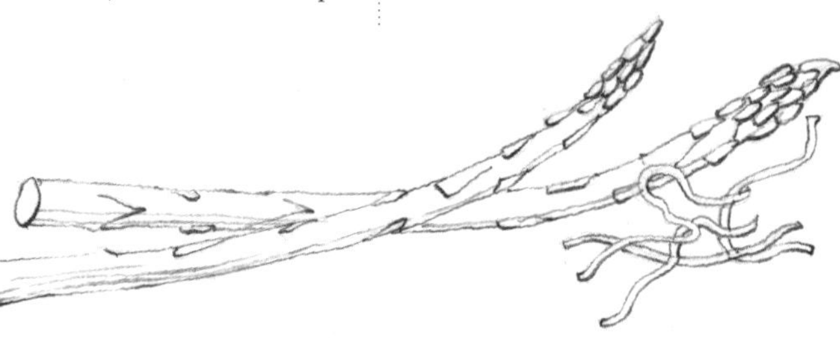

BROCCOLI AND HAZELNUT TERRINE

Contrasting flavours, colours and textures in the broccoli and hazelnuts of this terrine make it an outstanding starter. It is quite filling so serve thinly sliced with a salad garnish or crispy melba toasts.

Serves 6-8

INGREDIENTS

6-8 large whole spinach leaves
460g/1lb broccoli
2 free-range eggs, beaten
175g/6oz low fat vegetarian curd cheese
280ml/½ pint double cream, lightly whipped
4 slices white bread, crusts removed, made into crumbs
1 shallot, finely chopped
Pinch dried thyme
Pinch ground nutmeg
Salt and freshly ground black pepper
120g/4oz hazelnuts, lightly toasted then finely chopped
280ml/½ pint mayonnaise
150ml/¼ pint natural yogurt
Grated rind and juice of 1 lemon
Pinch cayenne pepper

Preheat the oven to 160°C/325°F/Gas Mark 3. Trim away any coarse stalks from the spinach, taking care to keep the leaves whole. Wash the leaves, then blanch in boiling water for 1 minute, drain and refresh in cold water. Drain again and pat dry.

Leaving at least 5cm/2 inches of leaf hanging over the edges, carefully line a 900g/2lb loaf tin with the spinach leaves. Overlap each leaf slightly to ensure that no gap appears when the terrine is turned out.

Chop the broccoli finely. Place the eggs, cheese, cream, breadcrumbs, shallot, thyme, nutmeg, salt and pepper in a bowl and mix well. Stir in the broccoli and hazelnuts then spoon the mixture into the lined loaf tin, packing it down well but taking care not to dislodge the spinach leaves. Carefully fold the spinach over the top of the filling. Cover with a sheet of non-stick baking parchment and then foil. Place in a roasting tin filled with hot water. Bake for 1 hour or until the terrine feels firm to the touch.

Cool the terrine completely and chill before turning out. Mix together the mayonnaise, yogurt, lemon rind and juice, cayenne pepper and a little salt. Serve the sauce with slices of the terrine.

SALADS & VEGETABLE DISHES

There is an art to making a salad. With a little imagination one of the simplest and freshest of culinary collations may be transformed from a dull selection of lettuce, cucumber and tomato to a delight of varying flavours and textures, blended together with a dressing to drool for!

To Chill or not to Chill?

Is that a bit over the top? Well, I don't think so! Salads can be so varied that there really is no excuse at all for producing the same old combination of vegetables day after day. Nine times out of ten a salad is served cold but do remember that chilled is not always best. Think of delicious concoctions eaten abroad or on holiday – a Greek tomato salad enjoyed in the Mediterranean sunshine oozes with flavour to an extent which is seldom matched in more temperate zones. This is partly due to the natural ripening of the tomatoes by the sun, but also to the fact that such dishes are usually served at room temperature, allowing their flavours to shine through. Yes, do store or chill salads in the refrigerator, but I really do feel that they benefit from standing for 30 minutes in the kitchen before serving.

Salads play a very important part in the Vegetarian diet so experiment, incorporating wildly differing flavours, textures and colours. Never add the dressing to a green salad until just before serving – the leaves start to become slimy and do not store well once the dressing is added.

A Simple Lunch or a Special Treat?

Salads are a rich source of vitamins and minerals. With nuts, pulse vegetables or lentils added they also contribute protein to the diet. One of my favourite lunches is a large plate of Caesar Salad, now an international standard and originally created by Caesar Cardini for his restaurant in Tijuana, Mexico. It is simply a crisp lettuce, a Sweet Romaine or a Cos, with freshly grated Parmesan cheese, garlic flavoured croutons and a dressing of lightly cooked egg, olive oil, lemon juice, salt and pepper (with more garlic if you dare!). Nothing could be simpler or more satisfying.

An Ever Increasing Variety of Ingredients

Over the last fifteen to twenty years our ability to make interesting salads has been greatly improved by the wide selection of ingredients that are now available to us through greengrocers and supermarkets. When I was a girl I don't think we ever had sweet peppers at home but this vegetable is now considered commonplace. Lettuces are no longer round and limp: this is where the designer imagery of salads begins. Leaves are available in green or red, or even green tinged with red and how popular these varieties have become!

Dressing Up!

Once you have selected the best ingredients for your salad (and there is no question that the quality of these will govern the success of the final dish), choose your dressing. The most adaptable is a vinaigrette and my basic recipe for this is to mix two parts of extra virgin olive oil with one part of vinegar, made up of a mixture of sherry and white wine vinegars, mixed with a teaspoon of dry mustard or a tablespoon of French mustard, salt, pepper and sugar to taste. Creamy mayonnaise may be flavoured with so many delicious ingredients to make stunningly different dressings, such as blue cheese, lime zest and chopped tarragon, and curry paste. These are all, however, powerful in flavour and should only be used on salads that they will complement and not drown.

Down with School Dinners!

The most enduring memory of primary school days for me is the smell of over-cooked cabbage! I am certain that many generations have had their attitude towards vegetables severely misguided by the efforts of the school cooks of yesteryear.

Vegetables are now often dramatically undercooked, to retain more of the precious vitamins and minerals of which they are such a rich source, and to keep their colour and texture. I personally cannot abide broccoli which I can't get my fork into or potatoes still hard in the middle. Why should we be surprised when we have vegetables cooked well in restaurants? It is much better to enjoy your vegetables, to your own taste, at home!

A Dish in their Own Right

Vegetables are not simply accompaniments to main courses. With their rich diversity of flavours, colours and textures they demand experimentation, exploring the fun of turning them into dishes in their own right. After the first few joyous weeks of runner beans straight from the garden, how I appreciate a few recipes for serving them with tomato sauce or chopped mushrooms and cream! Suddenly they are new and exciting all over again! A light dressing of olive oil over freshly cooked vegetables just before serving enhances the flavours and brings them to glory. Experiment with sauces and stuffings for your vegetables but do think carefully about what goes with what. Too many flavours can spoil the dish.

SPROUTED ADUKI BEAN SALAD

Serve this as a side salad, or add cubes of cheese and serve with crusty bread, as a light meal.

Serves 4

INGREDIENTS
1 cucumber
1 green pepper
225g/8oz sprouted aduki beans
90g/3oz toasted peanuts

Dressing
3 tbsps sesame oil
2 tbsps white wine vinegar
1 tbsp shoyu sauce (Japanese soy sauce)
1 tsp brown sugar
Freshly ground black pepper to taste

Chop the cucumber into bite-sized chunks. Cut the pepper in half, de-seed and cut into pieces. Place the cucumber, pepper and beansprouts in a serving dish. Whisk the oil, vinegar, shoyu and sugar together until the sugar has dissolved, then add pepper to taste. Mix the dressing carefully into the salad and serve at once.

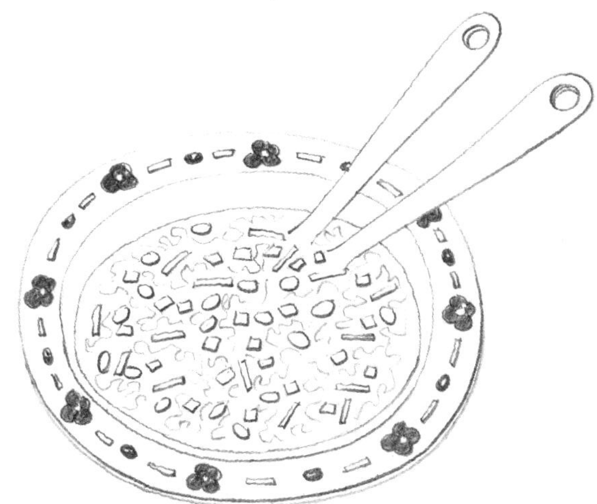

SALAD OF WILD MUSHROOMS AND ARTICHOKES

More and more varieties of mushrooms are now available in supermarkets and greengrocers; some even sell packs of mixed mushrooms. I love looking for wild mushrooms in the country but always go with someone who knows their mushrooms– mistakes can be upsetting.

Serves 4

INGREDIENTS

2-3 artichoke hearts, depending on size
1 slice lemon
1 bay leaf
6 black peppercorns
225g/8oz mixed wild mushrooms, eg shiitake or oyster, sliced
2 tbsps vegetable oil
Radicchio, iceberg lettuce and watercress leaves, mixed
2 tbsps freshly chopped chives
90ml/3fl oz olive oil
2 tbsps white wine vinegar
1 tbsp Dijon mustard
Salt and freshly ground black pepper
Sprigs fresh dill or chervil, to garnish

Trim the pointed leaves off the artichokes with a sharp knife. Remove the stems. Place the lemon slice, bay leaf and peppercorns in a saucepan of water and bring to the boil. Add the artichokes and cook for 30 to 40 minutes or until tender and the bottom leaves pull away easily. Stand each artichoke upside-down to drain completely.

Slice the mushrooms. Heat the vegetable oil in a frying pan and fry the mushrooms for 5 minutes until just tender. Set aside. Tear the salad leaves into small pieces and place in a bowl with the chives. Whisk together the olive oil, vinegar, mustard and seasoning with a fork or small whisk until the dressing is thick and pale in colour.

Remove the leaves from the drained artichokes and arrange them attractively on plates with the leaf salad over them. Cut away and discard the fluffy 'chokes' from the artichoke hearts, then trim the hearts and cut into pieces. Mix the artichoke hearts and mushrooms with about half of the dressing. Spoon equal amounts onto each plate. Garnish with sprigs of dill or chervil and serve the remaining dressing separately.

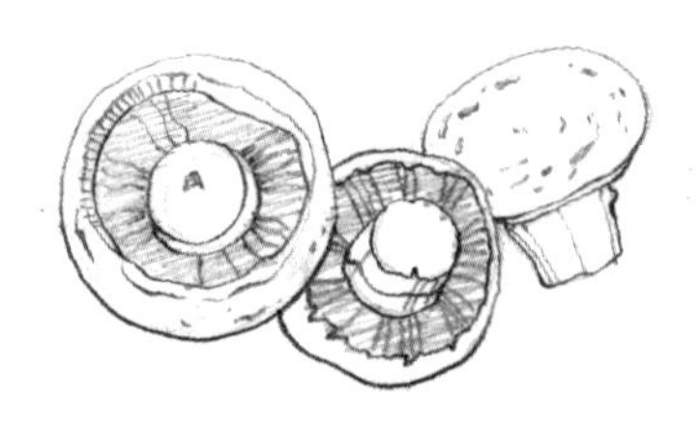

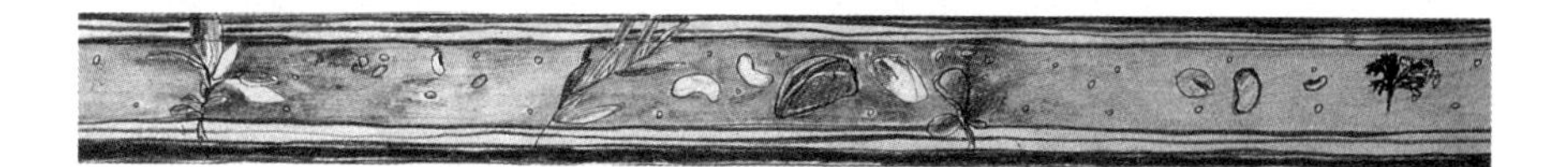

SEELI SALAD

An unusual and colourful coleslaw which would make a fine centrepiece for a buffet. The dressing could be very mildly flavoured with blue cheese.

Serves 4-6

Ingredients

1 large red cabbage
1 green pepper, deseeded and chopped
½ small pineapple, peeled and finely chopped
2 medium oranges, broken into segments
6 spring onions, finely chopped
3 sticks celery, chopped
90g/3oz hazelnuts, roughly chopped
90g/3oz sprouted aduki beans

Dressing

120ml/4fl oz mayonnaise
60ml/2fl oz Greek yogurt
Salt and freshly ground black pepper
Parsley to garnish

Remove any tough or discoloured outer leaves from the cabbage, then remove the base so that the cabbage will stand upright, and cut about a quarter off the top. Using a sharp knife, scoop out the inside of the cabbage leaving a 6mm/¼ inch thick shell. Set the shell aside.

Discard any tough pieces and shred the remaining cabbage very finely. Place in a large bowl together with the pepper, pineapple, orange segments, spring onions, celery, hazelnuts and bean sprouts. Mix the mayonnaise, yogurt and seasonings together and carefully fold into the vegetables and fruit. Pile the mixture into the cabbage shell and place on a serving dish. Garnish with parsley.

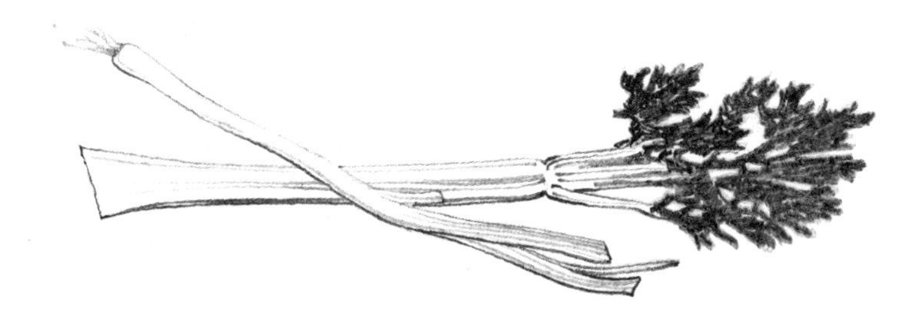

CARROT AND CELERY SALAD

This is another unusual salad variation on coleslaw. Add chopped hard boiled eggs and a few chives to make it more substantial.

Serves 4

Ingredients
225g/8oz carrots
120g/4oz celery
1 red pepper
90g/3oz walnuts
4 tbsps sweetcorn
1 tsp paprika
½ tsp chilli powder or a few drops of chilli sauce
4 tbsps French dressing

Scrub the carrots, then dice them. Slice the celery finely. Remove the core and seeds from the pepper and then dice the flesh. Place the carrots, celery and pepper in a serving bowl and add the walnuts and sweetcorn. Mix the paprika and chilli powder into the French dressing and pour over the salad. Toss well and refrigerate for 30 minutes. Toss again before serving.

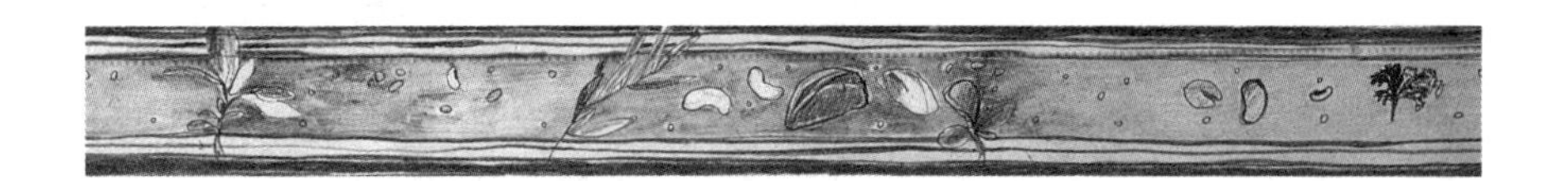

SPINACH SALAD

Use young tender leaves of spinach for salads. I frequently use spinach leaves in place of lettuce – they add an extra pepperiness to the salad bowl.

Serves 4-6

INGREDIENTS
460g/1lb spinach
1 medium red cabbage
1 medium onion
120g/4oz apricots
6 tbsps French dressing
60g/2oz toasted sunflower seeds

Wash the spinach and drain well. Remove the outer leaves and core of the cabbage then shred finely. Slice the onion finely and cut the apricots into slivers. Tear the spinach leaves into bite-sized pieces and place in a serving dish. Add the cabbage, onion and apricots. Pour the dressing over the salad and mix together thoroughly. Sprinkle with sunflower seeds and serve.

CUCUMBER AND PINEAPPLE SALAD

This is an excellent salad to serve with a green salad, providing contrasting flavours and textures. It is very bright and refreshing.

Serves 4

INGREDIENTS
1 tbsp raisins
2 tbsps pineapple juice
280g/10oz cucumber
1 red pepper
175g/6oz pineapple
3 tbsps French dressing
1 tsp freshly chopped mint
2 tsps sesame seeds

Soak the raisins in the pineapple juice for at least half an hour. Slice the cucumber finely, then cut the pepper in half, de-seed, remove the core and chop the flesh finely. Chop the pineapple into cubes.

Arrange the cucumber on a serving dish. Mix the pepper, pineapple and raisins together and pile into the centre of the cucumber. Mix the mint with the French dressing and pour over the salad just before serving. Sprinkle the sesame seeds over the top.

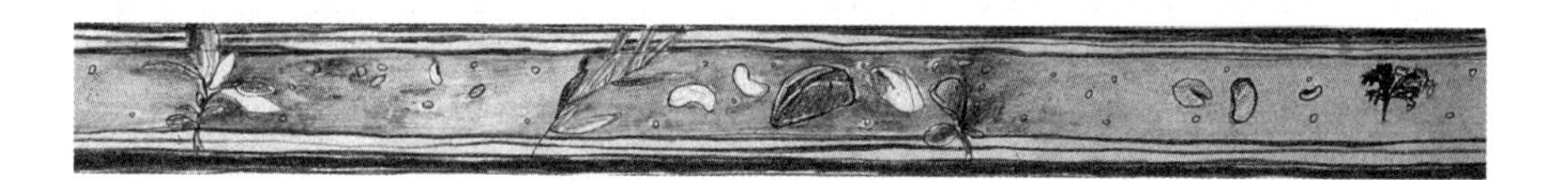

BAVARIAN POTATO SALAD

Serve with thinly sliced cheese and a cabbage salad. Potato salad always makes me think of exhibitions that I used to attend in Cologne, where standard lunchtime fare was potato salad and mustard.

Serves 4-6

INGREDIENTS
900g/2lbs tiny new potatoes
4 tbsps olive oil
4 spring onions, finely chopped
1 clove garlic, crushed
2 tbsps freshly chopped dill, or 1 tbsp dried
2 tbsp wine vinegar
½ tsp sugar
salt and freshly ground black pepper
2 tbsps freshly chopped parsley

Wash the potatoes but do not peel them. Place them in a pan, cover with water and boil until just tender. While the potatoes are cooking, heat the olive oil in a frying pan and cook the spring onions and garlic for 2-3 minutes until they have softened. Add the dill and cook gently for a further minute, then add the wine vinegar and sugar, and stir until the sugar melts. Remove from the heat and add a little seasoning. Drain the potatoes and pour the dressing over them while they are still hot. Allow to cool and sprinkle with the chopped parsley before serving.

MARINATED CARROT SALAD

This is best left to stand for 6-8 hours. If you should leave it overnight do stir it first thing in the morning, to help blend the flavours evenly.

Serves 4-5

Ingredients
460g/1lb carrots
1 medium onion
1 medium green pepper
Dressing
120ml/4fl oz tomato juice
120ml/4fl oz olive oil
120ml/4fl oz cider vinegar
2 tsps brown sugar
1 tsp dry mustard power
Salt and freshly ground black pepper

Peel the carrots and cut them into matchsticks. Place in a pan, cover with water, bring to the boil and simmer for 4-5 minutes. Drain and allow to cool a little. Slice the onion finely into rings, and cut the pepper into strips.

Mix together the dressing ingredients until well blended. Combine the carrots with the onion and pepper and pour the dressing over the top. Marinate for 6-8 hours, stirring occasionally. Serve garnished with chopped parsley and lemon slices.

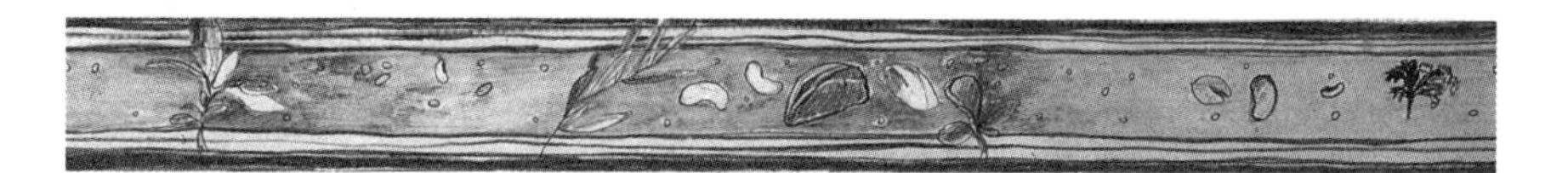

LOLLO ROSSO SALAD

Lollo Rosso is my favourite of the 'designer lettuces' – it is colourful and not at all bitter in flavour.

Serves 4

INGREDIENTS
½ Lollo Rosso lettuce
3 medium tomatoes, diced
1 red pepper, chopped
1 green pepper, chopped
3 sticks celery, diced
⅓ cucumber, diced
175g/6oz vegetarian Cheshire cheese
16 black olives

Dressing
1 tbsp tarragon vinegar
3 tbsps olive oil

Wash the lettuce and dry it well. Break into pieces and place it in a large bowl. Add the tomatoes, pepper, celery, cucumber and cheese. Mix together the vinegar and olive oil, and pour over the salad, then toss. Divide the salad between 4 individual dishes and place 4 olives on the top of each serving.

CUCUMBER SALAD

Fennel gives a deep, aniseed flavour to this unusual salad – you could use a head of celery if you do not like fennel.

Serves 6

Ingredients

1 whole cucumber
1 red apple
1 medium-sized bulb fennel, reserve feathery leaves for decoration
1 tbsp pine nuts

Dressing

3 tbsps corn oil or sunflower oil
2 tbsps cider vinegar
2 tbsps freshly chopped dill or 1 tsp dried dill
1 tsp caraway seeds
1-2 tsps paprika
Salt and freshly ground black pepper to taste

Wash the cucumber but do not peel. Slice very thinly and place the slices in a sieve. Leave to drain for about 20 minutes. Wash and core the apple, then slice thinly. Wash and trim the fennel, removing the tough outer leaves and stem, then slice finely. Combine all the ingredients for the dressing and mix well. Mix the dressing with the drained cucumber slices, apple and fennel. Place the salad in the refrigerator or keep in a cool place for about an hour before serving.

GLAZED VEGETABLES

This is a delicious way of serving almost any vegetable – I cook chestnuts in a similar way at Christmas. Glazed Vegetables make a super filling for baked potatoes.

Serves 4

INGREDIENTS

30g/1oz butter or vegetable margarine
1 tbsp muscovado sugar
4 tbsps vegetable stock
2 carrots, peeled and cut into sticks
2 salsify, peeled and cut into rounds
2 turnips, peeled and cut into wedges
175g/6oz pickling onions or shallots, peeled and cut in half if large
120g/4oz large mushrooms, quartered
1 tsp freshly chopped rosemary or thyme
Salt and freshly ground black pepper
2 tsps Dijon mustard
Fresh rosemary, to garnish

Melt the butter or margarine, add the sugar and stock, and stir until the sugar is dissolved. Add the carrots, salsify, turnips and onions or shallots and cook over a low heat, stirring frequently, until beginning to soften – this will take about 10 minutes. Add the mushrooms, herbs, seasoning and mustard. Cover and cook over a low heat for 10 minutes or until all the vegetables are tender, stirring occasionally. Serve garnished with fresh rosemary.

SESAME STIR-FRY

Don't forget to have everything prepared before starting to cook this stir-fry. Cut all the vegetables into similarly sized pieces for even cooking. Serve with rice or noodles for 4 people, or as a complete meal for 2.

Serves 4

INGREDIENTS

2 tbsps vegetable oil
1 tsp grated ginger root
15g/½oz sesame seeds
60g/2oz mangetout
1 stick celery, sliced
2 ears of baby corn, cut in half lengthways
60g/2oz water chestnuts, thinly sliced
30g/1oz mushrooms, thinly sliced
2 spring onions, sliced diagonally
½ red pepper, seeded and sliced
120g/4oz Chinese leaves, washed and shredded
120g/4oz bean sprouts
1 tbsp cornflour
2 tbsps soy sauce
1 tbsp sherry
½ tsp sesame oil
4 tbsps water

Heat the vegetable oil in a wok or large frying pan and fry the ginger and sesame seeds for 1 minute. Add the mangetout, celery, baby corn, water chestnuts, mushrooms, onions and pepper; stir-fry for 5 minutes or until the vegetables are beginning to soften slightly. Add the Chinese leaves and bean sprouts and stir over the heat for 1 to 2 minutes. Combine the remaining ingredients in a small bowl, then add to the pan. Continue cooking until the sauce thickens slightly. Serve immediately.

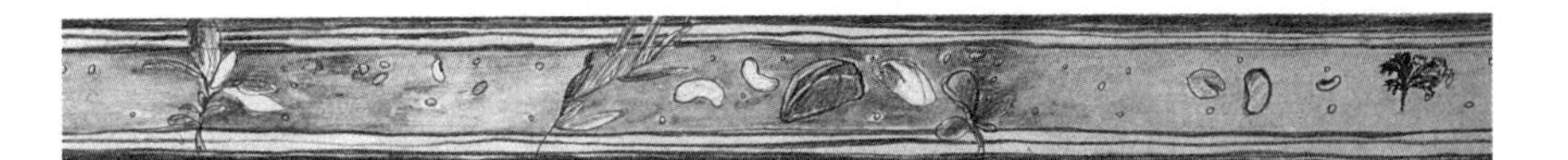

BUTTER BEAN, LEMON & FENNEL SALAD

I love this salad with its unusual combination of flavours and textures. Use a zester to pare the rind from the lemon to avoid any of the bitter pith, which could taint the otherwise bright flavours.

Serves 4

INGREDIENTS

225g/8oz butter beans, soaked overnight and drained
1 lemon
1 large bulb fennel, thinly sliced – reserve the green tops for garnish
4 tbsps vegetable or soya oil
Pinch unrefined sugar
Salt and freshly ground black pepper
Lettuce and radicchio leaves, to serve

Place the butter beans in a large pan with enough water to cover by 2.5cm/1 inch and bring to the boil. Boil rapidly for 10 minutes, then reduce the heat and simmer gently for about 2 hours or until the beans are tender. Drain well.

Pare the rind from the lemon taking care not to include any white pith. Cut the rind into very thin strips and blanch for 5 minutes in boling water. Remove from the water with a draining spoon. Add the fennel to the water (reserve the green tops) and blanch for 2 minutes – the fennel should be just cooked but still crunchy to the bite. Squeeze the juice from the lemons and place in a bowl with the blanched lemon rind, oil, sugar and seasoning – whisk together with a fork. Chop the reserved fennel tops and add to the dressing. Mix the cooked beans and fennel in a large bowl, then add the dressing and toss the salad to coat the vegetables. Serve on a bed of lettuce and radicchio leaves.

CAULIFLOWER AND CABBAGE IN WALNUT AND BLUE CHEESE SAUCE

Bored with Cauliflower Cheese? This unusual variation revives an old favourite, adding more than a touch of flair with the cabbage, walnuts and blue cheese. Delicious on its own or as a vegetable side dish for up to eight people.

Serves 4

INGREDIENTS
1 cauliflower
1 small green cabbage
60g/2oz butter
60g/2oz wholemeal flour
570ml/1 pint milk
120g/4oz vegetarian Cheddar cheese, grated
90g/3oz walnuts, finely chopped
Salt and freshly ground black pepper
Pinch ground nutmeg

Wash the cauliflower and break into small florets. Wash and thickly shred the cabbage. Bring a saucepan of water to the boil and add the cauliflower, cook for 5 minutes then add the cabbage. Cook for a further 5 minutes or until both the vegetables are just tender.

Meanwhile make the sauce: melt the butter in a small saucepan and stir in the flour. Cook for 1 minute. Remove from the heat and gradually add the milk, stirring well. Return to the heat and cook gently, stirring continuously, until the sauce boils and thickens. Add the cheese and walnuts and cook until the cheese melts. Season the sauce with salt and pepper and a little nutmeg.

When the vegetables are cooked, drain well and transfer to a serving dish. Pour the sauce over and sprinkle with a little more nutmeg. Serve immediately.

COURGETTE ROLLS

This is an elegant way of serving a side vegetable, but it works best (and is easiest to manage!) if the courgettes are large in width not length.

Serves 4

Ingredients
2 carrots, peeled and cut into matchsticks
2 green peppers, seeded and cut into strips
4 spring onions, trimmed
Salt and freshly ground black pepper
1 tsp freshly chopped basil or thyme
2 large, fat courgettes
Juice 1 lemon
Bunch fresh chives
30g/1oz butter or vegetable margarine
2 tbsps vegetable oil

Cook the carrots and green peppers for 5 minutes in boiling water until just softened. Drain well and place in a mixing bowl. Shred the spring onions lengthways and add to the carrots. Season the vegetables and add the chopped herbs, toss well.

Trim the courgettes and carefully cut lengthways into very thin slices. Sprinkle with lemon juice. Lay out the courgette strips on the work surface and arrange bundles of the vegetables in piles across them.

Carefully roll up the courgette strips around the vegetables. Secure them by tying at each end with chives.

Melt the butter or margarine with oil and sauté the vegetable bundles for 10 minutes, turning frequently until the courgettes are cooked and the vegetables are hot. Serve immediately.

BROCCOLI AND CAULIFLOWER MOULD WITH SALSA

A salsa is a spicy tomato sauce served in Mexico, and is usually quite chunky with pieces of pepper and tomato. It makes a colourful and unusual salad when served with a cold mould of cauliflower and broccoli. This would look good as part of a cold buffet.

Serves 4-6

Ingredients
1 small cauliflower
225g/8oz broccoli
3 tbsps walnut oil
1 tbsp white wine vinegar
1 tsp mustard powder
1 small clove garlic, crushed
Salt and freshly ground black pepper

Salsa
1 tbsp olive oil
1 green chilli, seeded and finely chopped
5 tomatoes, skinned, seeded and chopped
1 green pepper, seeded and finely chopped
1 tsp ground cumin
4 spring onions, finely chopped

Tomato quarters, to garnish

Divide the cauliflower into florets and discard the thick stalks. Trim the broccoli to within 5cm/2 inches of the florets. Bring a large saucepan of water to the boil and add the cauliflower, cook for 5 minutes then add the broccoli and cook for a further 10 minutes, drain well.

Combine the walnut oil, vinegar, mustard, garlic, salt and pepper in a small bowl and whisk with a fork. Pour the dressing over the warm vegetables and toss until well coated, taking care not to break up the vegetables. Carefully arrange the cauliflower and broccoli in a deep sided 570ml/1 pint bowl, alternating the vegetables and pressing them together to push them firmly into the bowl shape. Cover with a plate and weight lightly. Leave to cool before refrigerating, ready for serving.

Heat the olive oil in a small pan and fry the chilli for 2 to 3 minutes. Add the tomatoes, peppers, cumin and spring onions and cook for a further 5 minutes. Season with salt and pepper then allow to cool before chilling.

To serve, carefully turn out the cauliflower mould onto an inverted serving plate and spoon salsa around the base. Garnish with tomato quarters.

SWEET AND SOUR CABBAGE WITH APPLE

Braised red cabbage is always a popular vegetable and I certainly prefer it to pickled cabbage. This recipe has a most interesting combination of flavours.

Serves 4

INGREDIENTS
1.4kg/3lb red cabbage
1 onion, chopped
1 cooking apple, peeled, cored and chopped
60g/2oz light muscovado sugar
1 tsp ground mixed spice
Salt and freshly ground black pepper
150ml/¼ pint vegetable stock
2 tbsps red wine vinegar
1 tbsp walnut oil
1 dessert apple, cored and chopped
2 tsps freshly chopped parsley

Quarter, core and shred the cabbage and layer in a large saucepan with the onion and cooking apple. Sprinkle with the sugar and mixed spice and season with salt and pepper. Add the stock and vinegar and stir well. Cover and cook gently for 45 minutes, stirring occasionally. Just before the end of the cooking time, heat the walnut oil in a frying pan and cook the dessert apple for 2 to 3 minutes to partially soften. Remove from the heat and stir in the parsley. Transfer the cabbage to a serving dish and garnish with the apple and parsley mixture.

SPINACH WITH BLUE CHEESE AND WALNUTS

This is almost a hot salad and has a strong, dramatic blend of flavours. Work quickly, so that you serve the dish before the cheese melts too much.

Serves 4

INGREDIENTS
900g/2lbs spinach, washed
30g/1oz butter or vegetable margarine
Pinch nutmeg
Salt and freshly ground black pepper
120g/4oz walnuts, roughly chopped
120g/4oz vegetarian blue cheese, crumbled

Remove any tough stalks from the spinach and place in a saucepan with just the water left clinging to the leaves after washing. Cook over a low heat for 5 to 10 minutes, until the spinach wilts. Place the spinach between two plates and press firmly to remove excess water. Melt the butter or margarine in the pan and stir in the spinach with the nutmeg and seasoning. Stir well to coat evenly. Quickly add the walnuts and cheese, tossing the ingredients together lightly. Serve before the cheese melts too much.

BRAISED FENNEL

I always find fennel a most refreshing vegetable with its slightly aniseed flavour. I've got lovage in the garden but it is not easy to buy it in the shops – if unavailable, use a few leafy fennel tops to flavour the sliced vegetables.

Serves 4

INGREDIENTS

2 large bulbs fennel
2 tsps freshly chopped lovage
120ml/4fl oz vegetable stock
2 tbsps sherry
½ tsp celery seed or celery seasoning

With a sharp knife cut away the thick root end of the fennel bulbs. Trim away the upper stalks and reserve a little of the green top for a garnish. Slice the bulbs thickly, separating the strips from each other as you cut. Place the fennel, lovage, stock and sherry in a saucepan and bring slowly to the boil. Reduce the heat and simmer gently for about 15 minutes or until the fennel is tender. Drain and transfer to a warm serving dish. Sprinkle with celery seeds or seasoning and garnish with fennel tops.

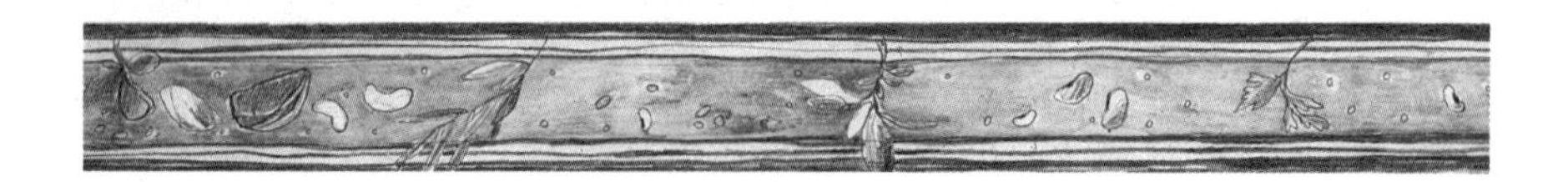

GREEN BEANS WITH MUSTARD SAUCE

Mustard sauce really emphasises the flavour of green beans and the pale yellow of the sauce sets off the colour of the beans – a winning combination!

Serves 4

INGREDIENTS
460g/1lb green beans, trimmed
150ml/¼ pint vegetable stock
Approximately 150ml/¼ pint milk
30g/1oz butter or vegetable margarine
30g/1oz plain flour
1 tsp dry mustard
Salt and ground white pepper
Freshly chopped chives, to garnish

Cut the beans into 5cm/2 inch lengths. Bring the stock to the boil and add the beans then simmer gently for 10 minutes or until tender. Drain, reserving the cooking liquid. Transfer the beans to a serving dish and keep warm.

Make the liquid up to 280ml/½ pint with milk. Melt the butter or margarine in a pan and stir in the flour and mustard. Cook for 1 minute. Remove from the heat and gradually add the stock and milk, stirring well. Cook slowly until the sauce boils and thickens, stirring continuously, and season well. Pour the sauce over the beans and garnish with chopped chives.

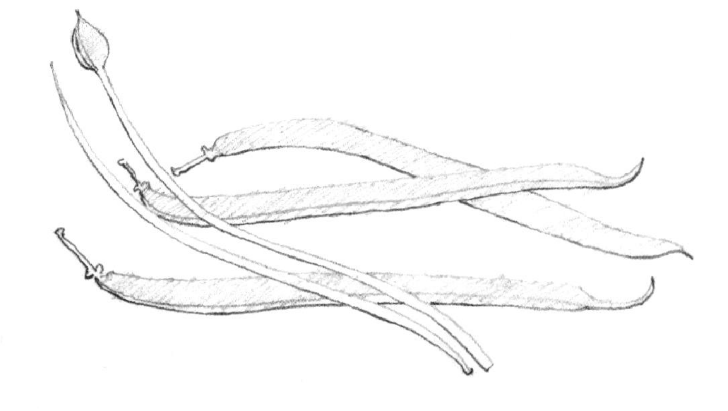

RED HOT SLAW

Hot and spicy as its name suggests, Red Hot Slaw is an unusual salad to serve with other highly flavoured foods.

Serves 4

INGREDIENTS
- 460g/1lb red cabbage, cored and shredded
- 2 red onions, sliced
- 1 small white daikon (mooli) radish, peeled and grated
- 4 tbsps mayonnaise
- 4 tbsps natural yogurt
- 2 tsps grated horseradish
- ½ tsp aniseed
- ½ tsp chilli powder

Combine the cabbage, onions and daikon radish in a large bowl. Mix the mayonnaise, yogurt, horseradish, aniseed and chilli powder in a small bowl and pour over the cabbage mixture. Toss until well coated then chill until ready to serve.

LEEKS PROVENÇALE

A basic Provençale sauce of tomatoes, garlic, and herbs goes well with most savoury dishes. With leeks it is exceptional.

Serves 4

INGREDIENTS

6 leeks, washed and trimmed
Salt
1 tbsp olive oil
2 cloves garlic, crushed
4 tomatoes, skinned, seeded and chopped
1 tsp dried thyme
2 tbsps freshly chopped parsley
4 tbsps dry white wine
Freshly ground black pepper
Sprigs of fresh parsley, to garnish

Cut the leeks into 5cm/2 inch pieces and cook for 10-15 minutes in lightly salted boiling water, until tender. Heat the oil in a small saucepan and fry the garlic until softened but not browned. Stir in the tomatoes, herbs and wine and simmer gently for 10 minutes until the tomatoes are soft, then season with salt and pepper.

Drain the cooked leeks and place in a serving dish with the tomato mixture, and toss to mix. Serve garnished with a sprig of parsley.

LIGHT LUNCHES & SUPPER DISHES

What's the difference between a light lunch dish and something more substantial? Well, that's a good question! I always think of a lunch or supper dish as a one course meal, to be served with just a little salad or a single fresh vegetable; something tasty and savoury but which is quick both to prepare and cook, and to eat.

Simple Preparation & Cooking

The benefits of such dishes are enormous for those who work all day and have little time during the week to indulge in creative hours in the kitchen. I work at home and am always pleased with simple dishes that I can prepare in the morning, almost whilst munching my muesli, and then just set aside until they need cooking around midday. An example of the perfect lunch dish for me is the Cheese Sandwich Soufflé on page 107. Left to stand throughout the morning the bread will absorb the eggy custard. It goes into the oven with no more attention required then, at the chosen time, there is lunch ready to be served with a couple of sliced tomatoes. The extra benefit of next-to-no washing up is also greatly appreciated in the middle of the working day!

Advance Preparation

Most of the recipes included in this chapter may be prepared in advance, ready for use when hunger strikes. Courgettes may be stuffed, nut roasts mixed and placed in their tins, and potato cakes and burgers shaped and chilled, ready for quick, shallow-frying when you are ready to eat. Quiches are also suitable for preparation in advance, but do not add the liquid filling until ready to bake, or the pastry will become soggy. Even vegetables for stir-fries may be peeled, chopped and stored in an air-tight box in the refrigerator until you are ready to cook them quickly in a wok or a frying pan.

One Large Meal a Day is Enough

Unless employed in a very physical job or profession, one large meal a day is generally enough for anyone. The recipes that I have selected for this chapter are, therefore, fairly light or, in the case of nut loaves, quiches and flans, they enable you to have a smaller helping than you might expect for your main meal of the day. It is especially important in a vegetarian diet to select contrasting meals, trying not to eat the same main ingredient twice. Beans are fine once a day, but eating them at lunchtime and for dinner might well lead to a dull diet and a certain thickening of the waistline!

It is true to say that anyone who is really hungry will eat anything, even the most unappealing and unappetising food. I have so often arrived home late at night and just eaten whatever was there and ready, rather than making what I actually needed. A peanut butter sandwich is okay (and highly nutritious), but a slice of quiche, a vegetable stir-fry or a grain salad provides a better light meal just before bed.

Do I Need a Pudding?

Perhaps that should read *do I want a pudding?!* For a light lunch or a supper the answer is probably 'no' but it is always so comforting and reassuring to have just a little yogurt or fruit. This is also a good way of balancing your meal, ensuring a good mix of proteins, fibre, fruit and vegetables. I always find an orange to be the most refreshing fruit, especially at lunchtime. Just as a glass of orange juice is a good start to the day at breakfast time, an orange after lunch gets me ready for an afternoon's work. Of course, there are plenty of occasions where I might prefer a helping of Sticky Toffee Pudding and Butterscotch Sauce, followed by an afternoon nap, but an orange ensures a more productive afternoon!

What About a Drink?

Yes, please! I like to have a drink with most meals and a glass of chilled mineral water, some elderflower cordial or a little fruit juice are all fine, but an alcoholic drink is probably my first choice! I do find that wine and I get on best in the evenings, rather than at lunchtime, so I tend to go for a beer in the middle of the day. As with other foodstuffs I like to choose a drink which has been produced in a traditional way from prime ingredients but, as with all things, do remember the adage *moderation in all things!*

SMOKED TOFU SALAD

This is a filling salad to serve as a main course with baked potatoes. Tofu, or bean curd, is rich in protein and very valuable in the vegetarian diet. It is available smoked in most healthfood shops.

Serves 4-6

INGREDIENTS
225g/8oz broccoli florets
120g/4oz mushrooms
120g/4oz pineapple
4 tbsps sweetcorn
4-6 tbsps French dressing
225g/8oz smoked tofu, cut into cubes

Cover the broccoli florets with boiling water and leave to stand for 5 minutes. Drain and allow to cool. Wipe the mushrooms with a clean cloth and slice thinly, and cut the pineapple into small pieces.

Place the broccoli, mushrooms, pineapple and sweetcorn in a large bowl together with the French dressing, and toss carefully. Divide the salad between 4 individual dishes and place the smoked tofu on top. Serve at once.

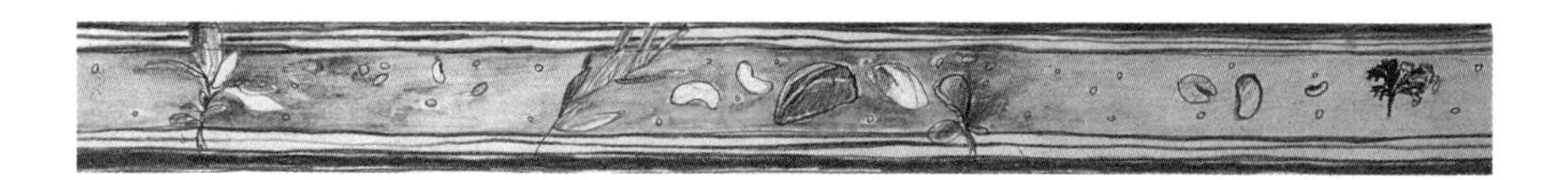

STUFFED COURGETTES

Asafetida powder is used to season food and bring out it's flavour - use salt and pepper if you prefer. This is an unusually spicy filling for courgettes.

Serves 4

INGREDIENTS
4 medium courgettes
2 tbsps olive oil
1 onion, very finely chopped
120g/4oz carrots, grated
½ tsp paprika
1 tsp cumin seeds
¼ tsp turmeric
¼ tsp asafetida powder (optional)
120g/4oz creamed coconut, grated

Preheat the oven to 190°C/375°F/Gas Mark 5. Wash the courgettes and cut in half lengthways. Using a teaspoon, remove the flesh leaving about a 5mm/¼ inch shell. Chop the flesh finely.

Heat the oil and sauté the onion for a few minutes. Add the carrots, courgette flesh and spices and cook, stirring frequently, for a further 5 minutes until softened. Remove from the heat and stir in the creamed coconut. Divide the mixture between the courgette shells, making sure that it covers the exposed part of the flesh. Place in a greased ovenproof casserole, cover and cook for 45 minutes until the courgette shells are soft. Serve immediately.

CARROT AND CASHEW NUT ROAST

This loaf has a delicious nutty flavour which is stronger when the nut roast is eaten cold. Cashew nuts are my favourites!

Serves 6

INGREDIENTS

1 medium onion, chopped
1-2 cloves garlic, crushed
1 tbsp olive or sunflower oil
460g/1lb carrots, cooked and mashed
225g/8oz cashew nuts, ground
120g/4oz wholewheat breadcrumbs
1 tbsp light tahini
1½ tsps caraway seeds
1 tsp yeast extract
Juice of ½ a lemon
75ml/2½fl oz stock from the carrots or water
Salt and freshly ground black pepper

Preheat the oven to 180°C/350°F/Gas Mark 4. Fry the onion and garlic in the oil until soft, then mix with all the other ingredients and season to taste. Place the mixture in a greased 900g/2lb loaf tin, and cover with foil then bake for 1 hour. Remove the foil and bake for a further 10 minutes. Leave to stand in the baking tin for at least 10 minutes before turning out.

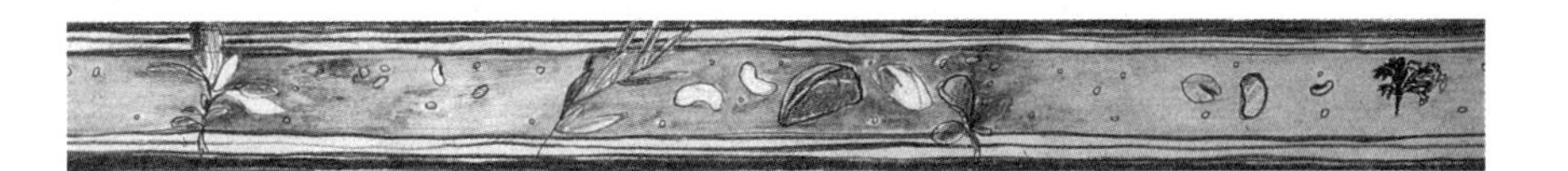

VALENCIA LOAF

I suggest you break the spaghetti into short lengths before cooking it for this recipe; it makes the loaf easier to cut neatly. Make an apple sauce, spiced with mace or nutmeg, to serve with it.

Serves 6

INGREDIENTS
2 large onions
90ml/3fl oz oil
90g/3oz spaghetti
60g/2oz wholewheat breadcrumbs
225g/8oz ground almonds
2 free-range eggs, beaten
1 tsp dried sage
Rind and juice of 1 lemon
Salt and freshly ground black pepper

Preheat the oven to 190°C/375°F/Gas Mark 5. Peel and slice the onions and fry in the oil for 10 minutes over a low heat. Cook the spaghetti in boiling, salted water until *al dente*, i.e. cooked but still with a bite. Drain the spaghetti and mix with the onion, breadcrumbs, almonds, eggs, sage, lemon juice and rind. Season to taste, then spoon into a greased and lined 900g/2lb loaf tin. Cover and bake for 1 hour. Turn out onto a serving dish and remove the lining paper carefully. Cut into thick slices and serve immediately.

SWEETCORN AND PARSNIP FLAN

The sweetcorn and parsnip filling of this flan is creamy and mild in flavour, so serve with a herby green salad, sprinkled with fresh chives.

Serves 6

INGREDIENTS

Base

90g/3oz soft margarine
175g/6oz wholewheat flour
1 tsp baking powder
Pinch of salt
4-6 tbsps ice-cold water
1 tbsp oil

Filling

1 large onion, finely chopped
1 clove garlic, crushed
30g/1oz butter or margarine
2 large parsnips, steamed and roughly mashed
175g/6oz sweetcorn, frozen or canned
1 tsp dried basil
Salt and freshly ground black pepper
3 free-range eggs
150ml/¼ pint milk
90g/3oz grated vegetarian Cheddar cheese
1 medium tomato, sliced

Preheat the oven to 220°C/425°F/Gas Mark 7. Rub the margarine into the flour, baking powder and salt until the mixture resembles fine breadcrumbs. Add the water and oil and work together lightly. The mixture should be fairly moist. Cover and chill for half an hour. Roll out the pastry and use to line a 25cm/10 inch flan tin. Prick the bottom and bake blind for about 8 minutes. Reduce the oven temperature to 190°C/375°F/Gas Mark 5.

Meanwhile, cook the onion and garlic in the butter or margarine until soft and golden. Add the parsnips, sweetcorn and basil and season to taste. Beat the eggs and add the milk, then add to the vegetable mixture and stir over a low heat until just beginning to set. Pour into the flan base and top with the grated cheese and sliced tomato. Bake for 15-20 minutes or until the cheese is golden brown.

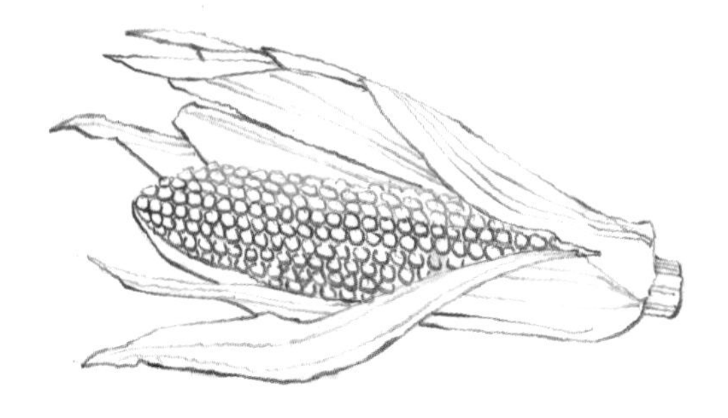

QUICK VEGETABLE CHILLI

Vegetable Chilli could be served with tortilla chips or in taco shells, with a salad garnish, as a change from rice. Make it as hot as you dare.

Serves 4

INGREDIENTS
2 large onions, sliced
1 tbsp olive oil
3-4 cloves garlic, crushed
1 tsp chilli powder
400g/14oz can tomatoes chopped
400g/14oz can red kidney beans
1 small red pepper, roughly chopped
1 medium courgette, cut into chunks
225g/8oz cauliflower florets
2 carrots, roughly chopped
2 tsps tomato purée
1 tsp dried basil
1 tsp dried oregano
150-280ml/¼-½ pint stock

Cook the onions in the oil until soft, add the garlic and cook for 1 minute, then stir in the chilli powder and cook for a further minute. Add the rest of the ingredients and simmer for 25-30 minutes. Serve on a bed of brown rice.

SAVOURY RICE CAKE

This is a substantial omelette, and a good way of using up left-over rice. It reminds me very much of Spanish Omelette, which is made with potato.

Serves 2-4

INGREDIENTS
1 medium onion, finely chopped
1 clove garlic, crushed
2 tbsps olive oil
1 tbsp freshly chopped thyme
1 red pepper, thinly sliced
1 green pepper, thinly sliced
4 free-range eggs, beaten
Salt and freshly ground black pepper
6 tbsps cooked brown rice
3 tbsps natural yogurt
90g/3oz vegetarian Cheddar cheese, grated

Fry the onion and garlic in the olive oil until soft, then add the thyme and peppers and fry gently for 4-5 minutes. Beat the eggs with the salt and pepper. Add the cooked rice to the thyme and peppers followed by the eggs. Cook over a moderate heat stirring from time to time, until the eggs are cooked underneath. Spoon the yogurt over the part-set eggs and sprinkle the cheese over the top. Place under a moderate grill and cook until puffed and golden. Serve immediately.

VEGETARIAN PAELLA

Paella originates from Spain so this recipe has lots of Mediterranean seasonings. Serve with crusty bread and a green salad.

Serves 4-6

INGREDIENTS
4 tbsps olive oil
1 large onion, chopped
2 cloves garlic, crushed
½ tsp paprika
340g/12oz long-grain brown rice
850ml/1½ pints stock
175ml/6fl oz dry white wine
400g/14oz can chopped tomatoes
1 tbsp tomato purée
½ tsp dried tarragon
1 tsp dried basil
1 tsp dried oregano
1 red pepper, seeded and roughly chopped
1 green pepper, seeded and roughly chopped
3 sticks celery, finely chopped
225g/8oz mushrooms, washed and sliced
60g/2oz mangetout, topped and tailed and cut into halves
120g/4oz frozen peas
60g/2oz cashew nut pieces
Salt and freshly ground black pepper
Lemon wedges and black olives for garnish

Heat the oil and fry the onion and garlic until soft. Add the paprika and rice and continue to cook for 4-5 minutes until the rice is transparent. Stir occasionally. Add the stock, wine, tomatoes, tomato purée and herbs and simmer for 10-15 minutes. Stir in the pepper, celery, mushrooms and mangetout and continue to cook for another 30 minutes, until the rice is cooked.

Add the peas, cashew nuts and seasoning to taste. Heat through and place on a large heated serving dish. Sprinkle the parsley over the top and garnish with lemon wedges and olives just before serving.

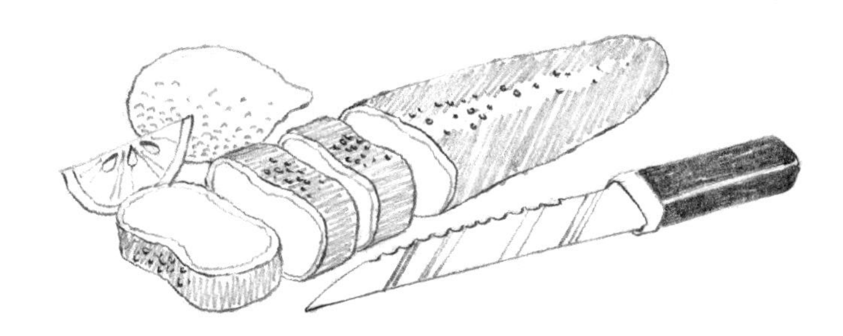

BULGAR RISOTTO

Bulgar, or cracked wheat, is quick to cook and makes a welcome change from rice for this easy lunch or supper dish. It requires only very brief cooking.

Serves 3-4

Ingredients

120g/4oz bulgar wheat
1 medium onion, finely chopped
2 sticks celery, finely chopped
1-2 cloves garlic, crushed
15g/½oz butter
1 small red pepper, diced
1 small green pepper, diced
½ tsp dried mixed herbs
60g/2oz peanuts, chopped
1 tsp vegetable extract dissolved in 60ml/2 fl oz boiling water
2 tsps shoyu sauce (Japanese soy sauce)
90g/3oz sweetcorn
90g/3oz peas
Salt and freshly ground black pepper
Juice of half a lemon

Place the bulgar wheat in a bowl and cover with boiling water. Leave for about 10 minutes, after which time the water will have been absorbed and the wheat will have swollen.

Meanwhile, place the onion, celery and garlic in a saucepan and cook for a few minutes in the butter. Add the peppers, herbs, nuts and vegetable extract, then simmer over a low heat for about 8 minutes. Add the bulgar wheat, shoyu, sweetcorn, peas and seasoning and mix together well. Continue cooking for a further 5 minutes, then add the lemon juice and transfer to a heated serving dish. Serve immediately.

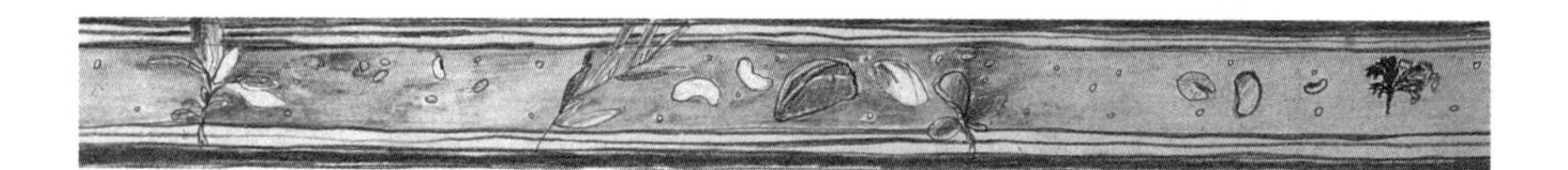

BUCKWHEAT SAVOURY

Buckwheat can be purchased either raw or roasted – the grains are called groats. The roasted variety has a slightly deeper flavour and crunchier texture.

Serves 4

INGREDIENTS
1 tbsp sultanas
1 medium onion, finely chopped
1-2 cloves garlic, crushed
2 sticks celery, finely chopped
3 tbsps oil
1-2 tsps garam masala
¼ tsp ground cumin
120g/4oz buckwheat
2 medium carrots, diced
1 small red pepper, diced
90g/3oz cashew nuts, roughly chopped
2 tsps tomato purée
1 tsp yeast extract or bouillon powder dissolved in 150ml/¼ pint boiling water
Salt and freshly ground black pepper
2 courgettes, cut into bite-sized pieces

Soak the sultanas in a little water for about 1 hour. Place the onion, garlic and celery in a saucepan with the oil and cook together for about 4 minutes. Add the garam masala and cumin and cook for a further minute, then add the remaining ingredients, except the sultanas and courgettes. Simmer for about 20 minutes or until the buckwheat is soft and chewy but do not allow the mixture to become too dry. Add the sultanas and courgettes and cook for a further 5 minutes. The courgettes should not be allowed to become too soft. Transfer to a heated dish and serve at once.

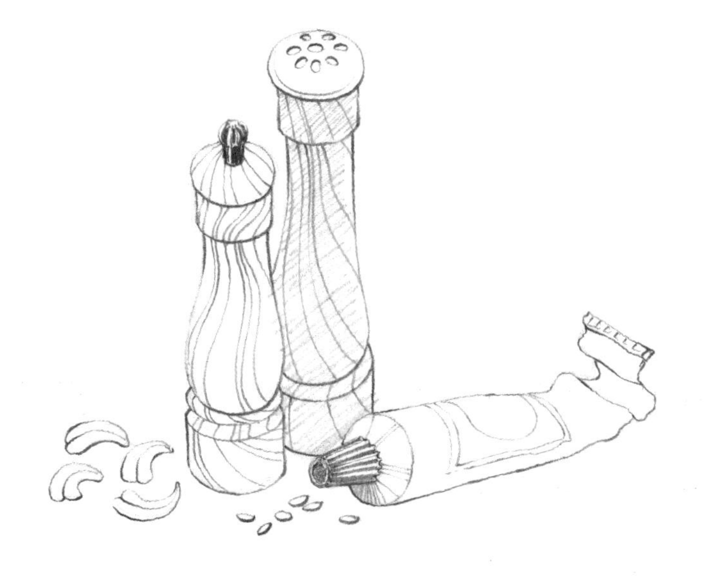

SWEET AND SOUR PEANUTS

Peanuts make this a highly nutritious dish – and what an unusual way to serve them! It tastes good, it does you good and is really quick and easy to prepare!

Serves4

Ingredients
90g/3oz light muscovado sugar
5 tbsps white wine vinegar
3 tbsps soy sauce
120ml/4fl oz vegetable stock
1 tbsp arrowroot
1 red pepper, seeded and sliced
120g/4oz bean sprouts
120g/4oz unsalted roasted peanuts
225g/8oz can bamboo shoots, drained and sliced

Combine the sugar, vinegar, soy sauce, vegetable stock and arrowroot in a saucepan. Heat gently, stirring all the time, until the mixture thickens slightly. Add the remaining ingredients and cook gently for 5 minutes or until the pepper strips are tender.

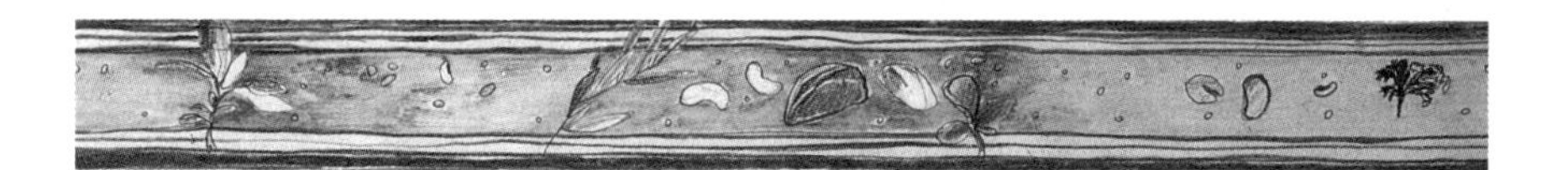

CHEESE SANDWICH SOUFFLÉ

This is not a real soufflé. An aunt of mine who hates cooking first showed me this dish – you can use any filling you like for the sandwiches.

Serves 4

INGREDIENTS

1 tbsp wholegrain mustard
8 slices wholemeal bread
2 tomatoes, sliced
175g/6oz vegetarian Cheddar cheese, grated
2 free-range eggs (size 2), beaten
570ml/1 pint milk
1 tsp dried basil
Salt and freshly ground black pepper
Parsley sprigs, to garnish

Preheat the oven to 180°C/350°F/Gas Mark 4. Spread equal amounts of mustard over four slices of bread. Arrange the tomato slices over the mustard-spread bread and sprinkle with the grated cheese, then use the remaining four slices of bread to cover the cheese. Place the cheese and tomato sandwiches in a shallow dish which they will just fit.

Beat together the eggs, milk and basil, season well. Pour over the bread and leave to stand for 30 minutes to allow the bread to soak up the milk mixture. Bake for 40-45 minutes or until set. Serve garnished with sprigs of parsley.

STIR-FRIED BEANS & SPROUTS

I think that aduki beans are very underrated; they have an attractive deep red colour and a very nutty flavour, whereas some other beans have very little flavour at all. The aduki beans may be cooked in advance and reheated from cold by adding them to the vegetables a minute or two before the bean sprouts.

Serves 4

INGREDIENTS

225g/8oz dried aduki beans, soaked overnight
2 tbsps vegetable oil
1 large onion, sliced
1 green pepper, seeded and sliced
225g/8oz bean sprouts
4 tbsps soy sauce

Drain the beans and place in a saucepan with enough water to cover them by 2.5cm/1 inch. Bring to the boil and boil rapidly for 10 minutes. Reduce the heat and simmer gently for about 30 minutes or until the beans are soft. Drain the beans and rinse in cold water. Leave them in a colander to drain completely.

Heat the oil in a wok or large frying pan and stir fry the onion and pepper for 4 minutes or until beginning to soften. Add the bean sprouts and stir fry for 1 minute, then add the cooked beans and soy sauce and fry for a few minutes to warm through. Serve immediately.

KIDNEY BEAN CURRY

Curries are traditionally served with rice, but I prefer to serve Naan breads, especially if I'm in a hurry. Pickles and chutneys add extra spice and flavour.

Serves 4

INGREDIENTS

2 tbsps vegetable oil
1 large onion, sliced
2 cloves garlic, crushed
2 green chillies, seeded and chopped
2 tsps grated root ginger
1 tsp chilli powder
1 tsp ground coriander
1 tsp ground cumin
1 tsp garam masala
1 cinnamon stick
400g/14oz can chopped tomatoes
1 bay leaf
430g/15oz can red kidney beans, drained weight
Salt and freshly ground black pepper
Chopped fresh coriander, to garnish

Heat the oil in a large saucepan and fry the onion, garlic and fresh chillies for 5 minutes. Stir in the spices and cook for 1 minute to bring out the flavours. Add the tomatoes, bay leaf and kidney beans and season to taste. Cover and simmer gently for 30 minutes or until the flavours are well blended. Season and garnish with chopped coriander.

FRESH AND DRIED BEANS PROVENÇALE

Flageolet beans are one of my favourite pulses – I often use the canned beans when time is short. With their pretty pale green colour the flageolets provide a tasty and attractive base for this colourful dish.

Serves 4

Ingredients

225g/8oz dried flageolet beans, soaked
460g/1lb tomatoes, chopped
1 clove garlic, crushed
2 tsps dried basil
1 tsp dried oregano
½ tsp dried rosemary
460g/1lb fresh or frozen green beans, trimmed
Salt and freshly ground black pepper

Drain the beans and place in a saucepan with enough fresh water to cover them by 2.5cm/1 inch. Bring to the boil, boil rapidly for 10 minutes, then reduce the heat and simmer gently for 2 hours or until the beans are soft. Drain and set aside until required.

Place the tomatoes, garlic and herbs in a saucepan and cook over a low heat for 10 minutes or until the tomatoes soften and the juices begin to flow. Cut the green beans into 2.5cm/1 inch lengths and add to the pan with the cooked flageolet beans. Cook gently for 15 minutes or until the flavours are well combined. Season to taste before serving.

BEANS WITH TREE EARS & BAMBOO SHOOTS

Listen to this: tree ears are Chinese black fungi! They are available dried from most good delicatessens and from Chinese supermarkets. Serve this unusual dish with plain boiled rice.

Serves 4

INGREDIENTS
6 Chinese tree ears, broken into small pieces
2 whole pieces canned bamboo shoots OR 225g/8oz can sliced bamboo shoots
2 tbsps vegetable oil
340g/¾lb green beans, trimmed
2 tsps cornflour
2 tbsps soy sauce
4 tbsps vegetable stock
Dash sesame oil
Salt and freshly ground black pepper

Place the tree ears in a bowl and add enough hot water to cover them. Allow to stand for 30 minutes.

Slice the bamboo shoots. Cut the slices into thin triangular pieces with a sharp knife. Heat the oil in a large frying pan and cook the beans and bamboo shoots for 3 minutes. Stir in the drained tree ears and cook for another couple of minutes. Mix together the cornflour and soy sauce then stir in the stock, add to the pan and stir fry until the sauce thickens. Add a dash of sesame oil and season with salt and pepper. Serve immediately.

VEGETABLE STIR-FRY WITH TOFU

As I have mentioned before, tofu is an excellent source of protein for all vegetarians. Including it in this Oriental stir-fry makes a much more nutritious and substantial meal than the vegetables would provide alone.

Serves 4

INGREDIENTS
4 heads of broccoli
120g/4oz baby corn
4 tbsps vegetable oil
30g/1oz blanched almonds
1 clove garlic, crushed
1 red pepper, seeded and sliced
120g/4oz mangetout, trimmed
60g/2oz water chestnuts, sliced
4 tbsps soy sauce
1 tsp sesame oil
1 tsp sherry
150ml/¼ pint vegetable stock
2 tsps cornflour
120g/4oz bean sprouts
4 spring onions, cut into thin diagonal slices
225g/8oz tofu, cut into small dice
Salt and freshly ground black pepper

Remove the florets from the broccoli and set aside. Trim the broccoli stems and slice thinly. Cut the baby corn in half lengthways.

Heat the oil in a wok or large frying pan and fry the almonds until browned. Remove with a draining spoon and set aside. Add the garlic, broccoli stems and baby corn to the pan and stir fry for 1 minute. Stir in the pepper, mangetout, water chestnuts and broccoli florets and stir fry for 4 minutes.

Mix the soy sauce, sesame oil, sherry, stock and cornflour together in a small dish until blended. Add to the vegetables in the pan and stir until the sauce thickens. Finally, add the bean sprouts, browned almonds, spring onions and tofu and cook for 3 minutes. Season to taste and serve at once.

MIXED GRAINS AND SEEDS

This could be served as a simple supper dish with a green vegetable but I prefer to present it as a base for curry or tomato sauces. Season with salt and pepper if required just before serving.

Serves 4

INGREDIENTS
120g/4oz brown rice
60g/2oz wheat grains
90g/3oz rye grains or buckwheat
90g/3oz barley or oat groats
90g/3oz sunflower seeds or pine nuts
90g/3oz sesame seeds
700ml/1¼ pints vegetable stock or water
120g/4oz vegetarian Cheddar cheese, grated
30g/1oz butter or vegetable margarine
Sprig of parsley, to garnish

Place the rice, wheat, rye and barley or oats in a colander and rinse well under running water. Drain and place in a large saucepan with the seeds, and pour in the stock or water. Bring slowly to the boil. Stir, cover and simmer gently for about 30 minutes or until the grains are tender and the liquid has been absorbed. Allow to stand for 5 minutes, then stir in the cheese and butter or margarine until well mixed. Serve garnished with a sprig of parsley.

PEASE PUDDING

Don't neglect Pease Pudding just because it is a traditional English accompaniment to boiled ham! These 'puddings' make a wonderful light snack and simply need to be served with a tossed green salad.

Serves 4

INGREDIENTS

225g/8oz dried yellow peas or green split peas, soaked overnight
1 carrot, peeled and finely chopped
1 onion, finely chopped
1 free-range egg, beaten
1 tsp dried marjoram
1 tsp dried savoury
Salt and freshly ground black pepper
1 tbsp arrowroot
150ml/¼ pint milk
30g/1oz butter
Tomato slices and chopped fresh parsley, to garnish

Drain the peas and place in a saucepan with enough fresh water to cover them by 2.5cm/1 inch. Bring to the boil, then reduce the heat and simmer gently for 1 hour or until the peas are soft. Drain, reserving some of the liquid. Blend in a food processor or liquidiser with sufficient liquid to form a thick purée.

Preheat the oven to 180°C/350°F/Gas Mark 4. Place the pea purée in a large bowl and add the carrot, onion, egg, herbs and seasoning. Mix the ingredients thoroughly. Blend the arrowroot with a little of the milk, then add the remaining milk, butter and arrowroot mixture to a small saucepan. Heat gently, stirring continuously, until thickened. Pour the sauce into the pea mixture and stir well. Season again.

Divide the mixture between four individual dishes and place in a roasting tin. Fill the tin with enough hot water to come halfway up the sides of the dishes and bake for 40 to 45 minutes, until the pease pudding has set and is firm to the touch. Turn out on to individual serving dishes and garnish with slices of tomato and chopped parsley.

VEGETARIAN GARBURE

Garbure is a French country stew; this vegetarian variation is made without meat. Served with fresh wholemeal bread it makes a warming lunch or supper dish. I like to place thick slices of bread in the bottom of some soup plates and then ladle the Garbure in over the bread – delicious!

Serves 4

Ingredients

225g/8oz haricot beans, soaked overnight
2 tbsps vegetable oil
1 large potato, scrubbed and diced
4 carrots, peeled and sliced
2 leeks, washed and chopped
1 tsp dried marjoram
1 tsp dried thyme
½ tsp paprika
850ml/1½ pints vegetable stock
Salt and freshly ground black pepper
1 small cabbage, finely shredded
Wholemeal bread for serving

Drain the beans and place them in a saucepan with enough fresh water to cover them by 2.5cm/1 inch. Bring to the boil, boil rapidly for 10 minutes, then reduce the heat and simmer gently for 1 hour or until the beans are soft. Drain and set aside until required.

Heat the oil and cook the potato, carrots and leeks for 5 minutes. Add the herbs and paprika and cook for 1 minute. Stir in the beans and vegetable stock and simmer gently for 20 minutes.

Stir the bean mixture and season to taste. Scatter the shredded cabbage over the beans, cover and continue cooking for 15 to 20 minutes or until the cabbage is cooked. Season and serve the Garbure ladled over slices of wholemeal bread.

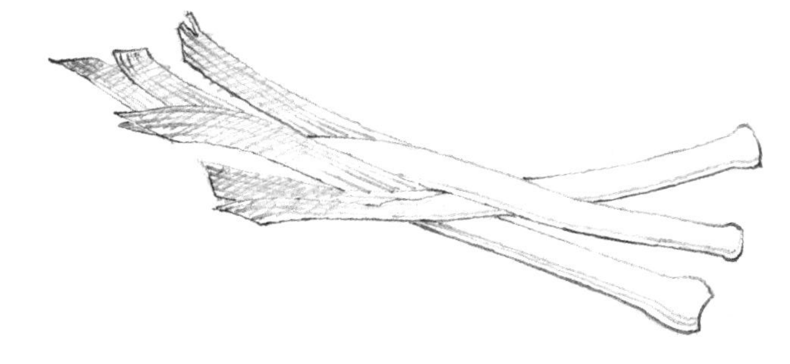

PANCAKES PROVENÇALE

Pancakes Provençale ooze Mediterranean sunshine onto your supper plate! They may be prepared and filled in advance, then heated through for 15-20 minutes in a moderate oven at 180°C/350°F/Gas Mark 4 when required.

Serves 4

INGREDIENTS

60g/2oz plain flour
Pinch salt
1 free-range egg, beaten
150ml/¼ pint milk
Oil for frying
2 green peppers, seeded and diced
1 red pepper, seeded and diced
1 large onion, peeled and finely chopped
1 clove garlic, crushed
1 small courgette, diced
3 tomatoes, skinned, seeded and chopped
1 tsp freshly chopped basil
2 tbsps tomato purée
30g/1oz vegetarian Cheshire or Wensleydale cheese, crumbled
Salt and freshly ground black pepper
Fresh herbs and tomato slices, to garnish

Place the flour and salt in a bowl. Make a well in the centre and add the egg with a little of the milk. Using a wooden spoon incorporate the flour into the egg mixture to form a smooth paste. Gradually beat in the remaining milk.

Heat a little oil in a heavy-based frying pan and spoon in a spoonful of the batter, then swirl to coat the base of the pan. Cook for about 1 minute or until the underside is golden. Flip or toss the pancake over and cook the other side. Slide the pancake out of the pan and keep warm. Repeat with the remaining batter. You should end up with 8 pancakes.

Heat 2 tbsps oil in a small pan and fry the peppers, onion and garlic until beginning to soften. Stir in the courgette and tomatoes, and cook for 2 minutes. Add the basil, tomato purée, cheese and seasoning, and cook gently until the cheese begins to melt.

Divide the vegetable mixture between the pancakes and roll or fold the pancakes to enclose the filling. Serve immediately, garnished with sprigs of fresh herbs and tomato slices.

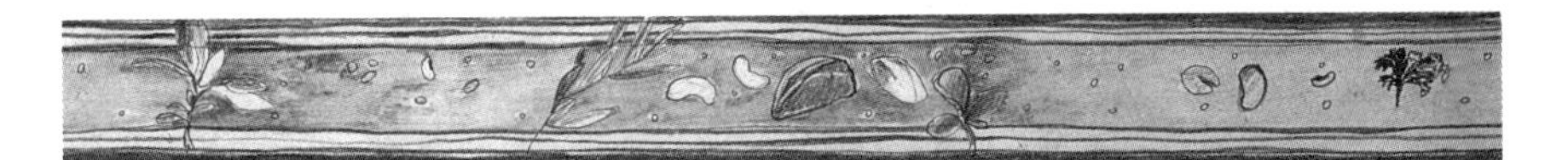

SPINACH AND PEPPER CASSEROLE

This subtly spiced casserole makes an excellent lunch or supper dish but may also be served as a mixed vegetable side dish with a main course. I love the combination of spinach and peppers, and the sultanas add just a little extra sweetness.

Serves 4

Ingredients
460g/1lb spinach, washed, trimmed and roughly chopped
2 tbsps oil
1 red pepper, seeded and sliced
1 green pepper, seeded and sliced
4 sticks celery, trimmed and thinly sliced
2 onions, finely chopped
30g/1oz sultanas
Pinch paprika
Pinch unrefined sugar
Pinch ground cinnamon
Salt
2 tbsps tomato purée
1 tsp cornflour
30g/1oz vegetarian Cheddar cheese
2 tbsps fresh breadcrumbs

Cook the spinach, with just the water that clings to the leaves after washing, in a covered pan until just wilted. Drain well, reserving the cooking liquid to make sauce.

Heat the oil in a frying pan and cook the peppers, celery and onion for about 10 minutes until softened. Mix together the sultanas, paprika, sugar, cinnamon, salt, tomato purée and cornflour. Make the reserved cooking liquid up to 150ml/¼ pint and add to the cornflour mixture. Add to the vegetables and cook until the sauce thickens. Pile into a flameproof casserole dish. Mix together the cheese and breadcrumbs and sprinkle over the vegetables. Place under a preheated grill until the cheese melts and the crumbs are golden.

WHOLEMEAL VEGETABLE QUICHE

The filling for this Wholemeal Quiche may be varied by using different vegetables but I always cook them before baking in the pastry case. I find they can be too crunchy within the custard filling if they are not pre-cooked.

Serves 4

Ingredients
175g/6oz wholemeal plain flour
90g/3oz vegetable margarine
About 2 tbsps cold water
2 tbsps oil
1 small red pepper, seeded and diced
120g/4oz courgettes, diced
2 spring onions, trimmed and sliced
1 tomato, skinned, seeded and chopped
2 free-range eggs, beaten
150ml/¼ pint milk
Salt and freshly ground black pepper
Tomato slices and chopped parsley, to garnish

Preheat the oven to 200°C/400°F/Gas Mark 6. Place the flour in a bowl and rub in the margarine until the mixture resembles fine breadcrumbs. Add enough cold water to mix to a firm dough, then roll out and use to line a 20cm/8 inch flan dish. Line the dish with a sheet of grease-proof paper and fill with baking beans. Bake for 16 minutes, removing the paper and beans half way through the cooking time.

Reduce the oven temperature to 180°C/350°F/Gas Mark 4. Heat the oil in a small pan and fry the pepper for 2 minutes, add the courgettes and fry for 2 minutes. Add the spring onions and tomato. Spoon the vegetable mixture into the flan case. Beat the eggs and milk together and season well. Pour over the vegetables. Return to the oven and bake for 30 minutes or until the filling is just set. Garnish with sliced tomatoes and chopped parsley

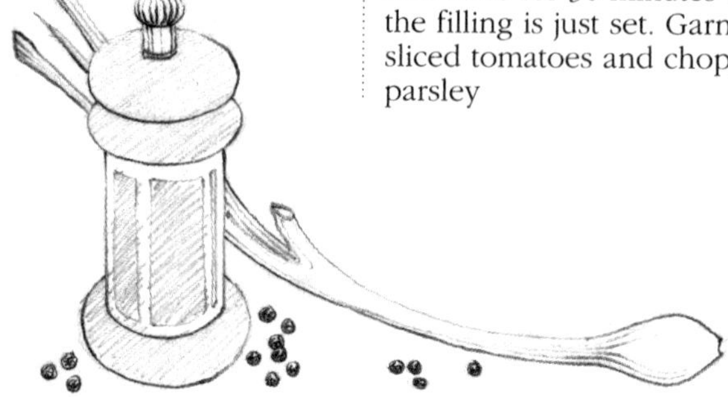

WATERCRESS STUFFED POTATOES

If you feel that baked potatoes have become too mainstream and boring, think again! This is a wonderfully different way of serving them and the egg, hidden inside the potato shell, is a real surprise!

Serves 4

INGREDIENTS

4 large baking potatoes, scrubbed
4 free-range eggs
60g/2oz butter or vegetable margarine
120g/4oz button mushrooms, sliced
1 shallot, finely chopped
45g/1½oz plain flour
430ml/¾ pint milk
60g/2oz vegetarian Cheddar cheese, grated
Pinch dry mustard
Pinch cayenne pepper
Salt and freshly ground black pepper
1 bunch watercress, chopped
Grated vegetarian cheese, cayenne pepper and watercress sprigs, to garnish

Preheat the oven to 200°C/400°F/Gas Mark 6. Prick the potatoes with a fork and place them directly on the oven shelves. Bake for 45-60 minutes, depending on size, until they are soft when squeezed. Reduce the oven temperature to 160°C/325°F/Gas Mark 3 and keep the potatoes warm while completing the dish.

Poach the eggs in gently simmering water for 3½ to 5 minutes until the white and yolk are just set. Remove from the pan and keep in cold water until required. Melt 15g/½oz of the butter in a small pan and fry the mushrooms and shallot for 5 minutes until just beginning to soften. Add the remaining butter, stir in the flour and cook for about 1 minute. Remove from the heat and gradually add 280ml/½ pint of the milk, stirring well after each addition. Return to the heat and cook gently until the sauce thickens. Stir in the cheese and continue cooking until the cheese melts. Season with the mustard, cayenne, salt and pepper.

When the potatoes are cooked cut a slice off the top of each and scoop out the flesh with a spoon, taking care to leave a border inside each skin to form a firm shell. Place equal amounts of the mushroom mixture into each potato and top with a well drained egg. Spoon the cheese sauce mixture over the top.

Heat the remaining milk until almost boiling. Mash the potato flesh, then gradually beat in the hot milk and chopped watercress. Pipe or spoon the potato over the sauce in the potato shells. Sprinkle the top of each with a little extra cheese and return to the oven for 15 minutes to warm through. Serve garnished with a sprinkling of cayenne pepper and sprigs of watercress.

ASPARAGUS AND OLIVE QUICHE

Always serve quiche warm, not hot – this prevents the filling becoming watery when cut.

Serves 6

INGREDIENTS

25 cm/10 inch part baked pastry case
3 free-range eggs
280ml/½ pint single cream
½ tsp salt
Pinch of nutmeg
Freshly ground black pepper
1 tbsp flour
298g/10½oz can green asparagus tips
90g/3oz green olives
1 onion, finely chopped
Knob of butter
45g/1½oz vegetarian Cheddar cheese, grated
1 tbsp grated vegetarian Parmesan cheese
30g/1oz butter

Preheat the oven to 200°C/400°F/Gas Mark 6. Whisk the eggs with the cream, and add the salt, nutmeg and seasoning. Mix a little with the flour to make a smooth paste, then add to the cream mixture.

Arrange the asparagus tips and olives in the pastry case. Cook the chopped onion in the butter until soft, add to the asparagus and pour the cream mixture over the top. Sprinkle with the grated Cheddar and Parmesan, then dot with the 30g/1oz butter and bake for 25 minutes. Turn down the oven to 180°C/350°F/Mark 4 for a further 15 minutes until the quiche is golden and set.

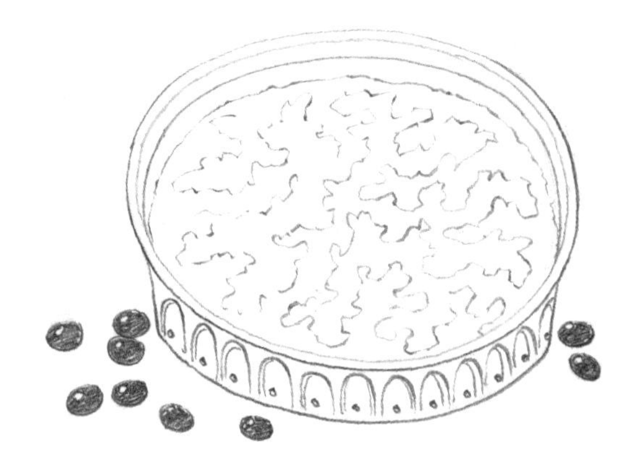

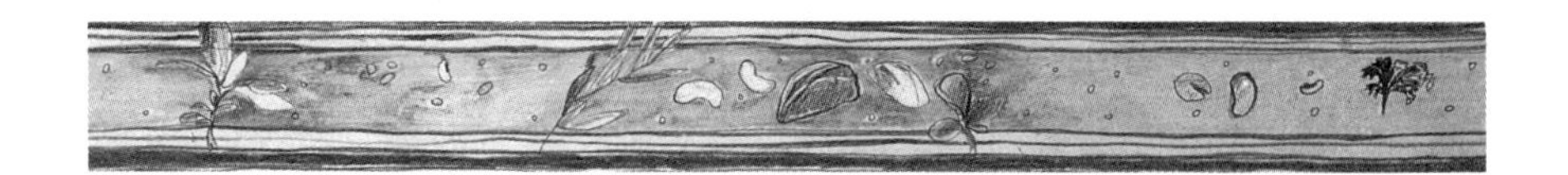

TOFU SPINACH FLAN

The filling of this flan may develop slight cracks on cooling – don't worry; it's quite normal.

Serves 4

INGREDIENTS

Pastry

1 tsp brown sugar
2-3 tbsps water
2 tsps oil
120g/4oz wholemeal flour
½ tsp baking powder
Pinch of salt
60g/2oz hard margarine

Filling

225g/8oz spinach
275g/10oz tofu
Juice of 1 lemon
2 tbsps shoyu (Japanese soy sauce)
4 tbsps sunflower oil
150ml/¼ pint soya milk
Salt
175g/6oz onions, chopped

Dissolve the sugar in the water in a pan and mix in the oil. Keep cool. Mix the flour, baking powder and salt together in a large bowl, then rub in the margarine until the mixture resembles fine breadcrumbs. Add the liquid mixture and mix into the flour, adding more water if necessary. The dough should be of a wettish consistency. Leave to rest under the upturned bowl for half an hour.

Preheat the oven to 190°C/375°F/Gas Mark 5. Roll out the pastry and use to line a 20cm/8 inch flan dish. Prick the base all over and bake blind for 5-6 minutes. Wash the spinach, shake dry and cook in its own juices in a covered pan until soft – about 5-8 minutes. Drain, chop and set aside.

Crumble the tofu into a liquidiser or food processor, add the lemon juice, shoyu, 2 tbsps of the oil, the soya milk and salt. Blend to a thick, creamy consistency. Adjust the seasoning if necessary. Chop the onions and fry them in the remaining oil until lightly browned, then add the spinach and fold in the tofu cream. Pour the mixture into the prepared flan case and bake in the middle of the oven for 30 minutes or until set. Allow to cool for about 10 minutes before serving.

MUSHROOMS FLORENTINE

I like to use fresh field mushrooms for this recipe whenever possible but the large, open, flat mushrooms now available in supermarkets are a good alternative.

Serves 4

INGREDIENTS
150g/5oz vegetable margarine
2 shallots, finely chopped
900g/2lbs spinach, stalks removed, washed and roughly shredded
4 tomatoes, skinned, seeded and chopped
Salt and freshly ground black pepper
Pinch nutmeg
460g/1lb open cap mushrooms
45g/1½oz plain flour
½ tsp dry mustard
Pinch cayenne pepper
570ml/1 pint milk
225g/8oz vegetarian Cheddar cheese, grated
Paprika, to garnish

Melt 30g/1oz of the margarine in a large pan and fry the shallots until softened. Add the spinach with just the water that is left clinging to the leaves, cover and cook for 5 minutes or until wilted. Add the tomatoes, seasoning and nutmeg and mix well. Spread the spinach mixture in a shallow flame-proof dish and keep warm.

Melt the remaining margarine and cook the mushrooms for 6 minutes until just soft. Remove with a draining spoon and arrange on the spinach. Stir in the flour and cook for 1 minute, then remove from the heat and gradually add the milk, stirring after each addition. Cook slowly, stirring, until boiling and thickened. Add 175g/6oz of the cheese and cook until melted. Season with salt, pepper and nutmeg. Spoon the sauce over the mushrooms and sprinkle with the remaining cheese. Flash under a preheated grill to melt the cheese and serve sprinkled with a little paprika.

VINAIGRETTE DE JARDIN

There are times when I just want a plate of fresh vegetables and this is a delicious way of preparing them. Vary the vegetables according to what is in season.

Serves 4

Ingredients
120g/4oz mangetout
2 courgettes, washed and sliced
120g/4oz broccoli florets
120g/4oz cauliflower florets
2 carrots, peeled and sliced
4 tomatoes
1 yellow pepper, deseeded and diced
4 spring onions, trimmed and cut into diagonal strips
90ml/3fl oz olive oil
2 tbsps white wine vinegar
1 tbsp Dijon mustard
1 tbsp freshly chopped herbs (eg chives, parsley, basil)
Salt and freshly ground black pepper

Bring a pan of lightly salted water to the boil and cook the mangetout for 3 minutes or until just tender. Remove them with a draining spoon and place in a bowl of iced water. Cook the courgettes in the water for 2 minutes, remove and add to the mangetout, then cook the broccoli, cauliflower and carrots for 5 minutes. The vegetables should be tender but still crisp to the bite. Once cool drain completely and set aside.

Skin the tomatoes by cutting a small cross in the stalk end and plunging into boiling water for about a minute. Quarter the tomatoes, remove and discard the seeds, then cut the tomato flesh into thin slices. Place the tomatoes, pepper and spring onions in a large bowl, add the drained, blanched vegetables and toss to mix well. Place the oil, vinegar, mustard, herbs and seasoning in a small bowl and mix together with a small whisk or fork, until thick and pale. Pour the dressing over the vegetables and toss again. Leave to marinate for 3 to 4 hours before serving.

CHEESE HOT POT

I suggest serving fresh green vegetables in season with this savoury Hot Pot.

Serves4

INGREDIENTS

570g/1¼lb potatoes
175g/6oz onions
175g/6oz carrots
250g/9oz grated vegetarian cheese
Salt and freshly ground black pepper
150ml/¼ pint water
Freshly chopped parsley to garnish

Preheat the oven to 230°C/450°F/Gas Mark 8. Peel the potatoes, onions and carrots, and cut into thin slices. Place in layers in a deep dish, with the cheese and a little seasoning between layers. Continue until all the vegetables are used, finishing with a layer of cheese. Pour the water into the dish, then cover with a greased lid and cook for 30 minutes. Reduce the temperature to 190°C/375°F/Gas Mark 5 for 1½ hours. Remove the lid and allow to brown for about 5 minutes. Garnish with chopped parsley.

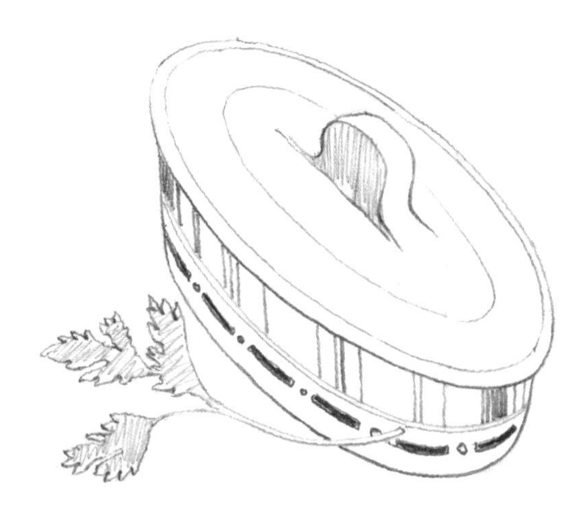

MAIN COURSES

Most people judge a style or a type of cookery on the strength of the main courses, the principal dishes or entrées. I have said before that a criticism of vegetarian food is that it is stodgy in texture, dull to look at and insipid in taste. Well, with that reputation it could be considered damned for all time! It need not, however, be like that at all, and as we move further into an established tradition of classic vegetarian recipes, tried, tested and enjoyed by an increasingly large number of people, vegetarian food is very definitely on the change, embracing the lighter, brighter colours and textures of today's cuisine.

The Flavours & Textures of the 'Nineties Cuisine

The most recent movement in inspirational cookery has been to lighter, more digestible textures with brighter seasonings and colours from vegetables and garnishes. This should be, and is becoming, the perfect way of cooking for the vegetarian. There is so much to be experimented with in the way of seasonings and, without the expense of traditional protein foods (by far the most expensive items in the usual shopping basket) we all have the opportunity to experiment with seasoning our meals, drawing out the natural tastes of the ingredients and adding that final flourish of flavouring.

Be Saucy!

One of the most dramatic changes in presentation and flavourings in recent years has been the introduction of many sauces, which are based on reduced stock, puréed vegetables and a little double cream. Don't think that the cream must make the final result heavy. Far from it! I find that such sauces are not only delightful in flavour but also much lighter in texture that their traditional counterparts made with the addition of flour to give a roux to thicken the sauce. To get the very best results from a sauce simply fry a few vegetables (onions, leeks, carrots etc.) until soft in a little olive oil, then add some wine and reduce to a thick syrup. Add some well flavoured vegetable stock and reduce that again until it has thickened and has a good flavour. Press the sauce through a fine sieve, pressing hard on the vegetables to extract all the colour and flavour, and return the sauce to the pan, rinsing it first to get rid of any sediment. Check the seasoning then add two or three tablespoons of double cream and boil again until the sauce is of the desired consistency. Serve with vegetable roasts, pilaffs and other grain dishes, and also pour over accompanying vegetables.

Served with Style

The presentation of vegetarian food makes such a difference to its visual appeal and thus to the satisfaction of the consumer! You can pick up so many good ideas from stylish food photography in glossy magazines, whether the food features includes animal proteins or not. For example, a pilaff with pieces of vegetables propped up in the middle of the rice, with a sauce poured round the whole dish looks more appetising than a great mound of rice with a heap of vegetables to the side of it. This method of serving can simply be adapted to the recipes in the chapter of main course suggestions. For example, try serving the Mushroom Stroganoff on page 131 on a bed of plain rice or pilaff, with the creamy sauce from the stroganoff spooned round the outside of the dish. Even shaped dishes such as Aubergine Rolls (page 161) and Chick Pea Burgers (page 148) can be served in this way, on a bed of accompanying vegetables arranged round a serving plate and with a sauce spooned over. It really is worth the effort.

Don't Be Overgenerous with the Helpings

Vegetarian food, based as it is on grains, nuts and pulse vegetables, takes a little getting used to! Do remember this when you entertain friends who are not vegetarians and don't overload their plates. Indeed, this is a good rule for everyone as it is much better to feel comfortable with the amount that you have on your plate and then to be able to enjoy going back for a little more, rather than having to struggle to get through the first plateful.

A Little Extra on the Side

Many vegetarian main courses have a sauce or juices with them which make them unsuitable for serving with salads; some people just don't relish their lettuce drowning in tomato juices! For this reason it is often wise practice to adopt the tradition of the French and to serve a salad either before or after the main course. This also helps to ensure that you don't have too big a helping, delicious as it will certainly be!

DEEP MUSHROOM PIE

I sometimes use ground mace instead of herbs with mushrooms, which brings out their slightly nutty flavour.

Serves 4

INGREDIENTS

Filling

1 tbsp vegetable oil
2 medium onions, finely chopped
340g/¾lb mushrooms, cleaned and chopped
225g/8oz mixed nuts, finely ground
120g/4oz wholewheat breadcrumbs
2 free-range eggs, beaten
1 tsp dried thyme or 2 tsps fresh
1 tsp dried marjoram or 2 tsps fresh
1 tbsp shoyu (Japanese soy sauce)
Salt and freshly ground black pepper to taste
Stock

Pastry

340g/¾lb wholewheat flour
Pinch of salt
1 tsp baking powder (optional)
120g/4oz solid vegetable fat
100ml/4fl oz water plus extra boiling water as necessary
Beaten egg to glaze

Preheat the oven to 220°C/425°F/Gas Mark 7. Heat the oil in a large saucepan and gently fry the onion until soft. Add the finely chopped mushrooms and cook until the juices begin to run. Remove the pan from the heat and add all the other filling ingredients to form a thick, but not dry, consistency, adding a little stock or water if necessary. Allow to cool.

To prepare the pastry, first sift the flour, salt and baking powder into a large mixing bowl. Cut the fat into small pieces and melt in a saucepan. Add the cold water and bring to a fierce bubbling boil. Immediately pour the liquid into the centre of the flour and mix vigorously with a wooden spoon until glossy. When the mixture is cool enough to handle, use your hands and knead it into a ball. Divide the mixture into two-thirds and one-third, placing the one-third portion in an oiled plastic bag to prevent it drying out.

Use two-thirds of the pastry to line the base and sides of a 17.5cm/7 inch spring-form cake tin, pressing it down and moulding it into position. Spoon in the mushroom filling, pressing down firmly to make a 'dome' shape. Roll out the remaining pastry to just larger than the tin and place on top of the pie, damping and pinching the edges together to seal, then glaze generously with beaten egg. Cut or prick vents in the lid to allow the steam to escape.

Bake for 20 minutes. Reduce the oven temperature to 190°C/375°F/Gas Mark 5 and bake for a further hour. Unmould and serve on an attractive platter surrounded by watercress and twists of lemon and cucumber.

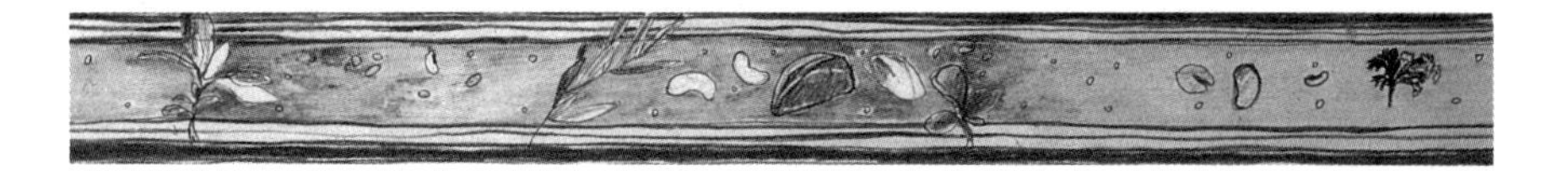

SPINACH, CORN & NUT RAISED PIE

A succulent pie which may be eaten hot or cold

Serves 6

INGREDIENTS
460g/1lb spinach
1 onion, chopped
2 tbsps oil
120g/4oz hazelnuts, finely chopped
120g/4oz brazil nuts, finely chopped
120g/4oz wholemeal breadcrumbs
120g/4oz sweetcorn
1 tsp dried oregano
½ tsp dried sage
1 tbsp freshly chopped parsley
1 tsp shoyu (Japanese soy sauce)
2 tbsps tahini
280ml/½ pint stock
Salt and freshly ground black pepper

Pastry
340g/¾lb wholemeal flour
1 tsp baking powder
120g/4oz vegetable fat
175ml/6fl oz water
Pinch salt

Preheat the oven to 220°C/425°F/Gas Mark 7. Wash the spinach and cook in the water left clinging to the leaves until soft. Drain well and chop finely. Fry the onion in the oil until soft.

Mix together all the dry ingredients, add the spinach and onions, the shoyu, tahini and sufficient stock to give a moist texture, then season to taste.

Mix together the dry ingredients for the pastry in a large bowl. Melt the fat in the water and heat until boiling. Pour the liquid on to the flour and mix well. Add extra boiling water if the mixture is too dry. Place two thirds of the dough in a 17.5cm/7 inch springform tin and push into shape. Spoon the filling into the pie case and press down well. Roll out the remaining dough to form a pie lid. Dampen and seal the two pastry edges. Glaze the top and make two small steam holes. Bake for 20 minutes, then reduce the heat to 190°C/375°F/Gas Mark 5 for a further 50 minutes or until golden brown.

FIFTEEN MINUTE GOULASH

The best and sweetest paprika is grown in Hungary, where goulash is the national dish.

Serves 4

Ingredients

1 onion, finely chopped
1 clove garlic, crushed
2 carrots, diced
3 medium courgettes, diced
2 tbsps olive oil
1 tbsp paprika
Pinch of nutmeg
1 tbsp freshly chopped parsley
1 tbsp tomato purée
225g/8oz cooked red kidney beans or 400g/14oz can, drained and rinsed
225g/8oz cooked white kidney beans or 400g/14oz can, drained and rinsed
150ml/¼ pint tomato juice or stock
Salt and freshly ground black pepper
Soured cream or yogurt to serve

Place the onion, garlic, carrots and courgettes in a pan with the olive oil and cook for 5 minutes until softened. Stir in the paprika, nutmeg, parsley and tomato purée, then add the rest of the ingredients except the cream or yogurt and cook over a low heat for 10 minutes. Turn onto a hot serving dish and top with a little soured cream or yogurt.

MUSHROOM STROGANOFF

The original recipe for stroganoff was created by a Russian count of that name – I think he would approve of this vegetarian version of his original dish.

Serves 4-6

INGREDIENTS
2 medium onions, sliced
5 sticks celery, chopped
60g/2oz butter or margarine
460g/1lb tiny button mushrooms
½ tsp dried mixed herbs
½ tsp dried basil
1 heaped tbsp unbleached flour
280ml/½ pint stock
Salt and freshly ground black pepper
75ml/2½fl oz soured cream or yogurt
Freshly chopped parsley

Place the onions and celery in a large pan together with the butter or margarine and cook over a low heat until the onions are transparent. Add the mushrooms and cook for 2-3 minutes until the juices run, then add the mixed herbs and basil. Stir in the flour and cook for 1 minute, then add the stock and seasoning and allow to cook gently for 8-10 minutes. Remove the pan from the heat, stir in the soured cream and adjust the seasoning if necessary. Heat very gently to serving temperature but do not allow to boil. Garnish with the chopped parsley and serve at once.

VEGETABLE STEW WITH HERB DUMPLINGS

I sometimes add 1 teaspoon of caraway seeds to the dumplings for a slightly more scented flavour.

Serves 4-6

INGREDIENTS

1 large onion
900g/2lbs mixed vegetables (carrot, swede, parsnips, turnips, cauliflower etc.)
570ml/1 pint stock or water plus a stock cube
Salt and freshly ground black pepper
Flour or gravy powder to thicken

Dumplings

120g/4oz wholewheat self-raising flour
60g/2oz vegetarian suet
1 tsp dried mixed herbs
¼ tsp salt

Chop the onion into large pieces. Peel and prepare the other vegetables and chop into bite-sized pieces. Place the onion and vegetables in a pan and cover with the stock. Bring to the boil and simmer for 20 minutes. Season to taste. Mix a little flour or gravy powder with a little water and stir into the stew to thicken.

Place the ingredients for the dumplings in a bowl and add just enough water to bind. Shape the mixture into 8 small dumplings – you may need to flour your hands to do this.

Bring the stew to the boil and drop in the dumplings. Cover and allow to simmer for 10 minutes.

Serve at once.

WINTER CRUMBLE

I suggest serving this with crusty bread and a glass of beer.

Serves 4-6

INGREDIENTS

Topping

90g/3oz butter or margarine
120g/4oz wholewheat flour
60g/2oz rolled oats
120g/4oz vegetarian Cheddar cheese, grated
¼ tsp salt

175ml/6fl oz stock or water
280ml/½ pint sweet cider
1 tsp brown sugar
2 carrots, chopped
2 large parsnips, cut into rings
2 sticks celery, chopped
2 heads broccoli, cut into florets
½ a small cauliflower, cut into florets
2 tsps wholewheat flour
2 tbsps chopped parsley
1 medium onion, chopped
4 large tomatoes, skinned and sliced
225g/8oz black-eyed beans
Salt and freshly ground black pepper

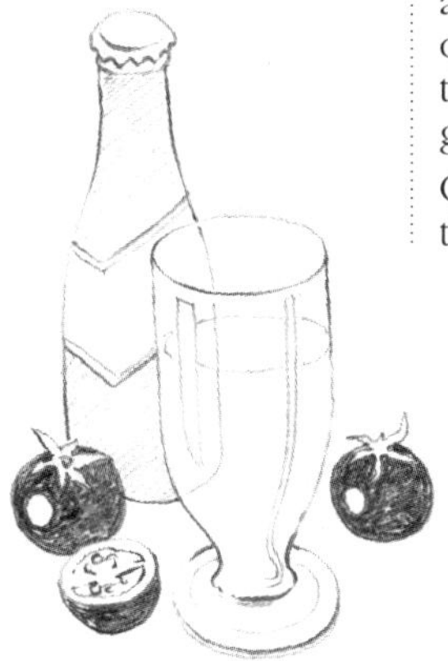

Preheat the oven to 200°C/400°F/Gas Mark 6. Make the topping by rubbing the butter into the flour and oats until the mixture resembles fine breadcrumbs, then stir in the cheese and salt. Set to one side.

Mix the stock with the cider and sugar and place in a large pan with the carrots and parsnips. Cook until tender, then remove the vegetables and put aside. Add the celery, broccoli and cauliflower to the pan, cook until tender, then remove and reserve with other vegetables. Mix the flour with a little water, add to the cider and cook until thickened, stirring all the time. Cook for 2-3 minutes, then remove from the heat and add the parsley.

Fry the onion in a little butter or oil until brown, then place in a greased casserole dish with the vegetables, tomatoes and beans and season well. Pour the sauce over the mixture. Sprinkle with the topping and press down gently.

Cook for 30-35 minutes or until the topping is golden brown.

COURGETTE AND SWEETCORN SAVOURY

This dish uses left-over pasta but you could use rice or other grains if preferred.

Serves 4

INGREDIENTS
1 tbsp oil
1 medium onion, chopped
225g/8oz courgettes, sliced
200g/7oz can sweetcorn
175g/6oz pasta shapes, cooked
Large pinch oregano
1 tbsp tomato purée
Salt and freshly ground black pepper

Sauce
30g/1oz margarine
30g/1oz wholewheat flour
280ml/½ pint milk
3 tbsps white wine
60g/2oz strong, vegetarian cheese, grated

Topping
30g/1oz wholemeal breadcrumbs
2 tsps sunflower seeds

Preheat the oven to 180°C/350°F/Gas Mark 4. Heat the oil in a frying pan and cook the chopped onion until soft. Add the sliced courgettes and brown lightly. Mix in the sweetcorn, cooked pasta, oregano and tomato purée, and stir. Season lightly and transfer the mixture to an oiled ovenproof dish.

Make the cheese sauce by melting the margarine and stirring in the flour to make a roux. Cook gently for a few minutes and then gradually add the milk and wine, stirring all the time, to make a smooth sauce. Heat until boiling and thickened. Add the grated cheese and stir until it melts into the sauce. Remove from the heat and pour over the vegetable mixture, then top with the breadcrumbs and sunflower seeds.

Bake for about 20 minutes until browned and bubbling.

SWEET POTATO AND FRENCH BEAN PASTIES

These are not typically Cornish but very delicious!

Serves 4

INGREDIENTS

225g/8oz wholemeal shortcrust pastry, made with 225g/8oz flour
½ medium onion, finely chopped
1 clove garlic, crushed
1 tbsp oil
½ tsp freshly grated root ginger
¼ to ½ tsp chilli powder
¼ tsp turmeric
½ tsp ground cumin
1 tsp ground coriander
¼ tsp mustard powder
1 medium-sized sweet potato, cooked and finely diced
120g/4oz French beans, chopped into 1.25cm/½ inch lengths
2 tbsps water or stock
Salt and freshly ground black pepper
Milk or beaten egg to glaze

Preheat the oven to 200°C/400°F/Gas Mark 6. Fry the onion and garlic in the oil until soft, then add the ginger and all the spices and stir. Add the diced cooked potato, beans and water or stock and cook gently for 4-5 minutes, until the beans begin to cook. Allow the mixture to cool and season well.

Roll the pastry out into 4 circles. Place a quarter of the filling in the centre of each and dampen the edges of the pastry with a little water. Join the pastry together over the filling, then make a small hole in each pasty and glaze with milk or beaten egg. Bake for 15-20 minutes until golden brown.

RATATOUILLE PIE WITH CHEESE AND PEANUT PASTRY

This autumnal pie has a delicious crunchy nut pastry.

Serves 4-6

INGREDIENTS

Ratatouille

2 tbsps olive oil
2 onions, chopped
4 tomatoes, sliced
1 aubergine, sliced
3 courgettes, finely sliced
2 sticks celery, chopped
Salt and freshly ground black pepper

White sauce

60g/2oz margarine
60g/2oz flour
430ml/¾ pint milk

Pastry

60g/2oz butter
120g/4oz self raising flour
60g/2oz finely grated vegetarian cheese
60g/2oz finely chopped salted peanuts
A little milk
Beaten egg

Preheat the oven to 190°C/375°F/Gas Mark 5. Place the oil and all the vegetables in a large pan and cook gently for about 20 minutes or until soft. To make the sauce, melt the margarine in a separate pan, stir in the flour and cook for 2 minutes, stirring all the time. Gradually add the milk and bring to boiling point. Stir the sauce into the vegetable mixture, season and pour into an ovenproof dish.

Rub the butter into the flour and add the cheese and peanuts. Mix with a little milk, then knead lightly and roll out the pastry. Place on top of the ratatouille mixture, trim and brush with beaten egg. Bake for about 30 minutes or until golden brown.

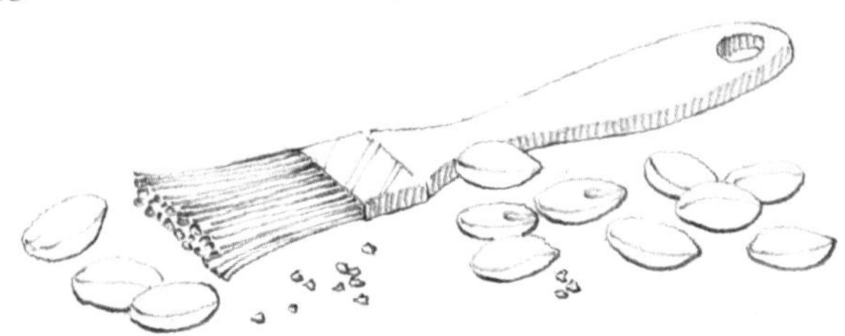

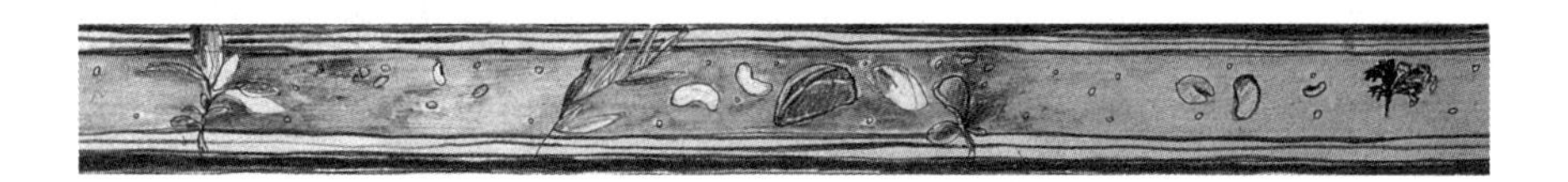

LENTIL MOUSSAKA

Soaking the lentils overnight will speed their cooking. Serve the Moussaka with a Greek-style tomato salad.

Serves 4-6

INGREDIENTS
150g/5oz green lentils
1 large aubergine, sliced
4-5 tbsps oil
1 large onion, chopped
1 clove garlic, crushed
1 large carrot, diced
4 sticks celery, finely chopped
1-2 tsps mixed herbs
400g/14oz can tomatoes
2 tsps shoyu sauce (Japanese soy sauce)
Freshly ground black pepper
2 medium potatoes, cooked and sliced
2 large tomatoes, sliced

Sauce
60g/2oz margarine
60g/2oz wholewheat flour
430ml/¾ pint milk
1 large free-range egg, separated
60g/2oz grated vegetarian Cheddar cheese
1 tsp nutmeg

Preheat the oven to 180°C/350°F/Gas Mark 4. Cook the lentils in plenty of water until soft. Drain and reserve the liquid. Fry the aubergine in the oil, drain well and set aside. Cook the onion, garlic, carrot and celery in a little of the lentil stock. Simmer, covered, until just tender, then add the lentils, mixed herbs and tomatoes. Simmer gently for 3-4 minutes, then season to taste with the shoyu and pepper.

Place a layer of the lentil mixture in a large casserole dish and cover with half of the aubergine slices. Cover the aubergine slices with half of the potato slices and all the tomato. Repeat with the remaining lentils, aubergines and potatoes.

To make the sauce, melt the margarine in a saucepan, remove from the heat and stir in the flour to make a roux. Cook for 1 minute then add the milk gradually, mixing well. Return to the heat and stir continuously until the sauce thickens. Remove the pan from the heat and cool slightly. Add the egg yolk, stir in the cheese and add the nutmeg. Whisk the egg white until it is stiff, then carefully fold in to the sauce. Pour the sauce over the moussaka, covering the dish completely.

Bake for about 40 minutes, until the top is golden brown and puffy.

MOORS AND CHRISTIANS

This dish gets its name from the use of black beans, representing the Moors, and white rice, symbolising the Christians.

Serves 4

Ingredients

225g/8oz black beans, soaked overnight and cooked until soft
2 tbsps vegetable oil
1 medium onion, chopped
4 cloves garlic, crushed
1 medium green pepper, finely chopped
2 large tomatoes, skinned and finely chopped
275g/10oz long grain rice
Salt and freshly ground black pepper
Little bean cooking water if required

Drain the cooked beans and mash 3 tablespoons of them to a paste with a fork, adding a little bean cooking water if necessary. Heat the oil and fry the onion, garlic and pepper until soft. Add the tomatoes and cook for a further 2 minutes, then add the bean paste and stir in the cooked beans and rice, and enough water to cover. Bring to the boil, cover and simmer for 20-25 minutes until the rice is *al dente.* Season to taste and serve hot.

CHICKPEA AND PEPPER CASSEROLE

Chick peas are used extensively in Middle Eastern and African cookery and are often flavoured with mild curry spices. I use ground cumin with chick peas and the addition of mint gives this colourful casserole a real North African flavour.

Serves 4

INGREDIENTS

225g/8oz dried chick peas, soaked overnight
2 tbsps vegetable oil
1 onion, sliced
1 clove garlic, crushed
1 green pepper, seeded and sliced
1 red pepper, seeded and sliced
½ tsp ground cumin
2 tsps freshly chopped parsley
1 tsp freshly chopped mint
4 tomatoes, seeded and cut into strips
Salt and freshly ground black pepper

Drain the chick peas and place in a saucepan with enough water to cover them by 2.5cm/1 inch. Bring to the boil and boil rapidly for 10 minutes. Reduce the heat and simmer gently for about 2 hours or until the chick peas are soft. Drain and reserve the liquid.

Heat the oil in a saucepan and fry the onion, garlic and peppers for 5 minutes, then stir in the cumin and fry for 1 minute. Make the reserved liquid up to 280ml/½ pint and add to the pan with the cooked beans. Add all the remaining ingredients and bring slowly to the boil. Cover and simmer for 30 minutes. Adjust the seasoning if necessary and serve.

VEGETABLE CASSOULET

Cassoulet is a traditional dish from France, where almost every region has its own recipe or variation on the basic theme of a stew of haricot beans. It is tasty and filling, requiring only a salad accompaniment. I often serve Cassoulet at big parties – it is always popular and very economical to prepare!

Serves 4

INGREDIENTS

225g/8oz haricot beans, soaked overnight
4 tbsps vegetable oil
2 cloves garlic, crushed
2 leeks, washed and cut into 2.5cm/1 inch pieces
3 carrots, peeled and sliced
4 sticks celery, trimmed and cut into 2.5cm/1 inch pieces
2 turnips, peeled and cut into 2.5cm/1 inch pieces
1 bay leaf
1 tbsp soy sauce
1 tbsp freshly chopped marjoram
Salt and freshly ground black pepper
430ml/¾ pint vegetable stock
30g/1oz vegetable margarine
90g/3oz wholemeal breadcrumbs

Drain the beans and place in a saucepan with enough water to cover them by 2.5cm/1 inch. Bring to the boil and boil rapidly for 10 minutes. Reduce the heat and simmer gently for about 1 hour or until the beans are soft. Drain.

Preheat the oven to 180°C/350°F/Gas Mark 4. Heat the oil in a large frying pan and fry the prepared vegetables, including the garlic, for 5 to 10 minutes until beginning to brown. Place the cooked beans, bay leaf, soy sauce, marjoram and seasoning in an ovenproof casserole and stir in the browned vegetables and stock. Cover and cook in the oven for 45 minutes.

Melt the margarine in the frying pan and stir in the breadcrumbs. Remove the lid from the casserole and sprinkle the breadcrumb mixture over the beans. Bake, uncovered, for 30 minutes or until the breadcrumb topping is crisp.

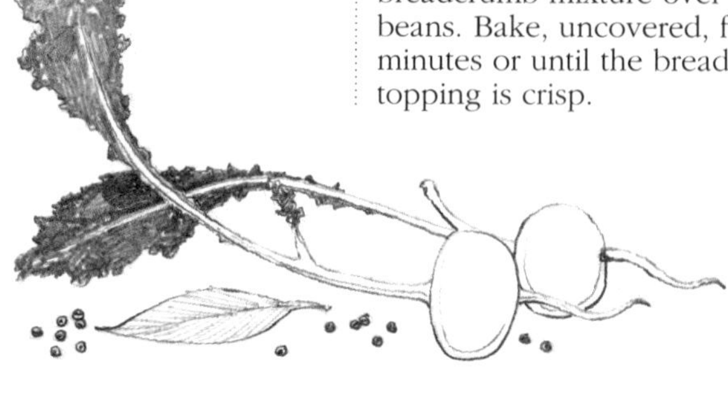

RED BEAN CREOLE

This colourful dish satisfied the eye as well as the appetite. Serve with a little side salad or a bowl of ratatouille – each is as good as the other.

Serves 4

INGREDIENTS

175g/6oz long-grain brown or white rice
30g/1oz butter or vegetable margarine
1 green pepper, seeded and sliced
120g/4oz mushrooms, sliced
Pinch cayenne pepper
Pinch ground nutmeg
340g/¾lb red kidney beans, cooked
150ml/¼ pint vegetable stock
4 firm tomatoes, skinned, seeded and cut into strips
4 spring onions, trimmed and chopped
Salt and freshly ground black pepper
Freshly chopped parsley, to garnish

Cook the rice in plenty of boiling water as directed on the packet. Drain and rinse with boiling water. Melt the butter in a large saucepan and cook the pepper and mushrooms for 5 minutes or until just beginning to soften. Add the rice, cayenne, nutmeg, beans and stock. Cook gently for 10 minutes, then stir in the remaining ingredients and cook for a further 5 minutes or until all the ingredients are heated through. Serve garnished with chopped parsley.

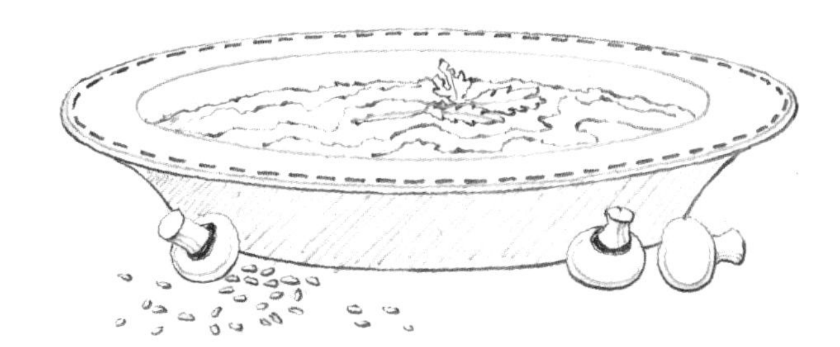

RED LENTIL AND MUSHROOM LOAF

This nutritious and tasty vegetable loaf is just as good served hot or cold. It also travels well for picnics. Chill well in the tin, transport it in a cool box and turn out on to a serving plate as you lay up your picnic.

Serves 4-6

INGREDIENTS
175g/6oz red lentils
340ml/12fl oz vegetable stock or water
1 free-range egg
2 tbsps double cream
90g/3oz mushrooms, chopped
120g/4oz vegetarian curd or cream cheese
1 clove garlic, crushed
1 tbsp freshly chopped parsley
Salt and freshly ground black pepper
400g/14oz can chopped tomatoes
1 tbsp tomato purée
Pinch unrefined sugar
1 tbsp freshly chopped tarragon

Preheat the oven to 180°C/350°F/Gas Mark 4. Rinse the lentils, then place them in a saucepan with the stock or water. Bring to the boil and boil rapidly for 10 minutes, then reduce the heat and continue to cook until the lentils are soft and the liquid has been absorbed. Use a potato masher to mash the lentils to a thick purée. Beat the egg and cream together and add to the lentil purée with the mushrooms, cheese, garlic, parsley and seasoning. Mix all the ingredients together thoroughly. Press into a greased and lined 460g/1lb loaf tin and bake for 1 hour, or until firm to the touch.

Put the tomatoes, tomato purée, sugar and half the tarragon into a small saucepan and cook for 5 minutes. Purée in a food processor or press through a sieve to form a smooth sauce. Stir in the remaining tarragon and season to taste. Slice the loaf and serve with the tomato sauce and a mixed salad.

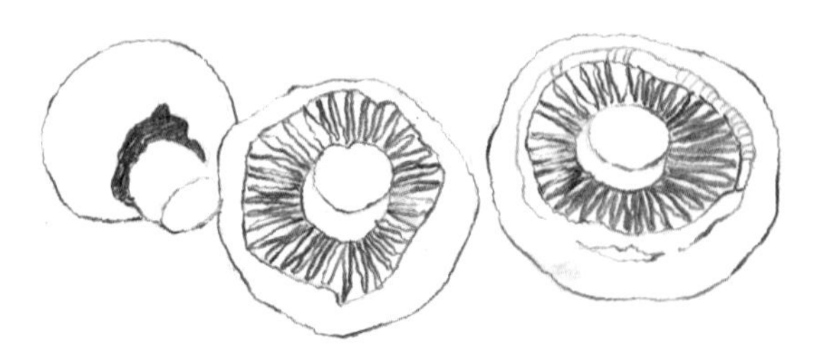

BUTTER BEANS IN TOMATO SAUCE

Serve with rice and green vegetables in season for a tasty and nutritious meal.

Serves 4-6

INGREDIENTS

175g/6oz butter beans, soaked overnight
60g/2oz vegetable margarine
1 onion, sliced
6 medium tomatoes, sliced
Bay leaf
60g/2oz flour
A little milk
Salt and freshly ground black pepper
Freshly chopped parsley

Drain the butter beans and place them in a pan with fresh water to cover, then cook slowly until soft. Melt the margarine in another pan and cook the onions with the tomatoes and bay leaf until soft. Stir in the flour, and add a little cooking water from the beans to make a thick sauce. Stir well and add about 280ml/½ pint milk and seasoning to taste. Remove the bay leaf and pour the sauce over the beans. Sprinkle with the chopped parsley before serving.

SWEET BEAN CURRY

Serve with boiled brown rice for a substantial and nutritious meal.

Serves 4

INGREDIENTS

175g/6oz red kidney beans, soaked overnight
30g/1oz butter or margarine
1 onion, sliced
1 apple, cored and chopped
175g/6oz mushrooms, sliced
1 tbsp curry powder
30g/1oz unbleached flour
570ml/1 pint bean stock or bean stock and water
Salt to taste
1 tbsp lemon juice
1 tbsp chutney
60g/2oz sultanas
60g/2oz creamed coconut, grated or chopped

Drain the beans, place in a large pan and cover with cold water. Bring to the boil and boil vigorously for 10-15 minutes, reduce the heat and simmer for about an hour until the beans are tender but still whole.

Melt the butter or margarine and cook the onion until it is very brown. Add the apple and mushrooms and cook for 2-3 minutes, then add the curry powder and flour and cook for 2-3 minutes, stirring all the time. Gradually add the bean stock and stir until smooth, then add the seasoning, lemon juice, chutney, sultanas and beans and cook for 10-15 minutes. Just before serving add the creamed coconut and stir until dissolved.

RED BEAN STEW WITH CHILLI SAUCE

I find that the flavour of kidney beans is much enhanced by chillies. Serving the sauce separately allows people to be as daring as they wish!

Serves 4

INGREDIENTS

175g/6oz dried red kidney beans, soaked overnight
2 tbsps oil
1 large onion, chopped
1 clove garlic, crushed
400g/14oz can tomatoes
½ tsp dried oregano
½ tsp dried basil
½ tsp shoyu sauce (Japanese soy sauce)
460g/1lb potatoes, peeled and diced
Salt and freshly ground black pepper

Chilli Sauce

30g/1oz butter or margarine
1 small clove garlic, crushed
1 small onion, grated
¾ tsp chilli powder
1 tbsp cider vinegar
90ml/3fl oz bean stock or water
A little salt
1 tsp tomato purée
1 tbsp freshly chopped coriander
1 tsp natural yogurt

Drain the beans, place in a large pan and cover with water. Boil vigorously for 10-15 minutes, then reduce the heat and cook for about an hour until the beans are tender but still whole.

Heat the oil and fry the onion and garlic until soft. Add the tomatoes, oregano, basil, shoyu and potatoes, cover and cook for 20 minutes until the potatoes are softened. Season to taste. Drain the beans, reserving a little stock, and add to the onion and tomato mixture – cook gently for a further 5-10 minutes.

Prepare the chilli sauce in a separate pan. Melt the butter or margarine and cook the garlic and onion until soft. Add the chilli powder and cook for a further 1-2 minutes, then add the vinegar, stock, salt, tomato purée and coriander and cook for 5 minutes. Remove from the heat and leave to cool slightly before stirring in the yogurt. Serve the Red Bean Stew with the sauce handed round separately.

PIPER'S PIE

Miso is a paste of fermented soya beans and is essential for Japanese cooking. It is available in delicatessens and specialist food shops.

Serves 4

INGREDIENTS

- 460g/1lb potatoes, peeled and diced
- Butter
- Salt and freshly ground black pepper
- 175g/6oz mung beans
- 225g/8oz leeks
- 1 onion, sliced
- ½ tsp dried dill
- 2.5cm/1 inch fresh root ginger, chopped or finely grated
- 1 tbsp apple juice
- 1 tsp miso

Preheat the oven to 200°C/400°F/Gas Mark 6. Boil the potatoes and mash with a little butter and seasoning.

Cover the mung beans with water in a separate pan and boil for 15-20 minutes until soft. Meanwhile, generously butter an ovenproof casserole dish and put in the leeks, onion, dill, ginger and apple juice. Mix well. Drain the beans, reserving the stock, and add them to the casserole dish. Dissolve the miso in a little of the bean stock and mix into the casserole which should be moist but not too wet.

Cover and cook for 30-45 minutes, stirring a couple of times during the cooking – add a little more bean stock if necessary. Remove from the oven and cover with a layer of the mashed potatoes. Return to the oven to brown or brown under the grill.

CHESTNUT HOT-POT

Chestnuts always make a filling casserole. In a hot-pot, with a potato topping, I suggest serving just a fresh green vegetable as an accompaniment. Use dried, canned or frozen chestnuts if fresh are unavailable.

Serves 4-6

Ingredients
680g/1½lb potatoes
3 medium onions
225g/8oz brown lentils, soaked overnight and then boiled
225g/8oz chestnuts
Salt and freshly ground black pepper
2 tsp yeast extract
430ml/¾ pint warm water
60g/2oz margarine

Preheat the oven to 190°C/375°F/Gas Mark 5. Peel and slice the potatoes and onions thinly. Layer the potatoes, onions, lentils and chestnuts in a greased pie dish, ending with a layer of potatoes. Season each layer well. Dissolve the yeast extract in the warm water and pour into the dish, then dot the potatoes with margarine and cover. Bake for an hour or until the potatoes are tender. Turn up the oven to 200°C/400°F/Gas Mark 6, remove the lid from the casserole and and bake for a further 10-15 minutes, until the potatoes are crispy and golden brown.

CHICKPEA BURGERS

I like to serve this with a spicy tomato dip. Small burgers make excellent dinner party food and are just as good cold as hot.

Serves 4

Ingredients

460g/1lb cooked chickpeas or 2 400g/14oz cans chickpeas
1 onion, finely chopped
2 cloves garlic, crushed
2 medium potatoes, cooked and mashed
2 tbsps shoyu sauce (Japanese soy sauce)
2 tsps lemon juice
Freshly ground black pepper
Wholewheat flour
Oil for frying

Place the chickpeas in a large bowl and mash well. Add the onion, garlic, potato, shoyu, lemon juice and pepper and mix together. With floured hands, shape heaped tablespoonfuls of the mixture into small burgers. Coat each burger with flour and refrigerate for 1 hour. Heat a little oil in a frying pan and gently fry the burgers on each side until golden brown.

BUTTER BEANS AND MUSHROOMS AU GRATIN

I like butter beans but a lot of people don't – too much like school dinners, I suspect! You can of course, use any type of bean for this dish.

Serves 4

INGREDIENTS
175g/6oz butter beans, soaked overnight and cooked until soft
90g/3oz butter
1 tbsp lemon juice
Salt and freshly ground black pepper
225g/8oz mushrooms, separate the caps from the stalks
30g/1oz wholemeal breadcrumbs
30g/1oz grated vegetarian cheese

Sauce
60g/2oz margarine
60g/2oz flour
280ml/½ pint milk

Preheat the oven to 190°C/375°F/Gas Mark 5. Mix the beans with 60g/2oz of the butter, the lemon juice and salt and pepper, then place the mixture in the bottom of a pie dish. Melt the remaining butter in a pan and fry the mushroom caps for about 5 minutes.

Make the sauce by melting the margarine in a separate pan and stirring in the flour. Cook for about 2 minutes and then gradually add the milk, stirring all the time until the sauce boils and thickens. Chop the mushroom stalks and add them to the sauce, then pour this over the beans. Place the cooked mushroom caps, undersides upwards, on the top and sprinkle with the breadcrumbs and cheese. Bake for about 15 minutes until the top is browned.

PEANUT RISOTTO

I suggest leaving the peanuts whole for a crunchier texture.

Serves 4

Ingredients
1 large onion, chopped
1 clove garlic, crushed
1 tbsp vegetable oil
175g/6oz short-grain brown rice
120g/4oz peanuts, roughly chopped
120g/4oz mushrooms, sliced
570ml/1 pint boiling water
120g/4oz fine green beans
30g/1oz raisins
2 tsps dried oregano
2 tsps lemon juice
Salt and freshly ground black pepper

Fry the onion and garlic in the oil in a large frying pan for 3-4 minutes. Add the rice and peanuts to cook for 1-2 minutes, then add the mushrooms and cook for a further 3-4 minutes. Add the boiling water, stir once and simmer for 30 minutes. Add the beans, raisins, herbs, lemon juice and seasoning and cook for a further 5-10 minutes.

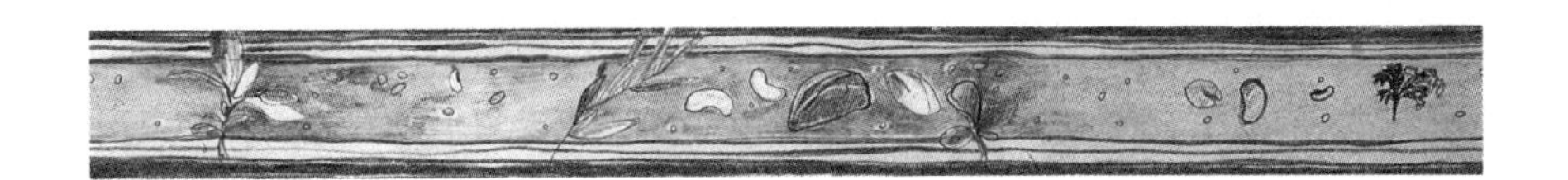

MILLET MEDLEY

This is just as good cold as hot if there are any leftovers! Millet has a sweet flavour and a nutty texture.

Serves 4

INGREDIENTS
1 medium onion, chopped
2 tbsps oil
225g/8oz millet
570ml/1 pint stock or water
Salt and freshly ground black pepper
90g/3oz cooked peas
90g/3oz sweetcorn
4 sticks celery, chopped
60g/2oz sunflower seeds
2 tbsps shoyu sauce (Japanese soy sauce)

Cook the onion in the oil until softened but not browned. Add the millet and cook for a few minutes, stirring all the time. Add the stock and seasoning, bring to the boil and simmer over a low heat for 30 minutes, then add the peas, sweetcorn and celery and mix well.

Place the sunflower seeds and shoyu into a frying pan and cook over a medium heat, stirring continuously until the seeds are dry. Sprinkle the millet with the toasted sunflower seeds just before serving.

FESTIVE ROAST

A good alternative to a traditional Christmas roast. Serve with bread sauce, cranberry sauce and the vegetables of your choice.

Serves 8

INGREDIENTS

- 2 tbsps sunflower oil
- 2 medium onions, finely chopped
- 2 cloves garlic, crushed
- 460g/1lb cashew nuts, finely ground
- 225g/8oz wholemeal breadcrumbs
- 2 free-range eggs beaten or 4 tbsps soya flour mixed with a little water
- 1 heaped tsp dried mixed herbs
- 2 tsps Marmite or yeast extract
- 280ml/½ pint boiling water
- Salt and freshly ground black pepper

Preheat the oven to 180°C/350°F/Gas Mark 4. Grease a 900g/2lb loaf tin. Heat the oil in a pan and fry the onion and garlic until soft. Place the onions and garlic in a large bowl, add all the other ingredients and mix well. Spoon the mixture into the prepared tin. Cover with a double thickness of foil and cook for about 1 hour 20 minutes, until firm. Allow to cool for about 10 minutes in the tin before turning out.

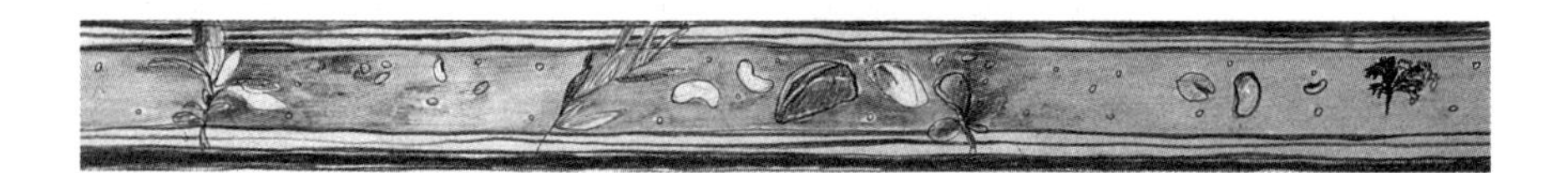

VEGETABLE COUSCOUS

Couscous is a popular dish in North Africa. It is usually steamed over a sauce or a stew, so that it can absorb the flavours. Cook the couscous over the vegetable sauce if you possibly can.

Serves 4

INGREDIENTS

2 tbsps vegetable oil
3 cloves garlic, crushed
2 onions, sliced
1 large potato, peeled and diced
4 carrots, peeled and sliced
2 small turnips, peeled and diced
1 green pepper, seeded and sliced
1 tsp ground cumin
1 tsp ground coriander
1 tsp tumeric
1 tsp chilli powder
425g/15oz can chickpeas, drained
570ml/1 pint vegetable stock
225g/8oz courgettes, trimmed and sliced
60g/2oz raisins or sultanas
60g/2oz no-soak dried apricots, chopped
Salt and freshly ground black pepper
460g/1lb couscous
2 tbsps natural yogurt (optional)

Heat the oil in a large saucepan and fry the garlic and onion until beginning to soften. Add the potato, carrot, turnip and green peppers and cook for 5 minutes, then stir in the spices and cook for 1 minute. Add the chick peas, stock, courgettes, raisins or sultanas and apricots, then season with salt and pepper. Bring slowly to the boil and simmer for 30 minutes.

Meanwhile, place the couscous in a large bowl and cover it with boiling water. Leave to stand for 15 minutes, then place in a steamer and steam for 15 minutes.

Pile the couscous on to a serving plate and serve the vegetables on top. Garnish with a little yogurt if desired.

CURRIED CASHEW NUTS

Cashews are my favourite nuts and I like to use them whenever I can in my cooking. They do not stay quite as crisp as some nuts, which is good in a curry when everything should have more or less the same texture.

Serves 4

Ingredients
3 tbsps vegetable oil
1 tbsp white mustard seeds
1 tsp ground cumin
1 tsp ground coriander
1 tsp garam masala
1 large onion, chopped
1 green pepper, seeded and sliced
120g/4oz cashew nuts, chopped
60g/2oz raisins
460ml/16fl oz tomato juice
225g/8oz bean sprouts
Cucumber slices and coriander leaves, to garnish

Heat the oil in a large frying pan and fry the mustard seed and spices for 30 seconds. Add the onion and pepper and cook for a few minutes until just beginning to soften. Add the nuts, raisins and tomato juice, and stir well. Simmer for 10 minutes, then add the bean sprouts and simmer for a further 5 minutes or until sauce has thickened. Serve the curry garnished with cucumber slices and coriander leaves.

BEANS BOURGUIGNON

Cooking 'à la Bourguignon' simply means in the style of Burgundy, so use a bottle of Burgundy wine. You won't need it all for the pot so there will be some left over for the cook!

Serves 4

INGREDIENTS

225g/8oz borlotti or red kidney beans, soaked overnight
1 bay leaf
4 tbsp olive or vegetable oil
225g/8oz shallots or baby onions, peeled
1 clove garlic, crushed
4 carrots, peeled and cut into 2.5cm/1 inch chunks
225g/8oz button mushrooms
150ml/¼ pint vegetable stock
280ml/½ pint red wine
1 tsp freshly chopped thyme
2 tsps freshly chopped parsley
Salt and freshly ground black pepper
4 slices wholemeal bread, crusts removed
30g/1oz butter or vegetable margarine
Freshly chopped parsley, to garnish

Drain the soaked beans and place in a saucepan with the bay leaf and enough water to cover by 2.5cm/1 inch and bring to the boil. Boil rapidly for 10 minutes, reduce the heat and cook for 2 to 3 hours or until the beans are very soft. Drain.

Preheat the oven to 190°C/375°F/Gas Mark 5. Heat half the oil in a frying pan and fry the shallots or onions, garlic and carrots for 5 minutes. Stir in the mushrooms and fry for 3 to 4 minutes. Transfer to an ovenproof casserole. Put the stock and wine in the pan and bring to the boil. Boil rapidly for 2 to 3 minutes, then pour over the vegetables. Stir the beans and herbs into the casserole and season well. Cook in the oven for 40 minutes. Just before the end of the cooking time, cut the bread into triangles. Heat the remaining oil with the butter or margarine and fry the bread until golden. Serve the casserole garnished with bread triangles and a sprinkling of freshly chopped parsley.

HAZELNUT ESCALOPES WITH PEAR BRANDY SAUCE

This elegant dish is ideal for entertaining – the hazelnut escalopes can be prepared well in advance and the sauce is very quick to prepare while the escalopes are frying. Use a mild cheese that will not mask the flavours of the other ingredients.

Serves 4

INGREDIENTS
- 30g/1oz butter or vegetable margarine
- 1 shallot, finely chopped
- 30g/1oz plain flour
- 150ml/¼ pint milk
- 120g/4oz lightly toasted ground hazelnuts
- 60g/2oz fresh breadcrumbs
- 1 tsp freshly chopped parsley
- 1 tsp freshly chopped thyme
- 1 free-range egg, beaten
- Salt and freshly ground black pepper
- Dry breadcrumbs, for coating
- Oil, for shallow frying
- 280ml/½ pint double cream
- 1 tbsp Calvados or brandy
- 60g/2oz vegetarian Cheddar cheese, grated
- 4 small ripe pears, halved and cored
- Lemon juice
- Fresh sage leaves, to garnish

Melt the margarine in a frying pan and fry the shallot for 2 minutes or until softened. Stir in the flour and cook for 1 minute. Remove from the heat and gradually beat in the milk. Cook slowly, stirring all the time, until thickened. Add the hazelnuts, breadcrumbs, parsley, thyme and half the egg. Season to taste and mix to form a thick paste. Add extra breadcrumbs if the paste is too thin, and chill well.

Divide the mixture into 8 and shape each piece into a round with lightly floured hands. Dip in the remaining egg and coat in dry breadcrumbs. Shallow fry for 3 minutes on each side until golden.

While the escalopes are cooking, place the cream and brandy in a small saucepan and bring to the boil. Boil for a few minutes or until the cream mixture thickens slightly. Stir in the cheese and season to taste, and cook until the cheese melts. Spoon some of the sauce on to 4 plates. Brush the cut side of the pear with lemon juice and arrange on the plate with a sprig of sage. Place 2 escalopes on each plate and serve immediately.

WALNUT CUTLETS WITH THREE PEPPER SALPICON

A salpicon is a preparation of one or more ingredients, cut into small dice and bound with a sauce. Walnut Cutlets and Three Pepper Salpicon sounds stylish and is an excellent dish for entertaining.

Serves 4

INGREDIENTS

60g/2oz vegetable margarine
1 shallot, finely chopped
45g/1½oz plain flour
150ml/¼ pint milk
120g/4oz walnuts, finely chopped or ground
60g/2oz fresh breadcrumbs
1 tsp freshly chopped parsley
1 tsp freshly chopped thyme
1 free-range egg, beaten
Dry breadcrumbs, for coating
Oil for shallow-frying
1 onion, peeled and finely diced
2 green peppers, seeded and diced
2 red peppers, seeded and diced
2 yellow peppers, seeded and diced
Juice of 1 lemon
90ml/3fl oz vegetable stock
2 tsps capers
Pinch cayenne pepper
Salt and freshly ground black pepper
Sprigs of watercress, to garnish

Melt 30g/1oz of the margarine in a frying pan and stir in the shallot, cook for 2 minutes or until softened. Stir in 30g/1oz flour and cook for 1 minute. Remove from the heat and gradually beat in the milk. Cook slowly, stirring all the time, until thickened. Add the nuts, breadcrumbs, parsley, thyme and half the egg. Season to taste and mix to form a thick paste. Add extra breadcrumbs if the paste is too thin, and chill well.

Divide the mixture into 8 and shape each piece into a cutlet with lightly floured hands. Dip each cutlet in the remaining egg and coat in dry breadcrumbs. Shallow-fry for 3 minutes on each side until golden.

While the cutlets are cooking, melt the remaining margarine in a frying pan and fry the onion until beginning to soften. Add the peppers and cook for 3 to 4 minutes. Stir in the remaining flour, then gradually add the lemon juice and stock, and cook until boiling and slightly thickened. Add the capers and season with cayenne, salt and pepper. Arrange the pepper salpicon on 4 serving plates and arrange the cutlets on top. Garnish with watercress.

MILLET RISSOLES WITH YOGURT SAUCE

Millet has a mild, buttery flavour so this yogurt sauce is a perfect accompaniment.

Makes about 15

INGREDIENTS

1 medium onion, finely chopped
1 clove garlic, crushed
1 tsp dried mixed herbs or 2 tbsps freshly chopped parsley
Oil
150g/5oz millet flakes
280-430ml/½-¾ pint water
1 tbsp tomato purée
1 tsp vegetable extract
90g/3oz vegetarian Cheddar cheese, grated
¼ tsp paprika
Salt and freshly ground black pepper
Wholemeal breadcrumbs

Sauce

280ml/½ pint Greek yogurt
2 tbsps freshly chopped parsley
Salt and pepper
Pinch of paprika
A little lemon juice (optional)

Cook the onion, garlic and mixed herbs in a pan with a little oil until soft. Place the millet flakes in a separate pan with the water, bring to the boil and simmer gently, stirring constantly until a thick mash results, then cool slightly. Combine the millet with the onion and add the remaining rissole ingredients, except the breadcrumbs; mix together well. Shape the mixture into rissoles and coat with the crumbs.

Fry the rissoles in very shallow oil on both sides until crisp and golden.

Make the yogurt sauce by mixing all the ingredients together and serve it with the rissoles.

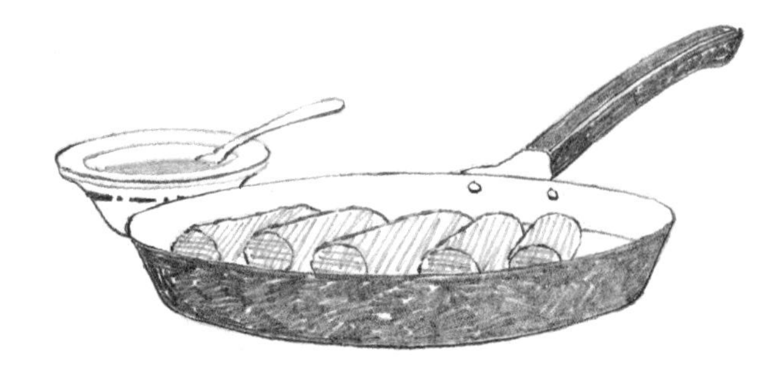

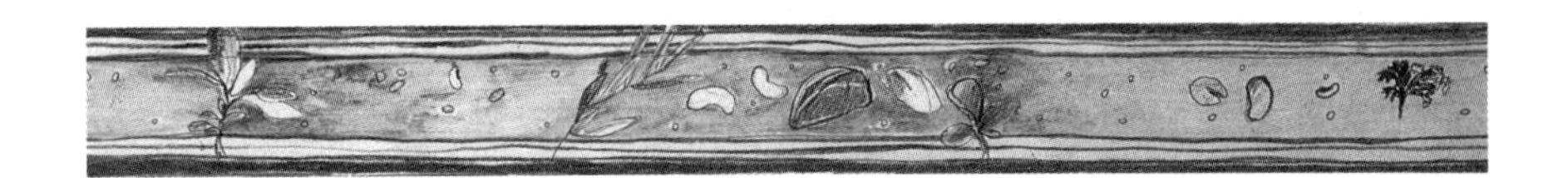

BUTTER BEAN AND SPINACH ROLL WITH LEMON CRUST

The lemon crust adds a real 'zing' to this dish, which should be served with a garlic-laden mixed pepper salad.

Serves 4

INGREDIENTS
225g/8oz butter beans, soaked overnight and cooked until tender
225g/8oz spinach
½ tsp freshly grated nutmeg
Salt and freshly ground black pepper
60g/2oz vegetarian Cheddar cheese, grated
1 free-range egg, beaten
1 tsp sunflower oil
60g/2oz fresh breadcrumbs
1 tbsp sesame seeds
Grated rind of 1 lemon
2 tsps lemon juice

Preheat the oven to 200°C/400°F/Gas Mark 6. Drain the cooked beans, transfer them to a large bowl and mash well. Wash and trim the spinach. Using a pan with a close fitting lid, cook the spinach, with no added water, for 5 minutes. When cooked and cool enough to handle, chop the spinach finely and add the nutmeg and seasoning. Stir the grated cheese and beaten egg into the mashed butter beans.

Place a sheet of clingfilm or foil on the working surface and spread the bean mixture over it in a rectangle measuring roughly 17.5cm × 27.5cm/7 × 11 inches. Cover the bean layer with the chopped spinach then, with the short end towards you, lift the edge of the cling film or foil and gently roll the mixture into a cylinder, using the wrapping to support the roll.

Rub the oil into the breadcrumbs in a bowl and stir in the sesame seeds and lemon rind. Spread the breadcrumb mixture over the working surface and roll the butter bean roll over it until it is well covered. Transfer the roll to a greased baking sheet, sprinkle with the lemon juice and bake for 15-20 minutes until the crust is crisp and golden.

MUSHROOM CROQUETTES WITH GREEN PEPPERCORN SAUCE

The spicy, green peppercorn sauce soaks into the mushroom croquettes to give a sophisticated blend of flavours. I suggest serving the croquettes with an orange and watercress salad.

Serves 4

INGREDIENTS

45g/1½oz vegetable margarine
2 shallots, finely chopped
120g/4oz mushrooms, finely chopped
45g/1½oz plain flour
150ml/¼ pint milk
90g/3oz fresh breadcrumbs
1 tsp freshly chopped parsley
1 tsp freshly chopped thyme
1 free-range egg, beaten
Salt and freshly ground black pepper
Dry breadcrumbs, for coating
Oil for shallow frying
2 tbsps dry vermouth or white wine
280ml/½ pint double cream
2 tbsps green peppercorns in brine, drained
½ red pepper, seeded and diced.

Melt 30g/1oz of the margarine in a frying pan and stir in one shallot and the mushrooms. Cook for 5 minutes or until softened. Stir in 30g/1oz flour and cook for 1 minute. Remove from the heat and gradually beat in the milk. Cook slowly, stirring all the time, until boiling and thickened. Add the breadcrumbs, parsley, thyme and half the egg. Season to taste and mix to form a thick paste. Add extra breadcrumbs if the paste is too thin, and chill well.

Divide the mixture into 12 and shape into small ovals with lightly floured hands. Dip each piece in the remaining egg and coat in dry breadcrumbs. Shallow fry for 3 minutes on each side until golden.

Meanwhile, melt the remaining margarine and add the remaining shallot, and fry until softened. Stir in the remaining flour, whisk in the vermouth or wine and cream. Season to taste, and cook until slightly thickened. Stir in the peppercorns and red pepper, and cook for a further minute. Serve the croquettes with a little of the sauce poured over.

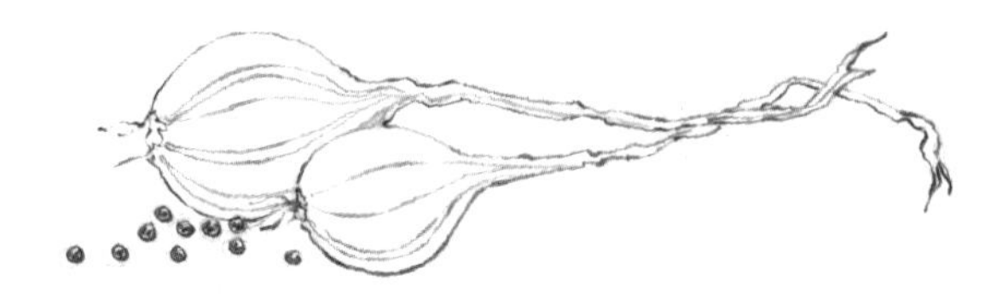

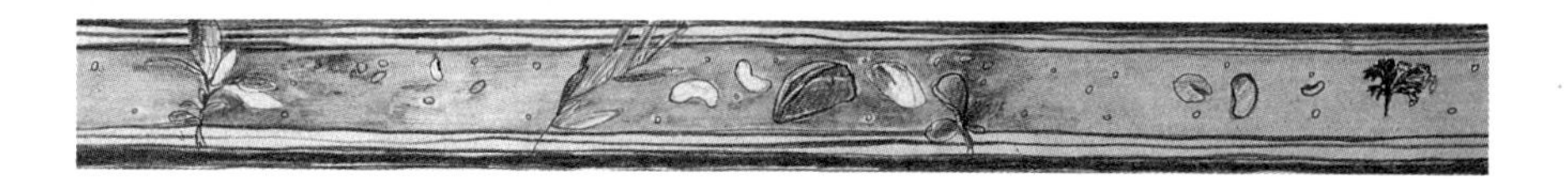

AUBERGINE ROLLS

The flavours of aubergines and tomatoes always go well together. I like this recipe because it is such an unusual way of serving aubergines.

Serves 4

INGREDIENTS
2 large aubergines
Salt
2 tbsps vegetable oil
1 onion, chopped
1 clove garlic, crushed
400g/14oz can tomatoes
2 tbsps tomato purée
Pinch unrefined sugar
Pinch dried oregano
1 bay leaf
2 sprigs fresh parsley
Freshly ground black pepper
About 3 tbsps olive oil
225g/8oz vegetarian Cheshire cheese, crumbled
120g/4oz black olives, pitted and chopped
175g/6oz vegetarian Cheddar cheese, grated
60g/2oz pine nuts
1 tbsp white wine
1 tsp freshly chopped parsley
1 tsp freshly chopped basil
Pinch nutmeg

Slice the aubergines, then lightly score the cut surfaces with a sharp knife. Sprinkle liberally with salt and leave to stand for 30 minutes. Rinse well and pat dry with absorbent kitchen paper.

Preheat the oven to 180°C/350°F/Gas Mark 4. Heat the vegetable oil and fry the onion and garlic until softened, stir in the tomatoes, tomato purée, sugar, oregano, bay leaf, parsley and seasoning. Bring to the boil and simmer gently for 10 minutes. Remove and discard the bay leaf and parsley then blend the sauce until smooth in a liquidiser or food processor. Press through a metal sieve to remove the tomato seeds.

Heat a little of the olive oil in a frying pan and fry the aubergine slices, in batches, for 1 minute each side, adding more oil if necessary. Remove and drain on kitchen paper. Place the Cheshire cheese, olives, 60g/2oz of the Cheddar cheese, pine nuts, white wine, herbs, nutmeg and a little seasoning in a bowl and mix well. Spoon about half of the tomato sauce into a shallow, oven-proof dish. Place equal amounts of cheese filling on to one half of each of the aubergine slices, roll up and place on the sauce in the dish. Secure the rolls with wooden cocktail sticks if necessary. Spoon the remaining sauce over the filled aubergine rolls and sprinkle with the remaining cheese. Cover with foil and bake for 20-25 minutes, or until piping hot and the cheese has melted. Serve at once.

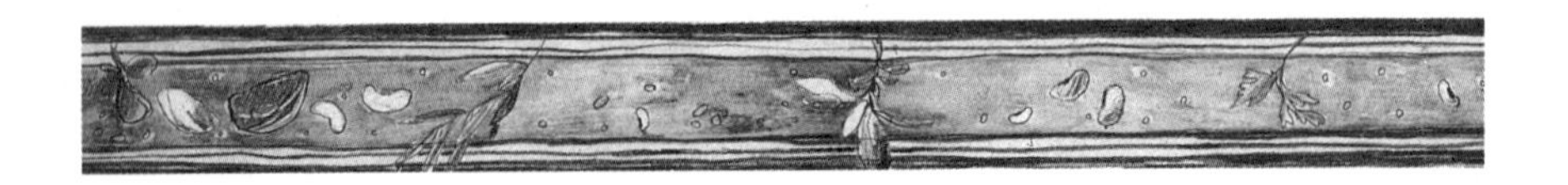

TASTY TOMATO SAUCE

This is a very versatile sauce for serving with numerous main courses, but also for pouring over vegetables before serving.

Serves 4

INGREDIENTS
30g/1oz pine nuts
Pinch salt
1 tsp sunflower oil
1 onion, chopped
pinch of chilli powder
3 cloves
400g/14oz can tomatoes

Place the pine nuts in a frying pan and dry roast. Remove when they are lightly browned and sprinkle with the salt. Fry the onion in the sunflower oil until soft, then add the chilli powder and cloves. Fry for 1 minute, then add the tomatoes, bring to the boil and simmer for 10 minutes. Cool slightly and remove the cloves. Blend the mixture in a liquidiser or food processor and return it to the pan. Add the pine nuts and reheat gently.

PUDDINGS & DESSERTS

By the time the end of the meal arrives one has to assume that appetites are pretty much satisfied – if they're not, even the most competent and experienced host or hostess would be beside themselves with worry! Well, that's the theory which applies in the middle of summer – when the temperature outside is sub-zero I guess it is acceptable to revel in chocolate pudding and chocolate sauce! What, therefore, is the culinary role of the pudding or dessert? Surely it can't really just be self-indulgence and luxury? No, I firmly believe that it is to place the food equivalent of a full-stop at the end of the meal, thus redressing the balance of the palate after what I hope have been startling and stimulating taste sensations from what has gone before. How often I have craved just a little chocolate mousse or ice cream ....

A wide and Varied Choice

For most vegetarians there is very little restriction on the ingredients that may be used in desserts and puddings. Gelatine, the standard setting agent for jellies, mousses and cold soufflés, presents the most problems, but these are easily overcome by the use of agar-agar, a plant-derived gelatine substitute. Some purists would tell you that it doesn't give the same shimmeringly clear set as leaf gelatine, but it is more than adequate in setting a wide range of desserts. Of course, if you do not eat eggs your choice will be more restricted but there are still many desserts and puddings that you will find suitable for your dietary regime.

It's Not a New Idea

With the recent emergence of interest in vegetarian and wholefood cookery there have been many more recipes produced using honey in place of sugar as a sweetener, it generally being a much purer and more natural product. This is very definitely not a new idea, as honey was used as the principal sweetener until sugar was introduced more widely in the 15th and 16th centuries. The amount of honey that you use is up to you but do taste each mixture very carefully so that you don't overdo the sweetness. It is also important to remember that if a recipe says 3 tablespoons of honey, you should level the top of the spoon with a knife and scrape away any honey left clinging to the underside of the bowl of the spoon – it's very easy to add too much!

Before or After the Cheese?

I doubt that this is an important issue for everyday eating but, when it comes to entertaining, when do you serve the dessert? In most countries it has traditionally been served straight after the main course. This is one move on from 14th century thinking, a time when sugar was a great luxury and to serve sweet dishes was a sign of great wealth, and when sweet and savoury dishes were often mixed up together. Serving the dessert straight after the main course came slightly later, but still served to impress guests with the financial abilities of the host

Cheese, or a savoury, was then served at the very end of the meal.

These days the choice is more open and I think it is almost down to do you enjoy red wines? If you have had a bottle of red with your main course it is now quite acceptable (and a habit of which I very much approve) to serve the cheese immediately after the main course, thus enabling it to be enjoyed with the remainder of the red wine. Then, once you move on to the pudding or dessert, a sweet wine may be served to accompany that and the meal will be ended in fine style.

Menu Planning Strikes Again!

As I have said countless times before, menu planning is so important for vegetarians and, of course, the sweet course must be included in the overall scheme of the meal. If you are having a relatively light main course, stuffed vegetables or a nut loaf, for example, choose a slightly more robust dessert such as Treasure Rice (page 179) or Rice Meringue (page 176). However, as most vegetarian main courses are fairly substantial, the majority of the desserts in this chapter are based on fruit and are bound to complement your meal plan.

How I wish I could eat a pudding every day ... but nature doesn't allow me to! However, never forget the abundance of fresh fruit that we have available all the year round. We are so lucky to be able to get mangoes, pineapples and kiwi fruits throughout the year and need never feel that we are missing out on a treat at the end of our meal.

CRANBERRY CRISP

Frozen cranberries are now available all the year round and may be used in both sweet and savoury dishes. This is a favourite variation on the theme of fruit crumble.

Serves 2

INGREDIENTS

150ml/¼ pint orange juice
120g/4oz fresh or frozen cranberries
2 tsps unrefined caster sugar
2 tsps cornflour
1 tsp ground cinnamon
30g/1oz vegetable margarine
225g/8oz crunchy oatmeal cereal
15g/½ oz plain flour
2 tbsps clear honey

Preheat the oven to 180°C/350°F/Gas Mark 4. Place the orange juice, cranberries and sugar in a small saucepan and cook gently for 10 minutes, stirring occasionally, until the fruit softens. Blend the cornflour with a little cold water and stir into the cranberries with the cinnamon. Cook until thickened, then pour into an ovenproof serving dish.

Melt the margarine and stir in the cereal and flour, mix well and pile on top of the cranberries. Drizzle the honey over the topping and bake for 15 minutes. Serve hot.

BAKED BANANAS SAUCE À LA POIRE

Baked bananas are often served with a sweet, sugary sauce, but I prefer them with this fruity accompaniment.

Serves 4

INGREDIENTS
2 small oranges
2 ripe pears, peeled and cored
Honey, to taste
4 bananas

Preheat the oven to 180°C/350°F/Gas Mark 4. Pare the rind from one of the oranges, using a potato peeler, taking care not to include any white pith. Cut the pared rind into very thin strips with a sharp knife and blanch in boiling water for 2 to 3 minutes, to soften. Drain and set aside. Peel and segment one orange and squeeze the juice from the other. Place the orange juice and pears in a liquidiser or food processor and blend until smooth. Sweeten to taste with honey.

Peel the bananas, place in an oven-proof dish and pour the pear purée over the top. Cover and bake for 15 minutes or until the bananas are soft. Decorate with orange segments and strips of orange rind. Serve immediately.

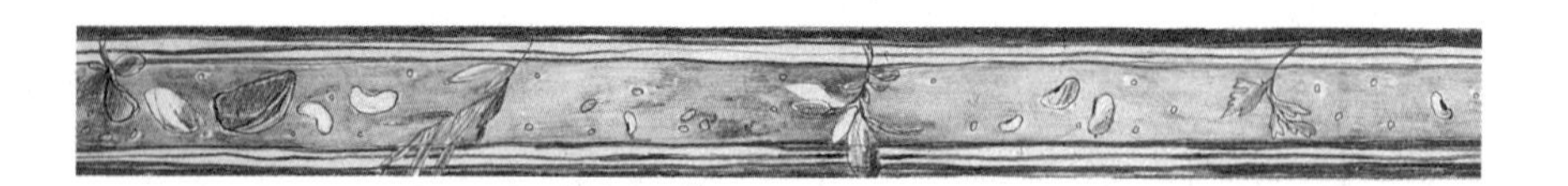

CHOCOLATE BRANDY CAKE

What can I say about this recipe? Except don't eat too much at once!

Serves 8

Ingredients
340g/12oz plain chocolate
120g/4oz unsalted vegetable margarine
2 free-range eggs, beaten
4 tbsps brandy
225g/8oz digestive sweetmeal biscuits, coarsely crushed
60g/2oz blanched almonds, chopped
150ml/¼ pint double cream, whipped
Candied rose petals, toasted flaked almonds and slivers of angelica to decorate

Break the chocolate into cubes and place in a bowl or the top of a double boiler with the margarine. Melt over a pan of hot water, stirring occasionally to combine. Remove from the heat and beat the eggs, a little at a time, into the chocolate mixture. Allow to cool slightly then beat in the brandy, biscuits and chopped almonds.

Lightly grease and base line a 17.5cm/7 inch spring form or loose-bottomed cake tin. Spoon the mixture into the prepared tin and chill until set. Remove the sides of the tin. Carefully slide the cake off the base of the tin onto a serving plate. Pipe swirls of whipped cream around the edge of the cake and decorate with the rose petals, almonds and angelica.

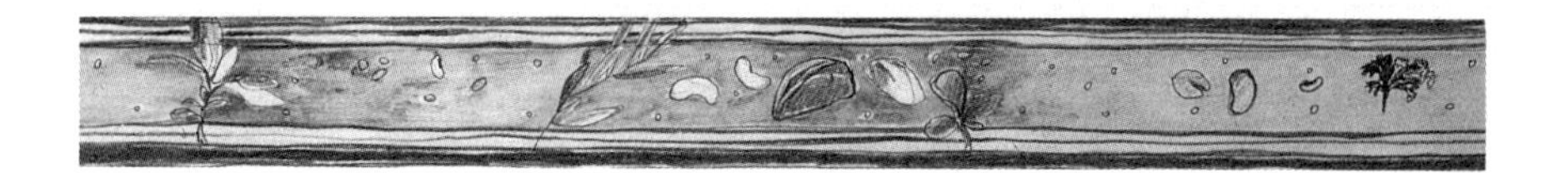

BAKED CARROT CUSTARD

Carrots are an unusual ingredient for a pudding but their natural sweetness does make them ideal for desserts. The younger the carrots, the sweeter they are.

Serves 4

Ingredients
460g/1lb young carrots, peeled
150ml/¼ pint water
120g/4oz stoned dates, finely chopped
1 tsp ground cinnamon
½ tsp ground nutmeg
¼ tsp ground ginger
¼ tsp ground cloves
3 free-range eggs (size 2), beaten
60g/2oz pistachio nuts, chopped
430ml/¾ pint milk
Pistachio nuts, to decorate

Preheat the oven to 160°C/325°F/Gas Mark 3. Grate the carrots coarsely and place in a saucepan. Add the water and simmer gently for 5 minutes or until soft, then add the dates and cook for a further 3 minutes. Place the carrot mixture in a liquidiser or food processor and blend to a fine purée. Transfer it to a large mixing bowl and stir in the spices, then beat in the eggs and pistachios.

Heat the milk until almost boiling, then pour onto the carrot mixture and beat well. Transfer to a shallow, ovenproof serving dish and bake for 40-45 minutes or until set. Allow to cool slightly and serve warm, or chill completely before serving. Decorate with extra pistachio nuts.

BROWN BREAD CRUMBLE

I particularly like this crumble topping which is flavoured with ground cardamom and is very high in fibre.

Serves 4

Ingredients
225g/8oz cooking apples, cored and sliced
225g/8oz raspberries
90g/3oz fresh wholemeal breadcrumbs
90g/3oz rolled oats
60g/2oz light muscovado sugar
1 tsp ground cinnamon
½ tsp ground cardamom
60g/2oz vegetable margarine or butter

Preheat the oven to 190°C/375°F/Gas Mark 5. Arrange the apple slices in a pie dish and scatter the raspberries over the top. Place the breadcrumbs, oats, sugar and spices in a large bowl and mix well. Add the margarine and rub into the mixture then spoon the topping over the prepared fruit and smooth the top with a spoon. Bake for 20-25 minutes.

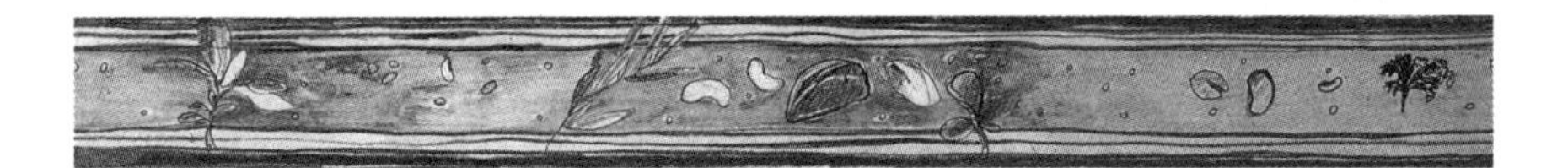

BAKED MANGO AND RICE

I think that mangoes are one of the most exotic tasting of all fruits. They certainly make a very special rice pudding!

Serves 4-6

Ingredients
2 large ripe mangoes
Juice of 1 lime
225g/8oz pudding rice
850ml/1½ pints water
60g/2oz unrefined caster sugar
411g/14½oz tin evaporated milk
Pinch ground nutmeg
Pinch ground cinnamon

Cut both mangoes in half lengthways, through the narrower sides of the fruit, and remove the stones. Cut one half of a mango into slices and reserve for decoration. Carefully scoop the flesh from the inside of the skin of the remaining 3 halves and place in a liquidiser or food processor with the lime juice and purée.

Place the rice in a saucepan with the water and sugar. Bring to the boil then reduce the heat and simmer for 10 to 15 minutes, or until the rice is tender and most of the liquid has been absorbed. Stir in the evaporated milk and spices and continue cooking for 5 to 10 minutes, stirring occasionally, until the mixture is thick and creamy.

If serving hot, heat the mango purée. Spoon a layer of the rice into a glass serving dish and cover with a layer of the purée. Repeat until all the rice and mango has been used. Serve hot or cold decorated with reserved mango slices.

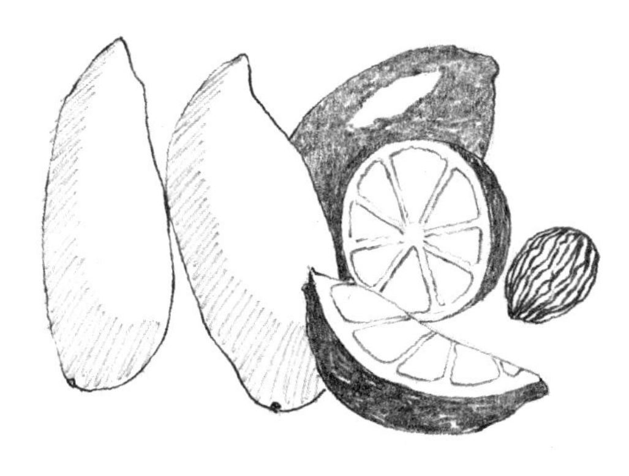

APPLEMINT PUDDING

Applemint is my favourite variety of mint – it has a slightly sweet flavour but any variety of garden mint may be used for this recipe. Serve the pudding with custard or cream.

Serves 4-6

INGREDIENTS
225g/8oz cooking apples, peeled, cored and sliced
Small knob butter
120g/4oz unrefined caster sugar
1 tbsp freshly chopped applemint
90g/3oz vegetable margarine
2 free-range eggs
120g/4oz self-raising flour
3 tbsps milk

Place the apples, butter and 30g/1oz of the caster sugar in a small saucepan and cook gently until the apples soften. Break up the fruit with the back of a wooden spoon. Stir in a teaspoon of the applemint and spoon into a 1.14 litre/2 pint pudding basin.

Place the margarine in a mixing bowl with the remaining caster sugar and beat until pale and creamy. Gradually add the eggs, beating well after each addition, then fold in the flour, the remaining applemint and milk. Spoon the sponge mixture into the pudding basin over the apple then cover with a piece of greased grease-proof paper and foil. Steam for 1½ hours, when the pudding will be just cooked or for up to 2 hours for a crisp, golden crust.

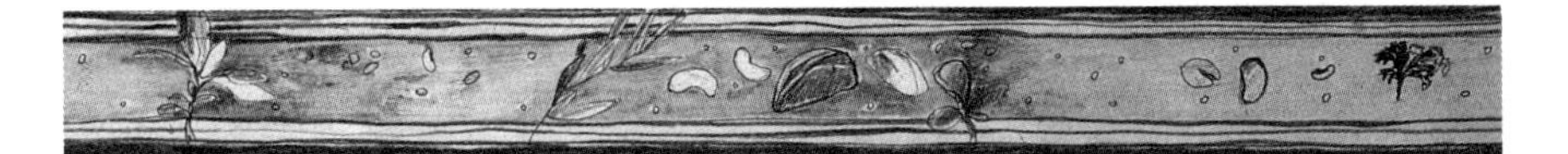

CARIBBEAN PINEAPPLE

This Caribbean Pineapple looks so impressive, especially when served flamed with the rum.

Serves 6-8

Ingredients
1 large fresh pineapple
150ml/¼ pint double cream
570ml/1 pint coffee ice-cream
60g/2oz raisins
120ml/4fl oz rum
2 tbsps chopped mixed nuts

Slice the top off the pineapple at the shoulder and scoop out the flesh from the top. Using a sharp knife, cut just within the skin until the bottom is almost reached. Insert the blade 2.5cm/1 inch up from the base and cut round in both directions just enough to loosen the flesh. Do not cut the bottom off. Insert a fork into the top of the pineapple flesh and twist to remove. Drain the shell and place in the freezer.

Remove the hard core from the pineapple and chop the flesh into tiny pieces, drain well. Whip the cream until stiff. Break up the ice-cream in a large bowl with a wooden spoon. Add the cream, raisins and nuts and mix well, then sprinkle the mixture with half the rum. Fill the frozen pineapple cask with the mixture, replace the top and wrap carefully in foil. Return to the deep freeze until required. Any extra mixture can be frozen in a separate bowl.

To serve, transfer the pineapple to the refrigerator three quarters of an hour before required. Place an ovenproof serving dish in the oven to become very hot. Place the pineapple on the hot dish, pour the rest of the rum into the dish and a little on the sides of the cask and light it. Scoop out portions of the ice-cream into individual serving dishes and spoon over a little burnt rum.

BAKED RASPBERRY APPLES

Raspberries are often used to stuff baked peaches – here they make an unusual topping for baked apples.

Serves 6

INGREDIENTS
2 tbsps apple juice
4 tbsps water
2 tbsps honey
1 tsp mixed spice
3 very large eating apples
225g/8oz raspberries

Preheat the oven to 200°C/400°F/Gas Mark 6. Mix the apple juice, water, honey and mixed spice in a large bowl. Wash the apples and, with a sharp knife, make deep zig-zag cuts around them. Take one half of the apple in each hand and twist gently until the two halves come apart. Remove the core and dip each apple in the apple juice mixture. Place the apples in an ovenproof dish and bake for 20-25 minutes until just soft. Remove from the oven and top with the raspberries. Reduce the oven temperature to 150°C/300°F/Gas Mark 2. Pour the remaining apple juice mixture over the raspberries and return the apples to the oven for a further 10 minutes. Serve at once.

PEAR AND APRICOT SLICE

Serve these slices warm as a dessert, topped with thick yogurt, or cold for afternoon tea.

Makes 8 slices

Ingredients
2 pears, approximately
340g/12oz in total
120g/4oz dried apricots, soaked
1 tbsp clear honey
2 tsps pear and apple spread
½ tbsp sunflower oil
1 free-range egg, beaten
120g/4oz wholemeal flour
1 tsp baking powder
Flaked almonds to decorate

Preheat the oven to 190°C/375°F/Gas Mark 5. Lightly grease a 15 × 20cm/6 × 8 inch tin. Peel and chop the pears into small pieces, and chop the apricots finely. Mix the honey with the pear and apple spread, then stir into the pears and apricots. Add the oil and egg and mix well. Mix together the flour and baking powder and fold into the pear and apricot mixture. Spread the mixture in the prepared tin and sprinkle with the flaked almonds. Bake for about 25 minutes or until risen and golden. Leave to cool then cut into 8 fingers.

RICE MERINGUE

Queen of Puddings is made with a breadcrumb base – this delicious variation is made with a rice pudding under the meringue.

Serves 4

INGREDIENTS
30g/1oz short grain pudding rice
570ml/1 pint milk
Few drops almond essence
5 tbsps soft brown sugar
A little butter
2 large dessert apples
2 tbsps raspberry jam
2 free-range egg whites

Preheat the oven to 160°C/325°F/Gas Mark 3. Wash the rice and place it in a shallow, buttered ovenproof dish. Add the milk, almond essence and 2 tbsps of soft brown sugar, then dot with a little butter and bake for 2½-3 hours stirring two or three times during cooking. Remove from the oven.

Meanwhile, peel and core the apples. Slice finely and place in a saucepan with 1 tbsp of water. Cook for 5-10 minutes until softened, then add a little of the sugar to sweeten. Cover the rice pudding with the raspberry jam and spread the apple purée over the top. Grind the remaining sugar finely and beat the egg whites until they are very stiff. Fold the remaining sugar into the egg whites and cover the pudding with the meringue mixture, pulling it up into peaks with a spoon or a fork. Bake for 20-30 minutes until heated through and golden on top. Serve immediately.

PEACHY CHEESECAKE

This cheesecake is just how I like them – baked and fairly rich! Use any fruit in season for decoration.

Serves 6

Ingredients

Base

12 digestive biscuits, crushed or liquidised until fine
45g/1½oz melted butter or margarine
1 tsp mixed spice

Topping

400g/14oz curd cheese
430ml/15fl oz soured cream or Greek yogurt
2 tbsps clear honey
1½ tsps vanilla essence or lemon juice
2 free-range eggs, beaten
1½ tbsps wholewheat self-raising flour
Sliced peaches to decorate

Preheat the oven to 150°C/300°F/Gas Mark 2. Lightly grease a 22.5cm/9 inch flan tin or dish. Combine the biscuit crumbs, melted butter and spices and press the mixture into the bottom of the prepared flan tin or dish.

Combine the curd cheese and 200ml/7fl oz of the soured cream or yogurt, 1 tbsp honey, ¾ tsp vanilla essence, the eggs and all the flour in a large bowl. Pour the mixture onto the biscuit base and bake in the preheated oven for approximately 20 minutes or until just set.

Remove from the oven and increase the oven temperature to 230°C/450°F/Gas Mark 8. Combine the remaining cream or yogurt with the rest of the honey and vanilla essence and spread over the top of the cake. Smooth over with a knife or spatula. Return the cheesecake to the oven and bake for a further 5 minutes. Allow to cool before decorating with sliced peaches then chill thoroughly before serving.

JAMAICAN MOUSSE CAKE

Rum, chocolate and bananas – true tastes of the Caribbean, combined in a wonderful dessert.

Serves 6-8

INGREDIENTS
175g/6oz plain chocolate
3 tbsps dark rum
280ml/½ pint double cream
2 large bananas, peeled and mashed until smooth
15g/½oz light muscovado sugar
1 tbsp strong black coffee
3 free-range eggs, separated
Chocolate curls, to decorate

Break the chocolate into cubes and place in a bowl over a pan of hot water or the top of a double boiler to melt, then stir in the rum and half of the cream, beating thoroughly until smooth. Put the mashed bananas, sugar and coffee in a large mixing bowl and beat until well combined. Add the egg yolks and mix well. Continue beating while adding all the chocolate mixture. Whisk the egg whites until stiff and forming peaks; fold into the banana mixture. Spoon the mixture into a lightly greased 20cm/8inch spring-form or loose bottomed cake tin. Chill for at least 2 hours or until completely set and firm.

Loosen the sides of the cake with a warm knife then remove the sides of the cake tin. Carefully slide the cake off the base of the tin on to a serving plate. Whip the remaining cream and decorate the cake with swirls of whipped cream and chocolate curls.

TREASURE RICE

The Chinese have very few traditional sweet dishes – this is a variation on one of the most popular.

Serves 4-6

INGREDIENTS

- 225g/8oz pudding rice
- 225g/8oz unrefined caster sugar
- 850ml/1½ pints water
- 150g/5oz red bean paste
- 1 tbsp candied lotus seeds (optional)
- 30g/1oz blanched almonds
- 4 red glacé cherries
- 4 green glacé cherries
- 2 rings glacé pineapple
- 2-3 stoned dates
- 4 glacé apricots

Place the rice in a saucepan with the sugar and water and bring slowly to the boil. Reduce the heat and simmer for 20 minutes or until rice is tender and the liquid has been absorbed. Stir occasionally. Spread half the cooked rice in a hot, shallow serving dish, then carefully spread with the red bean paste, taking care not to dislodge the rice. Spoon the remaining rice over the bean paste. Cut the fruit into pieces and arrange decoratively over the rice before serving. If the rice begins to get cold you can cover the dish with foil and heat it through in a warm oven.

PLUM AND GINGER CRISP

Plums and ginger are a winning combination, especially in this very quick dessert.

Serves 4-6

INGREDIENTS
460g/1lb dessert plums
60g/2oz light muscovado sugar
3 tbsps orange juice
75g/2½oz unsalted butter or vegetable margarine
225g/8oz ginger biscuits, crushed
60g/2oz flaked almonds

Preheat the oven to 180°C/350°F/Gas Mark 4. Wash and halve the plums and remove the stones, then place the fruit in a pie dish with the sugar and orange juice. Melt the butter or margarine and stir in the crushed biscuits and almonds. Sprinkle the biscuit topping over the fruit and level the top, then bake for 25 minutes. Cover with foil if the topping begins to brown too much.

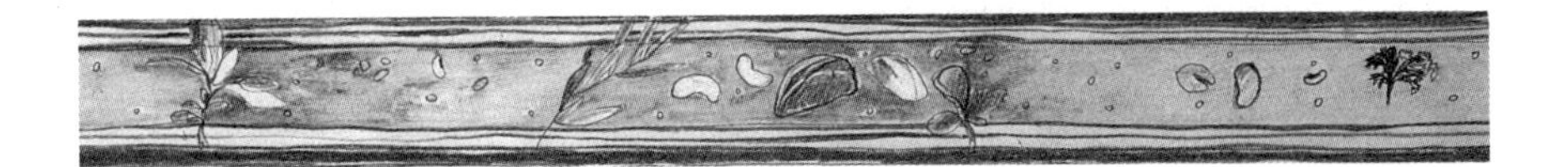

SWEET FRUIT PILAU

Sweet Fruit Pilau is fragrantly spiced and has a slightly crunchy texture from toasted nuts. Top with the fruits suggested or a selection of your own favourites.

Serves 6

INGREDIENTS
60g/2oz butter or vegetable margarine
30g/1oz cashew nuts
30g/1oz flaked almonds
9 cardamom pods, lightly crushed
4 cloves
½ tsp ground nutmeg
225g/8oz pudding rice
570ml/1 pint milk
120g/4oz unrefined caster sugar
Freshly grated rind of 1 orange
Few drops of orange flower water
60g/2oz black sesame seeds
1 small mango, peeled, stoned and sliced
60g/2oz seedless white grapes
1 orange, peeled and segmented
1 kiwi fruit, peeled and sliced

Melt the butter or margarine in a saucepan, add the nuts and cook until beginning to brown, then stir in the spices and cook for 30 seconds, stirring constantly. Stir in the rice, milk, sugar, orange rind and orange flower water and heat gently, stirring until the sugar dissolves. Bring the mixture to simmering point and cook over a low heat for about 20 minutes, or until the rice is tender and most of the liquid has been absorbed. Stir occasionally, and take care not to let the milk boil over. If the rice is not tender when the milk has been absorbed add a little extra. Stir in the sesame seeds and stand, covered, for 5 minutes; the rice will then fully absorb the liquid. Spoon the rice into a serving dish and decorate with the prepared fruit.

CHRISTMAS PUDDING

Christmas Pudding is traditionally served with brandy butter and cream – I like it with a strawberry coulis; try it!

Serves 8

INGREDIENTS

120g/4oz wholewheat self-raising flour
225g/8oz vegetarian suet
Grated rind of one small lemon
½ tsp grated nutmeg
120g/4oz sultanas
225g/8oz raisins
120g/4oz candied peel
30g/1oz chopped almonds
2 free-range eggs, beaten
2 tbsps clear honey
150ml/¼ pint milk

Combine the flour and suet in a large mixing bowl, add the lemon rind, nutmeg, fruit, peel and almonds. Beat the eggs and whisk in the honey. Add to the dry ingredients with the milk and mix well. Place in a greased pudding basin and cover with greaseproof paper and foil, tied securely. Place the pudding basin in a saucepan with about 2.5cm/1 inch of boiling water and steam for 3 hours, topping up with more water as required.

Cool the pudding completely and wrap in a clean tea towel. Store for between 4-6 weeks. On the day on which the pudding is to be eaten, steam for a further 1½ hours before serving.

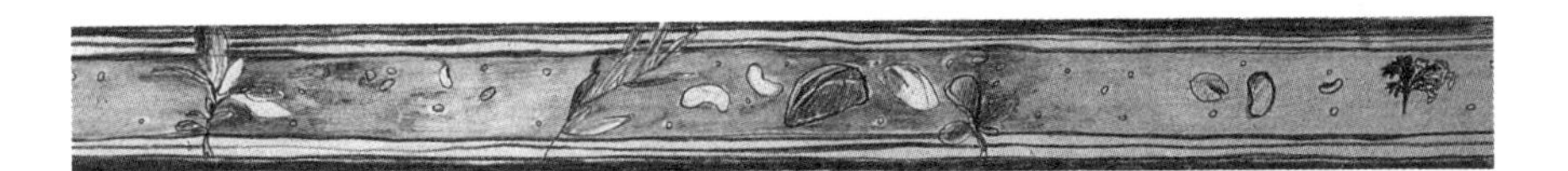

MINCE PIES

Mince pies used to be out-of-bounds for vegetarians because of the suet in the mincemeat. Vegetarian suet and prepared mincemeat are now, joyfully, widely available.

Makes about 16

INGREDIENTS
225g/8oz wholewheat self-raising flour
Pinch of salt
120g/4oz margarine or butter
90g/3oz soft brown sugar
1 egg yolk
2 tbsps cold water
175-225g/6-8oz vegetarian mincemeat
A little milk

Preheat the oven to 200°C/400°F/Gas Mark 6. Lightly grease two trays of patty tins. Combine the flour and salt in a bowl. Lightly rub in the margarine or butter until the mixture resembles fine breadcrumbs then mix in the sugar. Beat the egg yolk and water together and add to the flour mixture, mixing until a ball of dough is formed. Wrap in greaseproof paper or cling film and refrigerate for at least half an hour.

Roll out the pastry on a floured surface until about 6mm/¼ inch thick and cut out fifteen 7.5cm/3 inch rounds for the bases and fifteen 5cm/2 inch rounds for the lids. Line the patty tins with the larger rounds. Half fill with mincemeat and cover with the lids, having dampened the edges, pressing lightly to seal. Brush with milk. Bake for 20 minutes or until the pies are golden brown.

FILO CRACKERS

Take great care when working with filo pastry – it dries out very quickly. Either brush all the sheets with melted butter to keep them moist, or keep them covered until required.

Serves 4

INGREDIENTS
60g/2oz mixed dried fruit
30g/1oz figs, chopped
60g/2oz ground almonds
60g/2oz dates, chopped
60g/2oz walnuts, chopped
1 tbsp brown sugar
½ tsp ground cinnamon
zest and juice of 1 orange
60g/2oz butter, melted
16 sheets filo pastry, approximately 20cm x 8" square

Preheat the oven to 200°C/400°F/Gas Mark 6. Place the mixed fruit, figs, ground almonds, dates and walnuts in a mixing bowl, add the sugar, cinnamon, zest and juice of the orange and 30g/1oz of the melted butter. Mix together well and set to one side.

Use two sheets of pastry together for each cracker, buttering each one. Divide the mixture into 8 and place one portion of the filling in the centre of each double pastry sheet. Fold the base of the filo over the filling and roll up, then twist the ends of the filo roll where there is no filling, to form a cracker shape. Place on a greased baking tray and brush generously with the remaining melted butter. Cook for 20 minutes or until the crackers are golden brown and crisp.

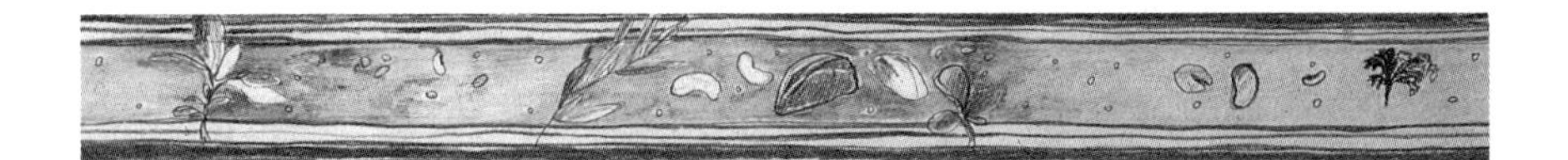

RASPBERRY MERINGUES

Raspberries are my favourite fruit and a perfect partner for meringues. Dredge the finished meringues with icing sugar instead of cocoa, if preferred.

Serves 4

Ingredients
2 free-range egg whites
120g/4oz unrefined caster sugar
Few drops raspberry flavouring
Few drops red food colouring (optional)
225g/8oz raspberries
4 tbsps raspberry liqueur or sherry
150ml/¼ pint double cream, whipped
Cocoa powder, for decoration

Line two baking sheets with non-stick baking parchment. Preheat the oven to 140°C/275°F/Gas Mark 1.

Whisk the egg whites until stiff then gradually whisk in two-thirds of the caster sugar.

Carefully fold in the remaining sugar, flavouring and food colouring, if used. Spoon the meringue into a piping bag fitted with a plain nozzle and pipe eight heart shapes or rounds. Place in the oven for 1½ hours to dry out. Remove from the oven and allow to cool completely.

Meanwhile, place the raspberries and liqueur or sherry in a bowl and allow to marinate until required. Whip the cream and use to sandwich two meringues together with a few of the soaked raspberries. Sprinkle the tops with a little cocoa powder and serve any remaining raspberries separately.

CELEBRATION PUDDING

Use Celebration Pudding as an alternative Christmas Pudding, and for any special occasion.

Serves 8

INGREDIENTS

First layer

175g/6oz sultanas
175g/6oz raisins
120g/4oz dates
2 tbsps apple juice
280ml/½ pint fresh orange juice
Juice of ½ lemon
¼ tsp grated nutmeg
2 tbsps rum or brandy
60g/2oz chopped almonds

Second layer

280ml/½ pint fresh orange juice
Juice of ½ lemon
2.5cm/1 inch cinnamon stick
60g/2oz ground almonds

Third layer

280ml/½ pint whipped cream
1 tbsp brandy (optional)

For the first layer, soak the sultanas, raisins and dates in orange and lemon juice for 2 hours. For the second layer, soak the apricots in the orange and lemon juice for 2 hours, then simmer the apricots and fruit juice with the cinnamon stick for about 40 minutes, until the apricots are soft. Remove the cinnamon stick, beat the apricots to a purée and stir in the ground almonds. Set to one side.

Simmer the sultanas, raisins and dates for the first layer in the apple juice, orange juice, lemon juice and nutmeg for about 40 minutes or until thick and syrupy, then stir in the rum or brandy and the chopped almonds. Stir the brandy into the whipped cream for the third layer.

Line a round pudding basin with cling film and build the pudding up in layers, beginning with the sultana and raisin mixture followed by the apricot mixture and lastly the whipped cream, making sure you end with a layer of the dark mixture on the top. Cover and chill well.

Turn out onto a serving dish, remove the cling film and flame before serving.

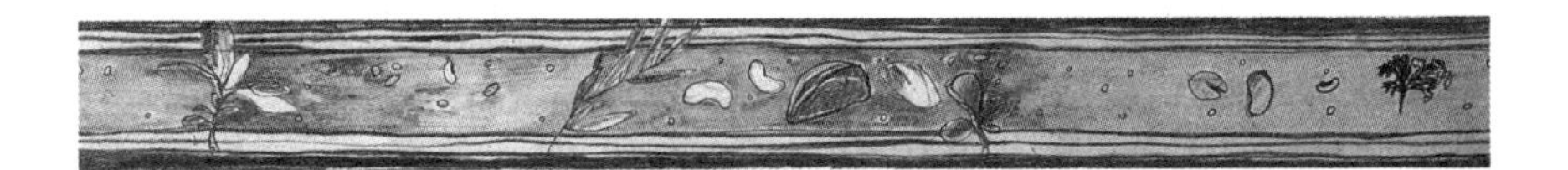

STRAWBERRY AND BANANA FROST

A thick, creamy sorbet.

Serves 4-6

INGREDIENTS
460g/1lb strawberries
1 large banana
175ml/6fl oz fromage frais
Few drops vanilla essence
1 tsp clear honey

Wash and hull the strawberries and keep half of them in the refrigerator. Peel the banana and cut into pieces, then cut the remaining strawberries in halves, or quarters if they are large, and freeze with the banana until solid.

Just before serving, remove the strawberries and banana from the freezer and place in a liquidiser or food processor with the fromage frais, vanilla essence and honey and blend until smooth. You will need to push the mixture down two or three times with a spatula or wooden spoon. Divide the mixture between 4 or 6 individual serving dishes and place the remaining strawberries around the 'frost' mixture. Serve at once.

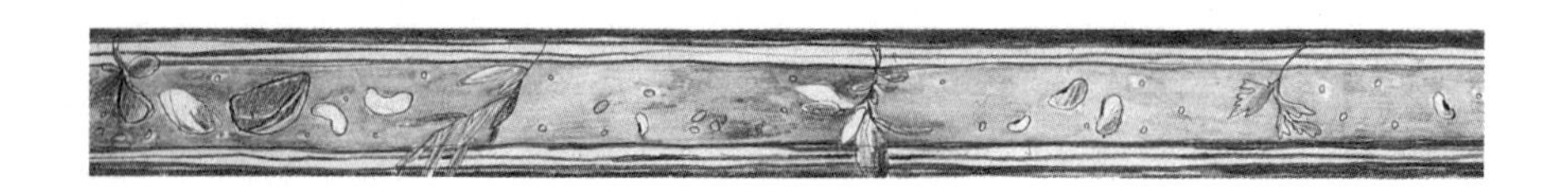

BRANDIED ORANGES WITH PEACH AND MANGO CREAM

A refreshing variation on caramelised oranges.

Serves 4

Ingredients
6 large Jaffa oranges
3 tbsps brandy
2 mangoes, peeled and cut into chunks
4 small ripe peaches, peeled and roughly chopped
3 tbsps double cream

Finely pare the zest from 3 of the oranges and boil in a little water for 2 minutes. Remove the zest and cool. Peel the oranges using a sharp knife, making sure that all the pith is removed. Slice them thinly then arrange the slices in a serving dish and sprinkle the zest over the top. Drizzle with the brandy and refrigerate for about an hour.

Place the mangoes and peaches in a liquidiser or food processor and blend until smooth. Stir in the cream and refrigerate until required. Hand round the peach and mango cream when serving the oranges.

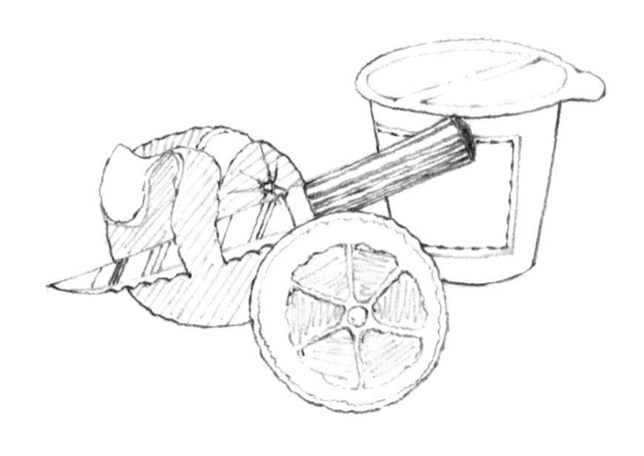

CAROB SUNDAE

The use of carob for this sundae instead of chocolate makes a much lighter dessert.

Serves 4

INGREDIENTS

Carob Dessert

225ml/8fl oz milk or soya milk
1 tsp vanilla essence
1 tbsp sunflower oil
2 tbsps honey
¼ tsp sea salt
1 tbsp cornflour
¼ tsp Caro (coffee substitute)
1 tbsp carob powder

Vanilla Custard

1 tbsp cornflour
120ml/4 fl oz milk or soya milk
1 tbsp honey
½ tsp pure vanilla essence

Filling

1 large banana, chopped
1 punnet of strawberries, hulled, washed and halved

Blend all the carob dessert ingredients together in a saucepan and cook until thick, stirring continuously, then leave to cool.

Mix the cornflour for the vanilla custard with a little of the milk to make a smooth paste then add the honey and vanilla essence. Heat the remaining milk until nearly boiling and pour over the cornflour mixture, stirring until smooth. Return the mixture to the pan and re-heat gently until thick, stirring constantly. Leave to cool.

Add half the carob dessert to the chopped banana and mix together carefully. Fill sundae glasses with layers of carob dessert, banana mixture, strawberries, vanilla custard and finally the plain carob dessert. Chill before serving.

MINTED GRAPES

This very refreshing fruit dessert is ideal after a large meal. You could use some chopped fresh mint in place of the Crême de Menthe – the colour is less violent.

Serves 4

INGREDIENTS
275g/10oz green grapes
A little Crême de Menthe
120ml/4fl oz soured cream
Soft brown sugar

Halve and pip the grapes, then divide them equally between four serving glasses, and sprinkle with a little Crême de Menthe. Top with soured cream and sprinkle a little brown sugar over. Serve at once.

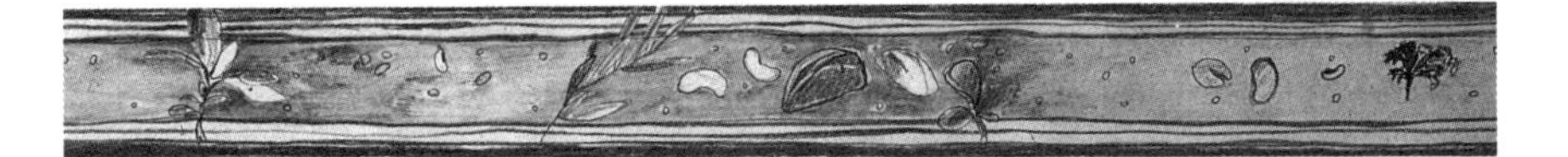

GINGER LOG

Chopped kiwi fruits may be used in place of the pineapple for this Ginger Log. For maximum effect when serving, slice the log diagonally to reveal layers of biscuit and fruit cream.

Serves 6

INGREDIENTS
200g/7oz ginger biscuits
60ml/2fl oz sherry
280ml/½ pint double cream
225g/8oz can pineapple chunks
Chopped nuts, toasted

Unwrap the ginger biscuits and set aside any broken ones. Pour a little sherry into a saucer. Whip the cream until thick and divide into two. Drain the pineapple chunks, divide into two and chop one half very finely, mixing into half of the cream.

Dip each biscuit briefly in the sherry and, using the cream and pineapple mixture, sandwich the ginger biscuits together to make a log. Lay the log on a serving dish and cover with the other half of the whipped cream spreading evenly with a knife. Using a fork, 'lift' the cream into peaks. Refrigerate for at least 2 hours. Sprinkle with chopped nuts and decorate with the remaining pineapple chunks before serving.

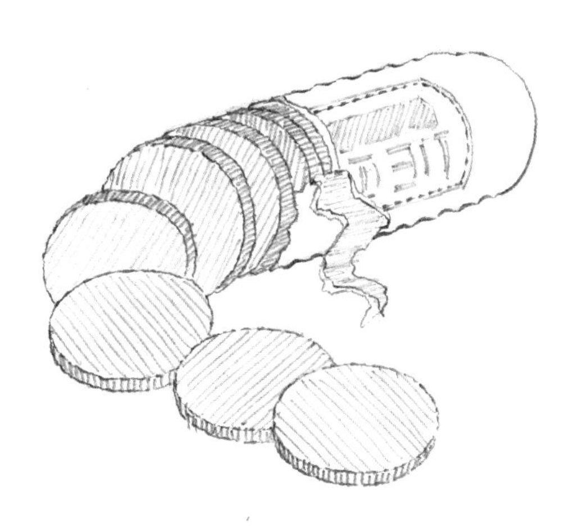

STRAWBERRY CLOUD

This is almost as quick to prepare as strawberries and cream!

Serves 4-6

INGREDIENTS
460g/1lb strawberries
275g/10oz silken tofu
Juice of ½ lemon
2 tbsps soft brown sugar
Few drops vanilla essence

Wash and hull the strawberries. Leave a few on one side for decoration. Drain the tofu and place in a liquidiser or food processor with the strawberries, lemon juice and sugar. Blend until smooth, then add the vanilla essence and blend again. Divide the mixture between 4-6 individual serving dishes and decorate with the reserved strawberries. Chill until required.

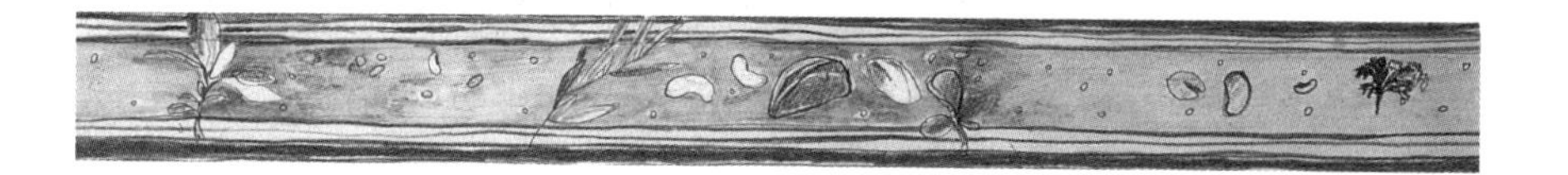

POACHED PEARS WITH RASPBERRY COULIS

Hyssop is easy to grow in the garden and is an attractive plant. If you don't have hyssop use a cinnamon stick to poach the pears and add a pinch of ground cinnamon to the raspberry coulis.

Serves 4

INGREDIENTS
280ml/½ pint water
4 tbsps clear honey
1 tbsp lemon juice
2 sprigs fresh hyssop or 1 stick cinnamon
4 pears
225g/8oz raspberries
1 tsp freshly chopped hyssop
Sprigs of fresh hyssop, to decorate (optional)

Place the water and honey in a large saucepan or frying pan and heat until the honey dissolves, then stir in the lemon juice and hyssop or cinnamon stick. Peel the pears and cut them in half lengthways with a sharp knife. Keeping the stalks intact, if possible, remove the cores with a grapefruit knife or teaspoon. Poach the pears in the syrup until tender. Cool, then chill until required.

Meanwhile, purée the raspberries and chopped hyssop in a liquidiser or food processor and press through a sieve to remove the seeds. Sweeten the raspberry coulis with a little of the honey syrup if necessary. Arrange the pears on a serving plate and pour a little raspberry coulis over each. Decorate with sprigs of hyssop and serve the remaining sauce separately.

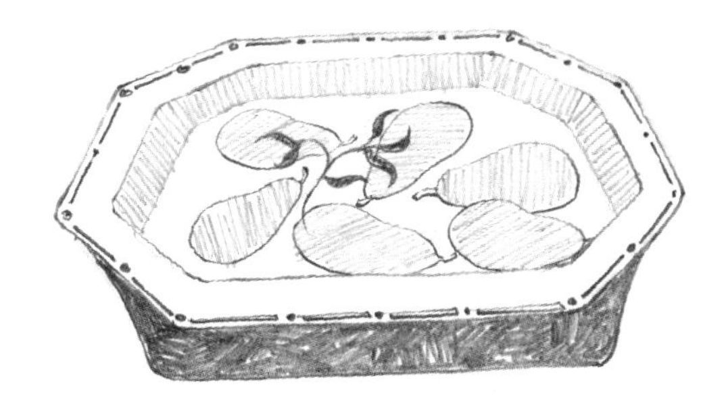

PARFAIT AU CASSIS

Parfaits are traditionally flavoured with coffee but this refreshing blackcurrant variation is particularly good, especially in the middle of summer.

Serves 4

INGREDIENTS
340g/12oz blackcurrants
2 tbsps crême de cassis
3 free-range egg yolks
120g/4oz light muscovado sugar
280g/½ pint single cream
280g/½ pint double cream, whipped
Blackcurrants and mint leaves, to decorate

Purée the blackcurrants in a liquidiser or food processor and press through a sieve with a wooden spoon to remove the skin and pips. Add the cassis to the fruit purée and freeze until it becomes slushy, stirring occasionally to prevent large ice crystals from forming.

Whisk the egg yolks and sugar together until they become very thick and creamy. Heat the single cream in a small pan until almost boiling. Gradually pour the scalded cream on to the egg mixture, stirring all the time. Place the bowl over a pan of gently simmering water and cook, stirring constantly, until the mixture thickens. Cool quickly by standing the bowl in iced water, then fold the whipped cream into the cooled egg mixture.

Freeze until the mixture is almost solid then whip with an electric mixer or in a food processor until slushy. Break up the blackcurrant mixture with a fork or electric whisk and fold into the cream mixture to give a marbled effect. Divide between 6 freezer-proof glasses and freeze until required. Move from the freezer to the refrigerator 30 minutes before serving, and decorate with blackcurrants and mint leaves.

WHITE COFFEE CREAMS

White Coffee Creams have a refreshing and most unusual flavour and make a welcome change from White Chocolate Mousse. Balance the flavour with a slightly sharp fruit sauce.

Serves 6-8

INGREDIENTS
8 coffee beans
280ml/½ pint milk
3 free-range eggs
60g/2oz unrefined caster sugar
150ml/¼ pint double cream
225g/8oz blackberries, blackcurrants or raspberries
1 tbsp lemon juice
Icing sugar to taste
Mint sprigs, to decorate

Preheat the oven to 160°C/325°F/Gas Mark 3. Place the coffee beans and milk in a small pan and simmer for 3 minutes, then allow to stand for 30 minutes to allow the flavour to infuse. Whisk the eggs and caster sugar together until they are thick, creamy and pale in colour. Strain the flavoured milk on to the egg mixture through a fine sieve, then stir in the cream and whisk to blend well. Pour equal amounts of the egg mixture into 6 to 8 lightly greased individual ramekin dishes or small bowls.

Place a few sheets of newspaper in a roasting tin and place the ramekin dishes on top. Fill with hot water to about half way up the dishes and bake for 25 minutes or until the custards are just set. Remove the dishes from the water bath and chill.

Reserve a few well shaped fruits for decoration and press the remaining fruit through a sieve into a small bowl. Stir in the lemon juice and enough icing sugar to sweeten to taste. Carefully loosen the sides of the chilled creams with a round-bladed knife. Invert a small plate over the top of each ramekin and turn the cream out, shaking to loosen if necessary. Pour a little fruit sauce around and partially over each cream. Decorate with the reserved fruit and mint sprigs.

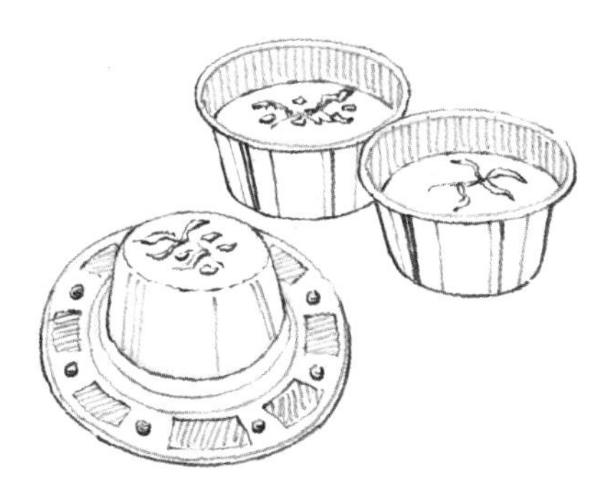

CAROB PEARS

There is a classic French dish where poached pears are coated with a thick chocolate sauce. Carob Pears are less rich but just as tasty.

Serves 4

INGREDIENTS
4 ripe dessert pears
1 tbsp maple syrup
Boiling water to cover
60g/2oz carob bar
30g/1oz desiccated coconut

Peel the pears thinly, leaving the stalks intact. Cut a small slice from the base of each so that they will stand upright and place them in a bowl. Mix the maple syrup with the boiling water and pour over the pears. Leave to go cold.

Remove the pears from the syrup and dry carefully. Place in one large or four small serving dishes. Break up the carob bar and put it into a heatproof bowl. Stand the bowl in a saucepan of boiling water until the carob is melted, stirring from time to time. Spoon the melted carob over the pears, allowing it to set a little before sprinkling the dessicated coconut over the top. Refrigerate for 2-3 hours before serving.

RHUBARB, ORANGE AND STRAWBERRY COMFORT

This 'comforting' dessert could easily be made with fresh rhubarb in season, but the ingredients listed will enable you to make it at any time of year.

Serves 4

INGREDIENTS
460g/1lb can rhubarb in natural juice
1 tsp ground ginger
298g/11oz can mandarin segments in natural juice
Liquid sweetener or honey to taste
2 tbsps low fat natural yogurt
175g/6oz strawberries, hulled and rinsed
2 tbsps crunchy oat cereal

Place the rhubarb and ginger in a saucepan. Strain the juice from the mandarins and add it to the pan, reserving the segments. Cook for about 10 minutes, stirring until mushy, then beat the rhubarb briskly until the fruit breaks up and the mixture becomes thicker. Sweeten with sweetener or honey to taste then stir in the yogurt with the mandarin segments, taking care not to break them up too much. Cover and allow to cool completely.

Slice the strawberries thinly and reserve a few slices for decoration. Mix most of the slices into the cooled rhubarb mixture and spoon into serving dishes. Just before serving sprinkle with the crunchy cereal and decorate with the reserved strawberry slices.

CHOCOLATE ORANGE CHEESECAKE

I love cheesecake and never tire of the endless variations. Chocolate Orange Cheesecake is refreshing, with the chocolate providing just a hint of wicked indulgence!

Serves 8-10

Ingredients

90g/3oz butter or vegetable margarine, melted
175g/6oz chocolate digestive biscuits, crushed
460g/1lb full fat vegetarian cream cheese
120g/4oz unrefined caster sugar
Grated rind and juice of 1 orange
280ml/½ pint Greek yogurt
1 tbsp agar-agar
3 tbsps water
60g/2oz plain chocolate, melted
2 oranges, peeled and segmented

Mix together the butter or margarine and biscuits and press into the bottom of a 20cm/8 inch loose bottomed cake tin. Chill. Beat together the cream cheese and sugar and then beat in the orange juice and rind and fold in the yogurt. Dissolve the agar-agar in the water and stir it into the mixture. Pile the filling on top of the base and level the top. Drizzle about two-thirds of the melted chocolate over the top and swirl a skewer through the mixture to form a marbled effect. Chill until set. Transfer to a serving dish and arrange the orange segments on top. Decorate with the remaining chocolate.

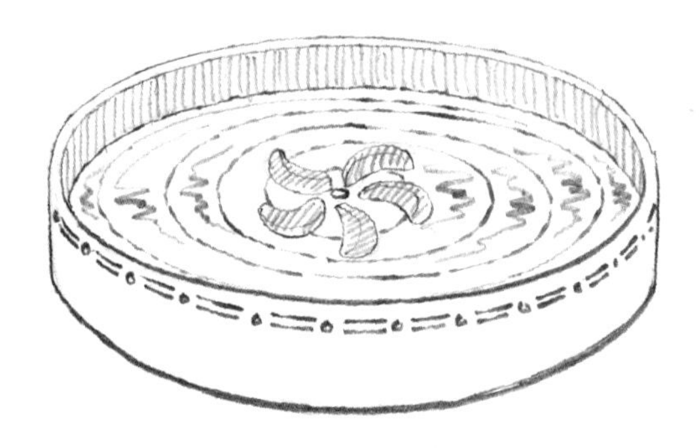

WHITE AND DARK CHOCOLATE BOMBE

A double treat for chocoholics and so easy to prepare! Use home-made ice cream if you have time to make it.

Serves 6-8

INGREDIENTS
280ml/½ pint dark chocolate ice cream
1 tbsp strong black coffee
570ml/1 pint vanilla ice cream
120g/4oz white chocolate
60g/2oz ratafia biscuits, coarsely crushed

Put a 1.14 litres/2 pints bombe mould or decorative mould into the freezer to chill. Allow the chocolate ice cream to stand at room temperature until just softened but not melted then beat in the coffee. Coat the base and sides of the chilled mould with the softened ice cream, leaving a hollow in the centre and refreeze the ice cream if it is too soft to stay up the sides of the mould. Freeze until solid.

Allow the vanilla ice cream to soften slightly at room temperature. Break the white chocolate into small cubes and melt in a bowl over a pan of simmering water. Beat the chocolate into the ice cream, then add the crushed biscuits, mixing until evenly distributed. Fill the centre of the mould with the white chocolate ice cream mixture, level the top then freeze until solid. About 30 minutes before required, remove the bombe from the freezer and stand in hot water for a few seconds. Upturn the mould onto a serving dish and shake the ice cream out. Leave to stand in the refrigerator to soften slightly.

LOW-FAT BROWN BREAD ICE CREAM

Brown Bread Ice Cream was popular in Victorian times and is now enjoying a revival!

Serves 4

INGREDIENTS
45g/1½oz brown breadcrumbs
45g/1½oz brown sugar
3 free-range eggs, separated
280ml/½ pint Greek yogurt
2 tsps honey (optional)

Preheat the oven to 190°C/375°F/Gas Mark 5. Place the breadcrumbs on a baking tray and cover with the sugar, then bake in the oven for 20 minutes or until they begin to brown and caramelise. Stir once or twice so that they brown evenly. Leave to cool.

Whisk the egg whites until stiff. Mix the egg yolks into the yogurt in a separate bowl and then fold in the egg whites. Add the honey if desired and fold in evenly. Add the cold breadcrumbs and mix well, then pour into a freezer container. Place in the freezer and, when starting to freeze, stir the sides to prevent ice crystals forming. Return to the freezer and leave until set. Leave to stand for 15-20 minutes at room temperature or for 20-30 minutes in the refrigerator before serving.

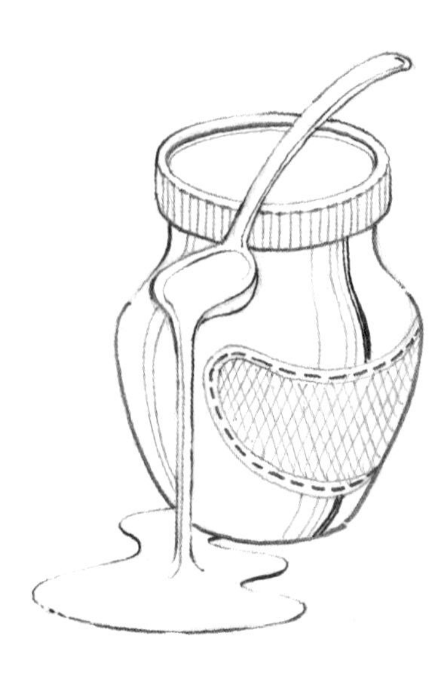

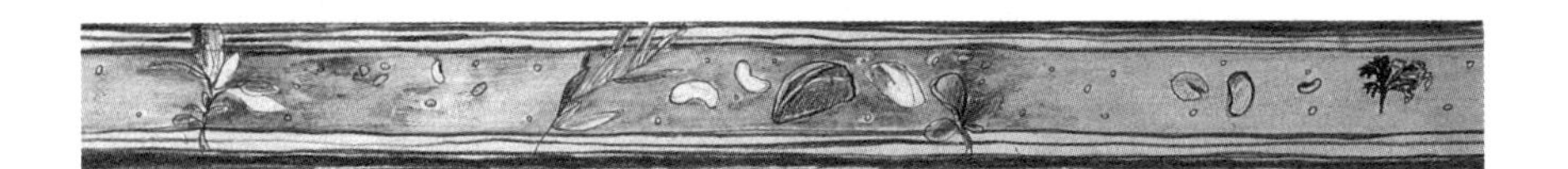

COFFEE AND RAISIN ICE CREAM

Make this luxury ice cream even more special by adding 2 tablespoons of rum

Serves 4

INGREDIENTS
280ml/½ pint full cream milk
120g/4oz sugar
6 tsps coffee granules or powder
1 tsp cocoa powder
1 free-range egg yolk
1 tsp vanilla essence
280ml/½ pint whipping or double cream
60g/2oz raisins

Heat the milk and sugar until almost boiling, then add the coffee and cocoa, stir and leave to cool. Beat the egg yolk with the vanilla essence until frothy and whip the cream until stiff. Pour the cream and coffee mixture into the egg mixture and stir well, then add the raisins and stir again. Freeze until firm (3-4 hours), stirring several times during freezing. Defrost in the refrigerator for 20-30 minutes before serving.

CASHEW ICE CREAM

Cashew nut is not a flavour immediately associated with ice cream – try it; you'll like it!

Serves 4

INGREDIENTS

- 1 large very ripe banana, peeled and roughly chopped
- 120g/4oz finely ground cashew nuts
- 150ml/¼ pint concentrated soya milk
- ½ tsp vanilla essence
- 2 tsps clear honey
- 2 rings unsweetened canned pineapple, diced

Place all the ingredients, apart from the pineapple, in a liquidiser or food processor and blend until smooth. Add the pineapple and blend briefly. Pour the mixture into a shallow container and freeze for 2 hours.

Cakes & Biscuits

In considering a vegetarian diet we so often think only of courses where animal proteins have to be exchanged for alternative forms of nourishment and forget that other things carry on as usual!

Baking with Better Ingredients

Experiment more with your baking! I believe that our interest in the high fibre foods such as oats and wholemeal flour, and unrefined sugar gives us the opportunity to create wonderfully varied and unusual cakes and biscuits. For those who eat them, the use of free-range eggs in baking adds an extra richness of flavour, but do be careful of the egg sizes. Most standard recipes assume a size 3, or occasionally a size 4 egg. Free-range eggs are seldom categorised by size, so for delicate mixtures adjust the number that you use. Too many cause heavy sponges and rather solid, over-moist fruit cakes.

Some lightly processed ingredients, available in health food shops, sound good for baking but, in practice, do not produce satisfactory results. A classic example is jumbo oats, which look large, luscious and perfect for flapjack. However, this is not so: because they are less refined than the traditional rolled oats the jumbo variety are unable to absorb as much of the buttery mixture used to bind flapjack together, resulting in a solid, brittle mass – great for the bird table if you can get it out of the tin!

Keeping Your Reputation as a Baker

The transition to wholemeal baker requires perseverance. There is a certain knack to keeping cakes, and especially sponges, light when made with wholemeal flour. I find that I need to keep at least two different grades of flour at home to ensure successful baking; 100% wholewheat for bread and an 80-85% flour for cakes and pastry making. The bread flour has 100 percent of the bran in it and is consequently coarse in texture. This is not suitable for pastry, which will not bind and roll out properly, or for light cakes, where the flour is too heavy for a good rise. I find it beneficial with most cakes to add tepid water, rather than milk, to the mixture to obtain the correct consistency before baking. This helps to produce almost instant steam when the cake is placed in the oven, thus aiding the crucial initial rising period.

Back to The Future?

Any problems that we have in adapting to wholemeal baking are not new! We have as standard ingredients refined flour and sugar and we have to learn to adapt to using the purer ingredients that were commonplace before progress arrived and set us back! There are references throughout history to baked goods: reliefs in the tomb of Rameses III at Thebes showing a variety of cakes produced by the royal bakery – these were carved more than 3,000 years ago; Aristophanes, the Greek playwright, referred to varieties of cakes and pastries in his plays; and in the earliest known cookbook, written in the first century AD, there are recipes for cakes made of honey, sesame, and fruit. Many of these early recipes were flavoured with spices such as black pepper, an idea which has been resurrected as new during the era of nouvelle cuisine.

Travel – the Traditional Broadening of our Horizons

Many classic cakes and biscuits were perfected in the religious houses of Euorpe, where monks experimented with new ingredients brought back from successful explorations overseas. How many countries would consider gingerbread to be traditional to their shores? Well, monasteries throughout France, Germany and Italy all became celebrated for their gingerbreads as their explorers returned with precious cargoes.

Once Columbus had opened up the West Indies and the cocoa bean was found the cooks of Spain had another vital ingredient for cooking (and, in my opinion, everyday living!) – chocolate. Knowledge of chocolate making was spread throughout Europe by travelling Spanish monks and, as the great cities grew and prospered, so experimentation in baking and the production of all sweet goods flourished, and more and more delicacies were produced, both to satisfy hunger and to show wealth.

Buying the Best

Now that all these once treasured ingredients are so much taken for granted it is vitally impotrant to understand that the best ingredients produce the best results. This is true in all cooking, but I feel especially strongly about using good quality chocolate with a high cocoa butter content, which should be above 50 per cent and is clearly indicated on the chocolate wrapper. I am also very selective when buying dried fruits, the best of which (in terms of vine fruits, or dried grapes) now come from some of the major wine producing areas of the world such as Australia, California and Greece. I thoroughly recommend Australian 5 Crown sultanas, Californian or Australian raisins and Greek currants, all of which, with their plump, juicy textures and intense flavours, will make a significant contribution to the success of your baking.

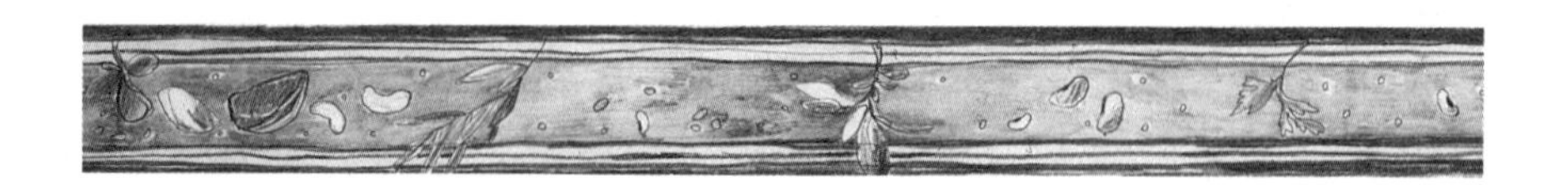

CAROB APPLE CAKE

You will need to exercise some self-control with this cake as it is better when stored for 24 hours in an airtight tin after baking!

Makes 1 20cm/8 inch cake

INGREDIENTS
150g/5oz soft margarine
120g/4oz light muscovado sugar
1 large free-range egg, beaten
175g/6oz fine wholemeal flour
75g/2½oz light carob powder
1½ tsps baking powder
1 tbsp Amontillado sherry
400g/14oz Bramley cooking apples, peeled and sliced

Topping
90g/3oz carob chips
Knob of butter
A little water

Preheat the oven to 160°C/325°F/Gas Mark 3. Lightly grease a deep, 20cm/8 inch cake tin. Cream the margarine and sugar together until fluffy. Add half of the beaten egg and continue creaming, then add the rest of the egg together with the sieved flour, carob, baking powder and sherry. Mix well. Place half the mixture in the prepared cake tin and cover with the sliced apples. Add the other half of the mixture and smooth the top. Bake for 1¼ hours or until firm to the touch. Melt the carob chips with the butter and water and drizzle over the top of the cake when cooled.

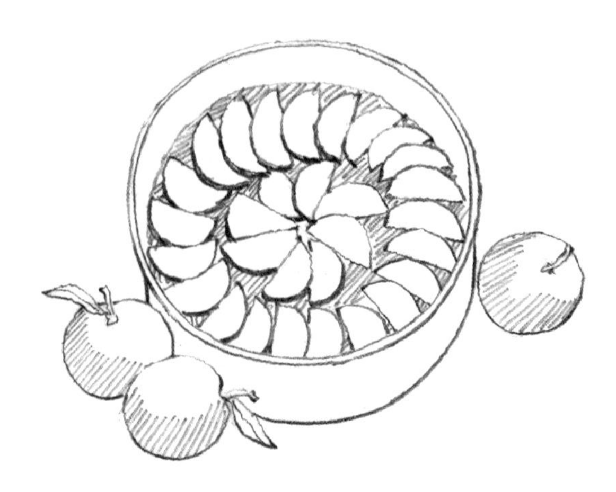

BANANA & DATE LOAF

Banana cakes are best made with the squashiest bananas available – those with really black skins are ideal! Choose a much firmer, yellow-skinned banana for decoration, dipping the slices in lemon juice to avoid discolouration.

Makes 1 900g/2lb loaf

INGREDIENTS
4 tbsps milk
1 tbsp treacle
120g/4oz vegetable margarine
90g/3oz light muscovado sugar
2 free-range eggs, beaten
175g/6oz self-raising flour, sieved
90g/3oz stoned dates, chopped
1 small ripe banana, peeled and sliced
60g/2oz walnuts, chopped
Glacé icing, walnut halves and banana slices, to decorate

Grease and base line a 900g/2lb loaf tin. Preheat the oven to 190°C/375°F/Gas Mark 5. Place the milk, treacle, margarine and sugar in a saucepan and heat, stirring, until the fat melts and the sugar dissolves. Cool slightly then beat in the eggs.

Place the flour, dates, banana and nuts in a large bowl and make a well in the centre. Pour the egg and treacle mixture into the centre and beat, gradually incorporating the flour, until a thick batter is formed. Pour the batter into the loaf tin and bake in the centre of the oven for 50 minutes, or until a skewer inserted into the loaf comes out clean. Cool slightly in the tin before transferring the loaf to a wire rack to cool completely. Cover with glacé icing and arrange walnut halves on top. Just before serving arrange banana slices, dipped in lemon juice, around the loaf.

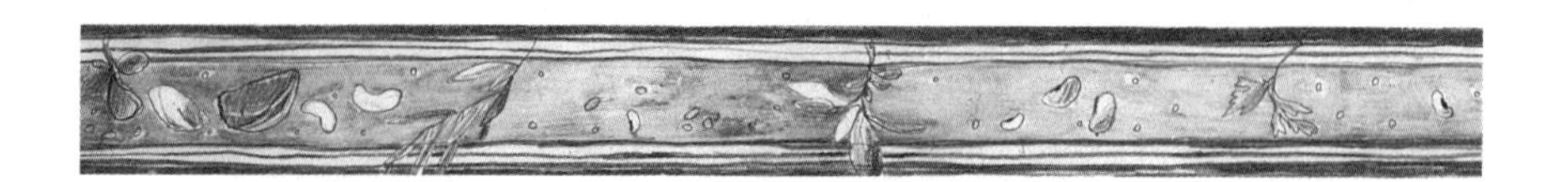

RICH FRUIT CAKE WITH GUINNESS

This cake requires self-control! It really is better if you leave it for a week or so before eating!

Makes 1 17.5cm/8 inch cake

INGREDIENTS
225g/8oz soft margarine
225g/8oz dark brown sugar
4 medium free-range eggs, beaten
275g/10oz wholemeal flour
2 tsps mixed spice
520g/18oz mixed dried fruit
10 tbsps Guinness

Preheat the oven to 160°C/325°F/Gas Mark 3. Lightly grease a 17.5cm/7 inch loose bottomed cake tin. Cream the margarine and sugar together until pale and fluffy, then beat in the eggs one at a time. Gradually stir in the flour and mixed spice, followed by the dried fruit. Add 4 tbsps Guinness to mix.

Place the mixture in the tin and make a deep well in the centre; this allows the finished cake to have a flat top. Bake for 1 hour then turn the temperature down to 150°C/300°F/Gas Mark 2 for a further 1½ hours. Allow the cake to cool in the tin.

Remove the cake from the tin and turn it upside down. Prick the base of the cake all over with a skewer and slowly pour in the remaining 6 tbsps of Guinness. Wrap in foil and store in a cool place for at least a week before eating.

VIENNA CAKE

Vienna Cake is made with dark brown, unrefined Barbados sugar, so it has a rich, dark colour.

Makes 1 17.5cm/7 inch cake

INGREDIENTS
225g/8oz butter or margarine
225g/8oz Barbados sugar
3 free-range eggs, separated
3 tbsps milk
90g/3oz carob powder
225g/8oz wholemeal flour
175g/6oz carob bar

Preheat the oven to 150°C/300°F/Gas Mark 2. Lightly grease a 17.5cm/7 inch cake tin. Place the butter and sugar in a mixing bowl and cream together until pale and fluffy. Add the egg yolks and beat well then mix in the milk. Combine the carob powder with the flour and fold into the creamed mixture, which will be very stiff at this stage. Whisk the egg whites until they are stiff and fold carefully into the mixture.

Spoon the cake mixture into the prepared tin and bake for 1½ hours, until a skewer inserted into the centre of the cake comes out clean. Turn out onto a wire rack to cool. When the cake is completely cold, melt the carob bar in a bowl over a pan of simmering water. Cover the cake with the melted carob, smoothing it with a knife dipped in boiling water. Leave the carob to harden before storing the cake in an airtight tin.

CARROT CAKE WITH APRICOT FILLING

Carrot cake should always be moist – with an apricot filling it is even more delicious.

Makes 1 17.5cm/7 inch cake

Ingredients
120g/4oz dried apricots
175g/6oz butter or margarine
175g/6oz soft brown sugar
2 free-range eggs, separated
200g/7oz plain flour
1 tsp baking powder
225g/8oz carrots (150g/5oz weight when peeled and finely grated)
60g/2oz sultanas
90g/3oz walnuts, finely chopped
2 tsps grated lemon rind
½ tsp ground cinnamon

Preheat the oven to 180°C/350°F/Gas Mark 4. Grease a 17.5cm/7 inch round springform or loose bottomed tin. Soak the apricots in water overnight, drain and purée until smooth in a liquidiser or food processor.

Beat the butter and sugar together until pale and creamy. Whisk the egg yolks with a fork and beat into the butter and sugar, then sieve the flour and baking powder and fold into the mixture. Add the rest of the ingredients except the egg whites. Whisk the egg whites until they form soft peaks, and fold into the mixture. Spoon into the greased tin and bake for 45-50 minutes. Cool in the tin for 10 minutes and then turn out onto a wire rack to cool completely.

Slice in half and spoon the apricot purée onto the bottom half of the cake. Place the other half on top.

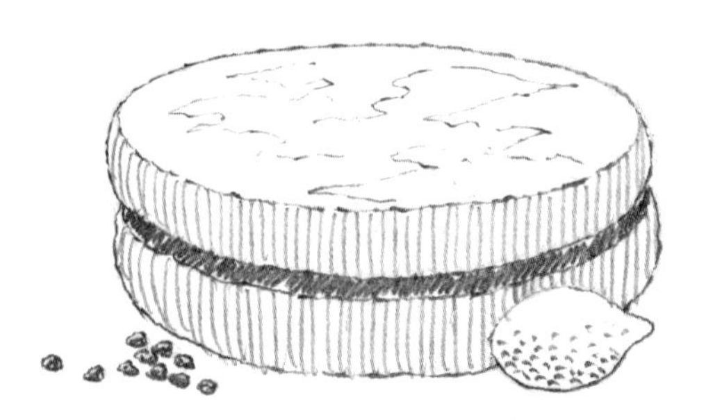

CARROB BISCUIT CAKE

This is a quick refrigerator cake, not quite so rich as some chocolate varieties, and suitable for eating as a snack at any time of day.

Makes 16 squares

Ingredients
225g/8oz digestive biscuits
120g/4oz margarine or butter
1 tbsp soft brown sugar
3 level tbsps carob powder
2 tbsps golden syrup
175g/6oz sultanas
225g/8oz carob bar

Lightly grease a 20cm/8 inch square tin or dish. Crush the biscuits with a rolling pin and place in a mixing bowl. Place the margarine, sugar, carob powder and syrup in a pan and melt over a low heat, stirring all the time. Add to the biscuit crumbs with the sultanas and mix well. Press the mixture into the prepared tin or dish. Break the carob bar into a heatproof bowl and place over a pan of simmering water until melted. Cover the cake with the melted carob and mark it attractively with the back of a fork. Refrigerate until cold then cut into squares. Store in an airtight tin.

PRUNE & WALNUT LOAF

This loaf may be made with either prunes or dates – they both taste good!

Makes 1 900g/2lb loaf

INGREDIENTS
340g/12oz prunes
175ml/6fl oz water
340g/12oz fine wholemeal flour
2 tsps baking powder
60g/2oz brown sugar
1 tsp mixed spice
120g/4oz walnuts, chopped
4 tbsps sunflower oil
1 free-range egg, beaten
Orange juice
Whole walnuts to decorate

Preheat the oven to 160°C/325°F/Gas Mark 3. Lightly grease a 900g/2lb loaf tin and line with greaseproof paper. Simmer the prunes in the water until soft. Allow to cool and retain the cooking liquid. Pit the prunes and chop finely. Mix the flour, baking powder, sugar, spice and walnuts together and in a separate bowl mix the prunes, cooking liquid, oil and egg. Fold together the flour mixture and the prune mixture, adding orange juice to give a soft dropping consistency. Pour into the prepared tin and decorate with walnuts. Bake for 1¼ hours, until a skewer inserted into the loaf comes out clean. Turn out and cool on a wire rack.

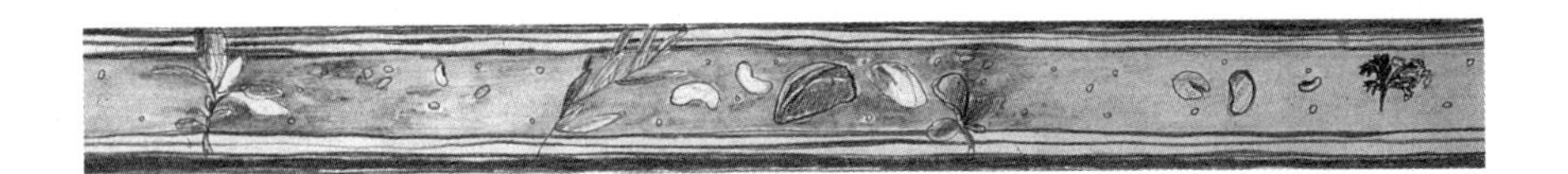

APPLE SPICE RING

This cake is equally delicious made with or without sugar – it's all a matter of diet and taste.

Makes 1 20cm/8 inch cake

INGREDIENTS

460g/1lb dessert apples, cored
90g/3oz ground hazelnuts
120g/4oz wholemeal flour
30g/1oz bran
60g/2oz light muscovado sugar (optional)
1½ tsps baking powder
1 tsp ground cinnamon
Pinch ground nutmeg
Pinch ground cardamom
30g/1oz vegetable margarine, melted
120ml/4fl oz milk
Dessert apple slices and icing sugar, to decorate

Preheat the oven to 180°C/350°F/Gas Mark 4. Lightly grease a 20cm/8inch ring tin. Coarsely grate the apples and place them in a mixing bowl with the hazelnuts, flour, bran, sugar (if using), baking powder and spices. Mix well. Add the margarine and beat until it is evenly blended, then stir in the milk and mix to a stiff batter.

Carefully spoon the mixture into the prepared tin and level the top. Bake for 45 minutes or until a skewer inserted into the centre of the cake comes out clean. Allow to cool slightly in the tin then transfer to a wire rack to cool. Dust with icing sugar and decorate with apple slices just before serving.

BANANA LOAF

I love the moist, sticky texture of Banana loaf, and serve it thinly sliced and buttered. Keep wrapped in foil for a day or two before cutting for maximum stickiness!

Makes 1 loaf

INGREDIENTS

60g/2oz porridge oats
175g/6oz soft brown sugar
150g/5oz mixed fruit
175ml/6fl oz Granose banana soya milk
175g/6oz self-raising flour
Pinch of nutmeg

Begin preparing the cake the day before it is to be cooked. Place all the ingredients except the self-raising flour and nutmeg into a large bowl and stir well. Cover and leave in the refrigerator overnight.

The following day, preheat the oven to 180°C/350°F/Gas Mark 4 and line or grease a 460g/1lb loaf tin. Mix the self-raising flour and the nutmeg gently into the mixture and pour into the loaf tin. Bake for an hour or until a skewer inserted into the loaf comes out clean. Cool on a wire rack.

CHOCOLATE PEAR SPONGE

This cake is moist and dense in texture – don't panic if it doesn't rise very much; it's meant to be like that!

Makes 1 × 18cm/7 inch cake

INGREDIENTS
120g/4oz vegetable margarine
120g/4oz unrefined caster sugar
1 tbsp milk
2 free-range eggs, size 2
100g/3½oz self-raising flour
15g/½oz cocoa powder
½ tsp baking powder
1 tsp mixed spice
1 small ripe pear, peeled, cored and diced

Lightly grease a 17.5cm/7 inch deep cake tin. Preheat the oven to 180°C/350°F/Gas Mark 4. Beat together the margarine and sugar until pale and creamy then beat in the eggs, one at a time, until well incorporated. Sieve the flour, cocoa powder, baking powder and mixed spice together and fold into the mixture with the milk. Add the diced pear and stir until evenly distributed through the sponge mixture. Carefully spoon into the prepared tin and level the top. Bake for 40 to 45 minutes or until springy to the touch. Allow to cool slightly in the tin then transfer to a wire rack to cool completely.

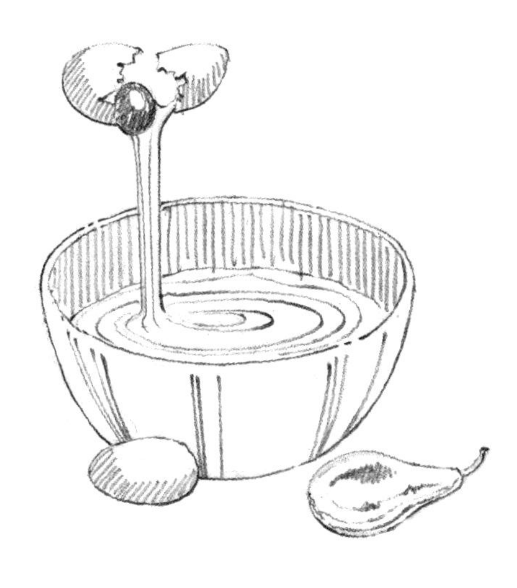

DATE & WALNUT CAKE

My Granny used to make us Date and Walnut cake - it has always been one of my favourites.

Makes 1 450g/1lb loaf

INGREDIENTS
150ml/¼ pint water
90g/3oz vegetable margarine
120g/4oz fresh or dried dates, stoned and chopped
120g/4oz wholemeal flour
1 tsp baking powder
½ tsp bicarbonate of soda
1 tsp ground cinnamon
60g/2oz walnuts, chopped
4 tbsps unrefined demerara sugar

Grease and base line a 460g/1lb loaf tin. Preheat the oven to 180°C/350°F/Gas Mark 4. Place the water, margarine and dates in a saucepan and heat gently until simmering. Simmer for 3 minutes or until the dates soften. Mash the dates roughly into the cooking liquid using a fork.

Place the flour, baking powder, soda, cinnamon and walnuts in a bowl and make a well in the centre. Pour the date mixture into the well and beat, gradually incorporating the flour, until well mixed. Pour the cake mixture into the prepared tin and level the top. Bake for 40 minutes, or until a skewer inserted into the cake comes out cleanly. Allow the cake to cool slightly in the tin before removing and transferring to a wire rack to cool completely. Sprinkle with demerara sugar just before serving.

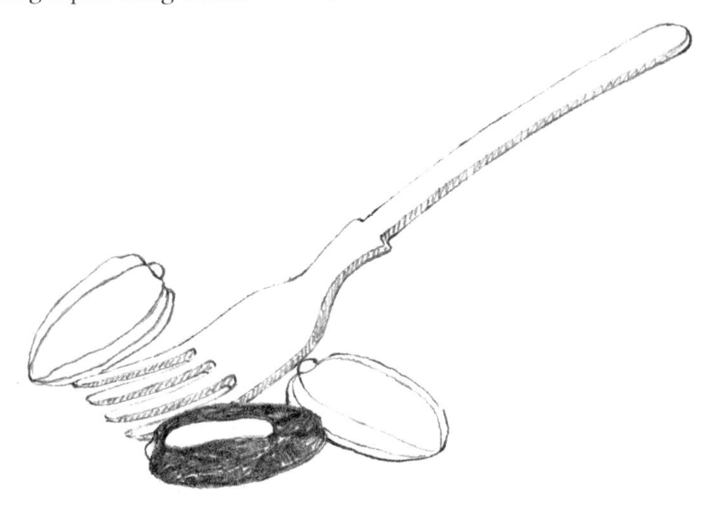

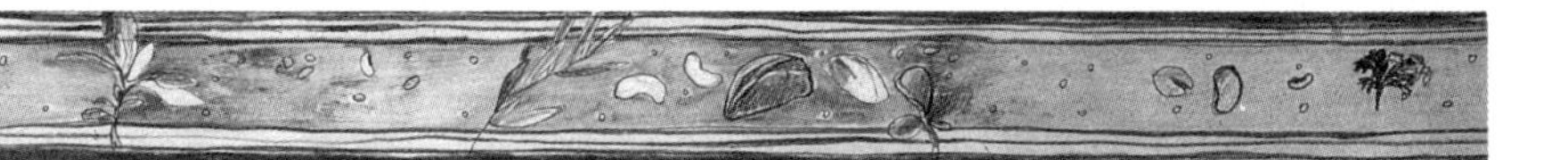

CORN CAKE

This unusual cake has a slightly grainy texture and freezes well. I like it toasted and spread with butter and honey.

Makes 1 cake

INGREDIENTS
660ml/23fl oz milk
60g/2oz brown sugar
½ tsp vanilla essence
160g/5½ oz fine cornmeal
2 free-range eggs
Pinch salt
60g/2oz margarine

Preheat the oven to 180°C/350°F/Gas Mark 4. Grease and line a 17.5cm/7 inch loose-bottomed cake tin. Place the milk, sugar and vanilla essence in a saucepan and bring to the boil. Stir in the cornmeal quickly to avoid forming lumps, then remove the pan from the heat and allow the mixture to cool slightly. Separate the eggs and whisk the egg whites with a pinch of salt until they form a soft peaks. Add the margarine and egg yolks, one at a time, to the cornmeal and beat well. Stir in one spoonful of the egg white and then carefully fold in the remainder with a metal spoon. Pour the mixture into the prepared tin and bake for about 40 minutes. Turn the cake onto a wire rack to cool.

CHRISTMAS CAKE

A Christmas Cake with no sugar or eggs which is suitable for vegans.

Makes 122.5cm/9 inch square cake

INGREDIENTS

120ml/4fl oz clear honey
175ml/6fl oz safflower or sunflower oil
90g/3oz soya flour
280ml/½ pint water
1 tbsp rum or 1 tsp rum essence
Grated rind and juice of 1 orange
Grated rind and juice of 1 lemon
60g/2oz flaked almonds
90g/3oz dried figs, chopped
90g/3oz dried dates, chopped
60g/2oz dried apricots, chopped
225g/8oz wholewheat self-raising flour
Pinch salt
2 level tsps mixed spice
225g/8oz currants
225g/8oz sultanas
225g/8oz raisins

Preheat the oven to 160°C/325°F/Gas Mark 3. Line a 22.5cm/9 inch square tin with greaseproof paper.

Cream the honey and the oil together. Mix the soya flour with the water and gradually add to the oil and honey mixture, beating well. Stir in the rum and the grated rind and juice of the orange and lemon. Add the almonds, figs, dates and apricots.

Mix the flour with the salt and spice and mix together the currants, sultanas and raisins. Stir half the flour and half the currant mixture into the soya cream, then stir in the remainder. Spoon the cake mixture into the prepared tin. Cover with two or three layers of brown paper and bake for 3¼ to 3½ hours, or until a skewer inserted into the centre of the cake comes out clean. Cool for 1 hour in the tin, then turn out on to a wire rack to cool. Store in an airtight tin.

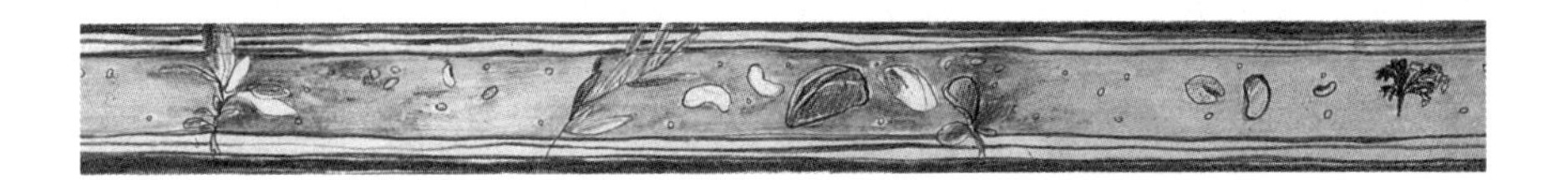

YOGURT SCONES

Scones always used to be made to use up soured milk. These are mixed with yogurt which gives the scones a slightly sour taste and a slightly denser texture.

Makes 10 scones

Ingredients

225g/8oz wholemeal self-raising flour
30g/1oz demerara sugar
60g/2oz butter or vegetable margarine
60g/1oz raisins
Natural yogurt to mix

Preheat the oven to 210°C/425°F/Gas Mark 7. Lightly grease a baking sheet. Place the flour and sugar in a large bowl and rub in the fat. Add the raisins and mix well, then add enough yogurt to make a fairly stiff dough. Turn the dough out onto a floured board and knead lightly. Make two large circles of dough or cut into 5cm/2 inch rounds. Place the scones on the baking sheet and bake for 15-17 minutes. Remove the scones and cool on a wire rack.

OATMEAL & TREACLE SCONES

These are darker in colour and coarser in texture than more traditional scones.

Makes about 12 scones

INGREDIENTS
120g/4oz plain wholemeal flour
2 tsps baking powder
Pinch of salt
30g/1oz margarine
120g/4oz oatmeal
1 tbsp molasses
Milk to bind

Preheat the oven to 220°C/425°F/Gas Mark 7. Lightly grease a baking sheet. Sieve the flour, baking powder and salt into a bowl three times then rub in the margarine and add the oatmeal. Warm the molasses and 1 tbsp of milk and use to bind the flour mixture, adding extra milk as necessary. Roll out to 6mm/¼ inch thick and cut into 5cm/2 inch rounds. Place on the baking sheet and cook for 10 minutes. Transfer to a wire rack to cool.

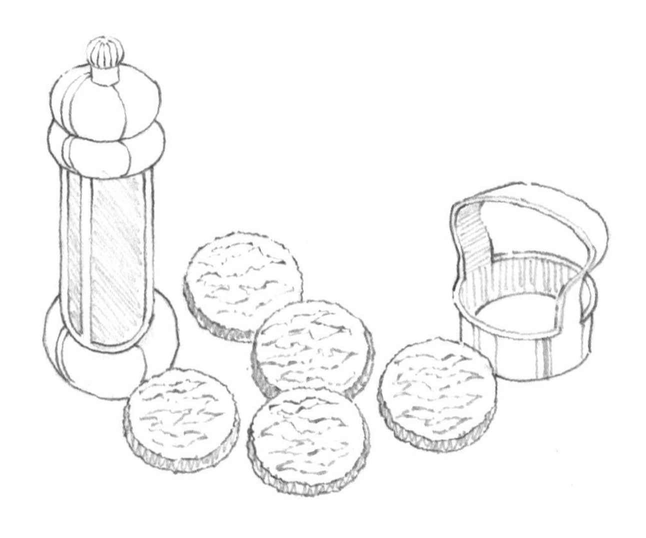

SUCCULENT SCONES

These substantial scones are good to serve in place of bread with soup or savoury snacks.

Makes 6-8 scones

INGREDIENTS
225g/8oz wholemeal flour
225g/8oz plain flour
1 tsp salt
1 tsp bicarbonate of soda
1 tsp cream of tartar
60g/2oz unsalted butter
150ml/¼ pint natural yogurt
Milk
1 free-range egg, well beaten

Preheat the oven to 220°C/425°F/Gas Mark 7. Lightly grease a baking tray. Sift the flours, salt, soda and cream of tartar twice and place into a mixing bowl then rub in the butter. Pour the yogurt into a measuring jug and make up to 280ml/½ pint with milk. Stir well to combine. Quickly stir the beaten egg into the flour followed by the yogurt and milk. Mix to form a soft dough, then knead for a few seconds until smooth. Divide the dough into 6 or 8 pieces and form into rough rounds on the baking sheet. Flatten the dough with your fingers and then prick with a fork. Bake for 8-10 minutes or until just coloured. Serve warm or cold.

FRUIT SCONES

I usually eat fruit scones with just butter, but have jam too if you like!

Makes about 8

Ingredients

- 225g/8oz unbleached plain flour, sieved
- 1 tbsp baking powder
- 60g/2oz vegetable margarine
- 30g/1oz unrefined caster sugar
- 30g/1oz sultanas
- 1 free-range egg, beaten
- About 4 tbsps milk
- 15g/½ oz unrefined granulated sugar
- 1 tsp ground cinnamon

Preheat the oven to 200°C/400°F/Gas Mark 6. Lightly grease a baking sheet. Place the flour and baking powder in a mixing bowl then rub in the margarine until the mixture resembles fine breadcrumbs. Stir in the sugar and sultanas, then add the egg and enough milk to form a soft dough.

Roll out the dough to about 1.25cm/½ inch thick and cut into rounds with a 5cm/2 inch plain cutter. Place on the baking sheet. Mix together the granulated sugar and cinnamon. Brush the tops of the scones with a little milk and sprinkle with the cinnamon mixture. Bake the scones for 10 to 15 minutes or until risen and golden, then transfer to a wire rack to cool.

CHEESE AND PAPRIKA SCONES

These savoury scones are made colourful by the addition of paprika and Red Leicester cheese. They are best eaten on the day that they are made, so indulge yourself.

Makes about 10

INGREDIENTS

225g/8oz self-raising flour, sieved
1 tsp paprika
Pinch salt
60g/2oz vegetarian Red Leicester cheese, grated
1 tsp English mustard
1 free-range egg, beaten
4 tbsps milk
1 tsp Marmite or yeast extract
Little boiling water

Preheat the oven to 200°C/400°F/Gas Mark 6. Lightly grease a baking sheet. Place the flour, paprika and salt in a mixing bowl and rub in the margarine until the mixture resembles fine breadcrumbs, then stir in the cheese. Beat the mustard, egg and milk together in a small bowl and pour into the flour and cheese. Mix well to form a soft dough, adding a little extra milk if necessary.

Roll out the dough to about 1.25cm/½ inch thick and cut into rounds with a 5cm/2 inch plain cutter and place on a baking sheet. Mix the Marmite or yeast extract with a little boiling water and brush over the tops of the scones. Bake for 10 to 15 minutes or until risen and golden. Transfer to a wire rack to cool.

CARROB-OAT SLICES

We all love flapjack – this is a delicious variation on the basic recipe.

Makes 12 slices

INGREDIENTS
120g/4oz carob bar
120g/4oz hard margarine
1 tbsp clear honey
225g/8oz porridge oats
120g/4oz sultanas
60g/2oz desiccated coconut

Preheat the oven to 180°C/350°F/Gas Mark 4. Lightly grease a baking tin about 22.5 × 27.5cm/9 × 11 inches. Break the carob into a pan and add the margarine and honey. Melt over a very low heat and stir until all the ingredients have melted. Remove from the heat and add the oats, sultanas and coconut. Mix well. Spread the mixture evenly in the baking tin and bake for 25-30 minutes. Cool slightly and cut into slices. When completely cold, cut again, remove from the tin and store in an airtight tin.

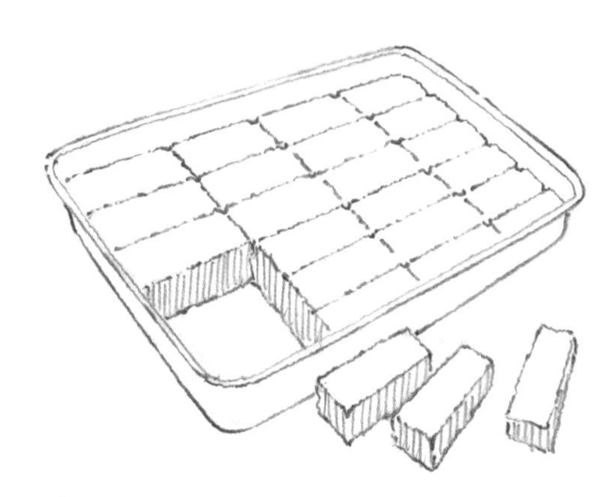

SUSAN'S OATIES

These biscuits may be varied by adding finely chopped nuts or a little desiccated coconut with the flour and oats.

Makes about 20 biscuits

Ingredients
120g/4oz margarine
120g/4oz soft brown sugar
1 tsp molasses
1 tsp boiling water
1 tsp bicarbonate of soda
120g/4oz wholemeal flour
120g/4oz porridge oats
½ tsp baking powder

Preheat the oven to 160°C/325°F/Gas Mark 3. Lightly grease two baking trays. Melt the margarine, sugar and molasses in a saucepan, then add the boiling water and bicarbonate of soda. Remove the pan from the heat and stir in the flour, oats and baking powder. Place teaspoons of the mixture on the greased baking sheets and bake for 20 minutes. Remove the biscuits from the baking sheets and place on a wire tray to cool.

SHORTBREAD BISCUITS

I like shortbread biscuits just as they are, but you could sandwich two together with jam if you wished.

Makes about 18

INGREDIENTS
150g/5oz plain flour
75g/2½ oz light muscovado sugar
120g/4oz soft margarine
½ tsp vanilla essence

Preheat the oven to 190°C/375°F/Gas Mark 5. Lightly grease two baking trays. Sieve the flour and sugar together and rub in the margarine. Add the vanilla essence and bind the mixture together with your hand. Form the mixture into small balls and place them on the baking trays a few inches apart. With the back of a fork, press the balls down making a criss-cross pattern. Bake for about 10-15 minutes until golden brown in colour. Cool slightly on the baking trays before transferring to a wire rack to cool completely.

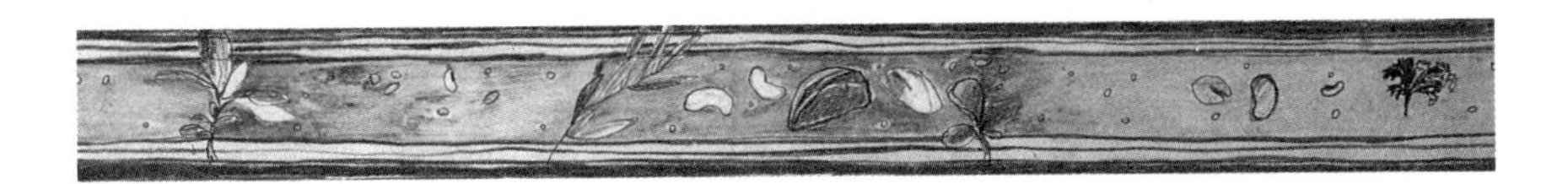

HAZELNUT BROWNIES

I always think that brownies are halfway between a cake and a biscuit. They should be moist and slightly heavy.

Makes 16

Ingredients

120g/4oz butter or vegetable margarine
175g/6oz light muscovado sugar
2 free-range eggs, beaten
½ tsp vanilla essence
90g/3oz wholemeal flour
½ tsp baking powder
Pinch salt
60g/2oz hazelnuts, chopped
Icing sugar, to dust

Grease and line a 20cm/8 inch square cake tin. Preheat the oven to 190°C/375°F/Gas Mark 5. Melt the margarine and beat in the sugar until smooth. Add the eggs and essence, beating well to prevent the mixture from curdling, then stir in all the remaining ingredients except the icing sugar, mixing well. Pour the mixture into the prepared tin and bake for 25 to 30 minutes or until springy to the touch. Allow the brownies to cool for 10 minutes in the tin, then turn out onto a wire rack to cool completely. Cut into 16 squares and dust with icing sugar before serving.

PEANUT BUTTER BRAN COOKIES

Peanut butter cookies are favourites with children of all ages.

Makes about 35

INGREDIENTS
120g/4oz vegetable margarine
120g/4oz light muscovado sugar
1 free-range egg, beaten
225g/8oz crunchy peanut butter
60g/2oz bran
60g/2oz wholemeal flour
Pinch salt
½ tsp baking powder
½ tsp vanilla essence

Grease two baking sheets. Preheat the oven to 190°C/375°F/Gas Mark 5. Beat the fat and sugar together until pale and creamy, then gradually add the egg, beating well after each addition. Beat in the peanut butter. Add the bran, flour, salt, baking powder and vanilla essence, mixing well to form a stiff dough.

Take small pieces of the dough and roll them into balls. Place them well apart on the baking sheets and flatten slightly with a fork or palette knife. Bake one tray of biscuits at a time for 5 to 10 minutes. Cool the biscuits slightly on the trays then transfer them to a wire rack to cool completely.

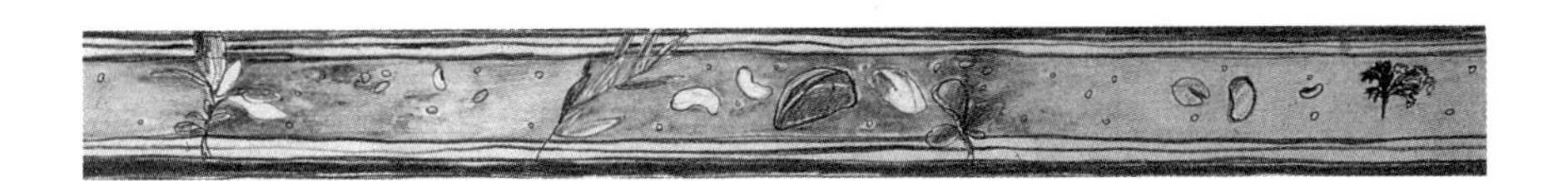

CRANBERRY BARS

I often make a 'flapjack sandwich' with a filling of dates or apples. This recipe uses cranberry sauce mixed with walnuts for a very bright, unusual flavour.

Makes 12-16 bars

INGREDIENTS
120g/4oz butter or vegetable margarine
150g/5oz light muscovado sugar
120g/4oz plain flour, sieved
Pinch salt
90g/3oz rolled oats
120g/4oz cranberry sauce
60g/2oz walnuts, chopped

Preheat the oven to 180°C/350°F/Gas Mark 4. Beat the butter or margine and sugar together in a bowl until pale and creamy, then stir in the flour, salt and oats and mix well. Spread two thirds of the mixture over the base of a well greased 20cm/8 inch square baking tin and press down firmly. Mix together the cranberry sauce and nuts and spread over the oat mixture, then crumble the remaining oat mixture over the top and spread out evenly with a knife. Bake for 20 minutes.

Allow the biscuit to cool for about 10 minutes, then mark into bars. Leave to cool completely in the tin before cutting.

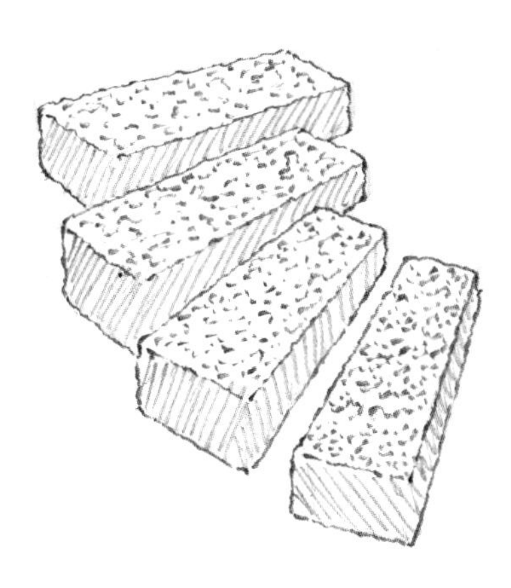

LEMON ICED TREACLE COOKIES

Homemade biscuits never last very long in our house! The lemon icing on these spicy cookies makes another winning combination.

Makes about 30

Ingredients

120g/4oz vegetable margarine
120g/4oz light muscovado sugar
1 free-range egg, beaten
2 tbsps treacle
2 tsps baking powder
1 tsp ground allspice
½ tsp ground ginger
225g/8oz wholemeal flour
Pinch salt
460g/1lb icing sugar
150ml/¼ pint water
Grated rind and juice of 1 lemon
Yellow food colouring (optional)
Candied lemon slices (optional)

Grease two baking sheets. Preheat the oven to 190°C/375°F/Gas Mark 5. Beat together the fat and sugar until pale and creamy, then gradually add the egg, beating well after each addition. Beat in the treacle then, using a metal spoon, fold in the baking powder, spices, flour and salt. Place spoonfuls of the mixture on the baking sheets and bake one tray at a time for 5 to 10 minutes. Cool the biscuits slightly on the trays then transfer them to a wire rack to cool completely.

Sieve the icing sugar into a bowl and add the lemon rind and juice, and colouring if used. Gradually stir in enough water to form a thin coating of icing and spread equal amounts on each cold biscuit. Decorate if desired and allow the icing to set before serving.

CRUNCH

Eat these biscuits freshly made to enjoy them as 'Crunch'. After a couple of days storage they become soft and sticky – different but, just as good!

Makes 24 squares

Ingredients
225g/8oz butter or margarine
2 tbsps golden syrup
275g/10oz oats
225g/8oz soft brown sugar

Preheat the oven to 180°C/350°F/Gas Mark 4. Lightly grease a 20 × 30cm/8 × 12 inch Swiss roll tin. Place the butter and syrup in a pan and melt gently over a low heat. Place the oats in a large mixing bowl and mix in the sugar, then pour in the melted butter and mix well with a wooden spoon. Transfer the mixture to the prepared tin and flatten well with the back of a spoon. Bake in the centre of the oven for 30-35 minutes until golden brown on top. Remove from the oven, allow the Crunch to cool for 2-3 minutes then mark into squares. Leave until nearly cold before cutting and removing from the tin.

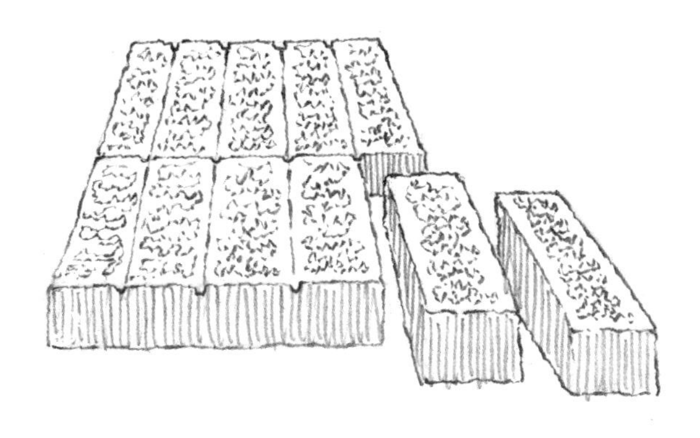

MUESLI COOKIES

Use an unsweetened flaky muesli for these biscuits and not one where the ingredients are stuck together in crunchy clusters.

Makes about 36

INGREDIENTS
120g/4oz butter or vegetable margarine
120g/4oz light muscovado sugar
1 free-range egg, beaten
1 tsp vanilla essence
1 tsp baking powder
225g/8oz wholemeal flour
Pinch salt
120g/4oz sugarless muesli
60g/2oz currants

Grease two baking sheets. Preheat the oven to 190°C/375°F/Gas Mark 5. Beat together the fat and sugar until pale and creamy, then gradually add the egg, beating well after each addition. Beat in the vanilla essence, then the baking powder, flour, salt, muesli and currants to make a stiff dough. Place heaped spoonfuls of the mixture on the baking sheets and bake for 5 to 10 minutes. Cool the biscuits slightly on the trays then transfer them to a wire rack to cool completely.

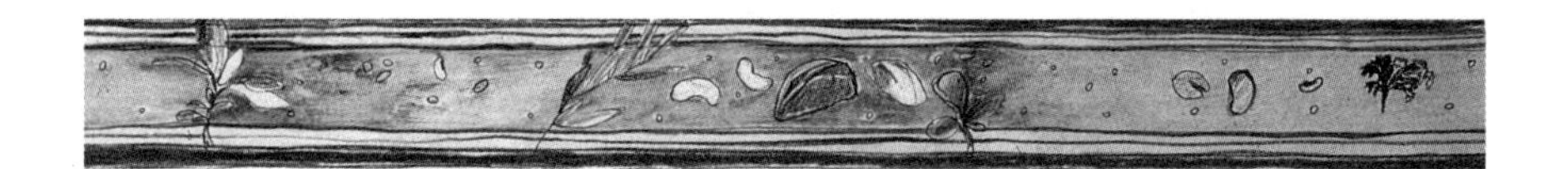

AMARETTI-ALMOND MACAROONS

Macaroons are easy to make at home. I prefer to make my own as shop ones are either huge or tiny – this way you can make the biscuits whatever size you want.

Makes about 24

INGREDIENTS
225g/8oz ground almonds
225g/8oz caster sugar
2 free-range egg whites
1 tsp almond essence

Preheat the oven to 180°C/350°F/Gas Mark 4. Lightly grease and flour 2 baking trays or line them with rice paper.

Mix the ground almonds and sugar together. Whisk the egg whites in a large bowl until stiff but not dry. Gradually fold in the almonds and sugar mixture and add the almond essence. Pipe or spoon the mixture on to the prepared baking sheets and leave to rest for as long as possible before baking. Bake for 15-20 minutes until golden brown. Cool slightly then transfer the macaroons to a cooling rack to cool completely.

BREADS, BON-BONS & BREAKFAST CEREALS

This chapter may appear to contain an odd mixture of recipes but I feel that here are two of the most important aspects of all diets; breads and breakfast ideas.

The Staff of Life

How many times has bread been described in glowing terms? I certainly can't claim that they have streamed in original flow from my word processor, but it is perfectly true that bread plays a most important dietary role in almost every culture throughout the modern world, certainly in all the temperate zones, and has done so throughout history.

The French agricultural expert Parmentier concluded in the 18th-century that: 'Bread is a generous gift of nature, a food that can be replaced by no other . . . It is suitable for every time of day, every age of life, and every temperament . . . It is so perfectly adapted to men that we turn our hearts to it almost as soon as we are born and never tire of it to the hour of our death.'

A Short History of Bread Making

Early arable farmers grew and milled wheat and prepared unleavened flat breads, which were suitable for baking on hot stones, warmed in the fire and then left to finish cooking in the heat of the sun. This method (from which pizza stones and Indian bread ovens are derived) was fine, but limiting in the thickness of breads which could be prepared. Once an inventive person considered the possibility of turning a cooking pot upside down over the hot stone, to create an early oven, the possibilities for baking breads were greatly increased.

Just as animal herders discovered that milk left in a skin would ferment and start to form cheese, so it was found that the thin meal porridge-like mixtures (which were the staple diet of the arable farmers) would eventually ferment and that this could be used as a starter for rising doughs, making them more palatable and lighter to eat. This was the beginning of sourdoughs, an alternative method of preparing bread which does not require yeast. We make a Russian-style sourdough at home with rye flour; it takes about 6 days to prepare as the starter has to be left for days at a time, but it makes an excellent alternative to the standard breads.

A Purpose-Built Oven

Over 4,000 years ago bakers in Egypt started to build bread ovens. These contained a fire beneath the baking shelf and were preheated by burning the fire down. The bread was then cooked in the residual heat.

The Romans went on to develop the early bread oven and started to produce long, tunnel-shaped ovens where the fire was actually burned on the brick floor, the embers being swept out before the bread was placed in the oven to cook. These ovens continued, virtually unchanged, until modern steam ovens were introduced for massive batch baking.

There is now a great movement to reintroduce wood fired bread ovens to achieve a traditional standard of bread baking. The ovens are fired up for the early morning baking process and are then gradually allowed to cool as biscuits and cakes are baked, leading to their label of 'morning goods'.

Travel – the Biggest Influence in Eating

Travel, years ago in terms of exploring and now by way of holidays abroad, has introduced us to so many ingredients that can be added to the standard bread dough, and so many different styles and shapes of bread. Five years ago who would have dreamed that most supermarkets would now be stocking sun-dried tomato and olive breads, as well as large ranges of Indian naans and chapatis?

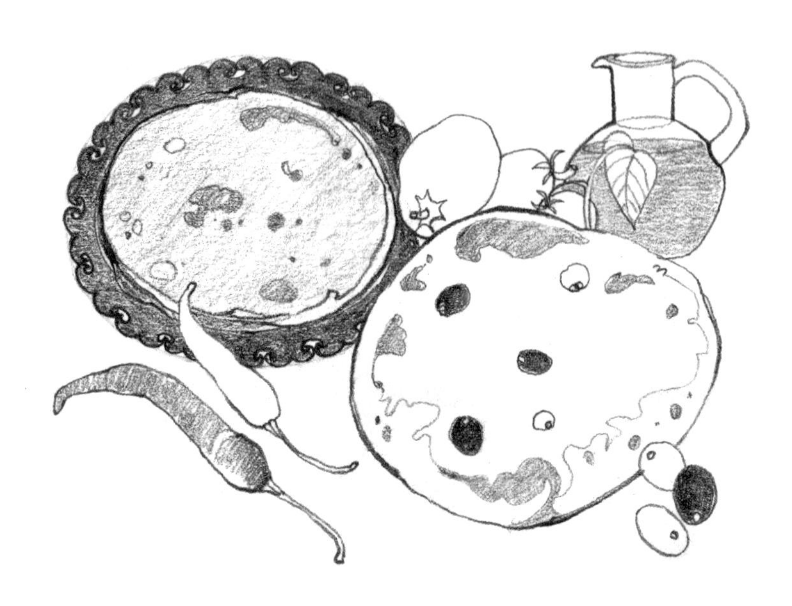

Home-made Bread is Best

I believe that all vegetarians care about the food that they eat and are more willing than most people to spend time in the preparation of their meals. Bread is one of the most rewarding foods to cook and it is such fun to experiment with flavourings, different flours and dough shapes. The recipes in this section include a traditional yeast dough made with malted grain 'Granary' flour which requires repeated kneading and proving periods, but it also includes rapid mix-and-bake doughs which take next to no time at all. Experiment with both, looking for variety in texture and flavour.

Breakfast Bonuses

I have included two recipes for breakfast dishes, one for home-made muesli which you can adapt as you will, and one for Granola which contains a wider variety of ingredients. A good start to the day is dependent on having a nourishing breakfast and both of these will set you on your way. Some commercially prepared breakfast cereals, even from a healthfood shop, lack variety in texture and too closely resemble sawdust! We want food to be good for us, but we jolly well want it to be enjoyable too!

And Finally

Sweets do not have to be forsaken just because you are vegetarian. There is nothing quite like a home-made truffle to end a memorable meal and I never cease to be impressed when a little saucer of home-made delicacies is produced without ceremony.

MRS MURPHY'S WHOLEWHEAT BROWN BREAD

Mrs. Murphy's Wholewheat Bread requires no kneading at all! It is a moist bread which keeps well but I suggest freezing one of the loaves until it is required.

Makes 2 loaves

INGREDIENTS
680g/1½lbs wholewheat flour
120g/4oz strong white flour
60g/2oz porridge oats
90g/3oz bran
150g/5oz pinhead oatmeal
90g/3oz wheatgerm
½ tsp baking powder
½ tsp sea salt
1.14 litres/2 pints milk
2 free-range reggs, beaten

Heat the oven to 180°C/350°F/Gas Mark 4. Mix all the dry ingredients together in a large bowl. Beat the eggs and milk and add to the dry ingredients, then mix thoroughly.

Spoon into 2 greased 900g/2lb loaf tins and bake in the centre of the oven for 1¼ to 1½ hours.

Turn out to cool on a wire rack.

SCOFA BREAD

This bread is quick to make and requires no yeast. It has an open texture and is ideal with cheese.

Makes 1 loaf

Ingredients
570g/1¼lbs self-raising wholemeal flour
225g/8oz bran
1 tsp salt
120g/4oz vegetable fat
Just under 570ml/1 pint water
1 tbsp vegetable oil

Preheat the oven to 200°C/400°F/Gas Mark 6. Lightly grease a baking tray. Place the flour, bran and salt in a large mixing bowl, then rub in the fat.

Make a well in the centre of the flour and pour in most of the water and the oil. Mix in the flour, drawing it into the liquid gradually from the sides, until a dough is formed – add more water if necessary. Shape into a 17.5cm/7 inch round and place on the greased baking tray. With a sharp knife cut to within 1.5cm/½ inch of the bottom, making four sections. Bake just above the centre of the oven for about 1 hour or until browned and 'hollow' sounding when the base is tapped with the back of your fingers. Remove from the oven and wrap in a clean tea towel to cool.

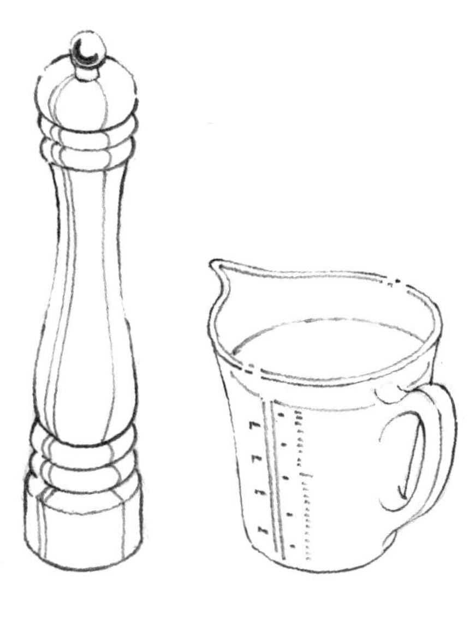

QUICK HOME-MADE BREAD

This is a very simple and quick method for making bread – the extra yeast dramatically cuts the rising time.

Makes 3 loaves

INGREDIENTS
1.14ml/2 pints hand hot water
1 tbsp molasses
1 tbsp sunflower oil
1kg/3lbs 100% wholemeal flour
2 sachets Easy-Blend yeast
3 tsps sea salt

Preheat the oven to 220°C/425°F/Gas Mark 7. Oil three 900g/2lb bread tins and place them on top of a warm cooker.

Fill two 570ml/1 pint jugs with the hand hot water, add the molasses and oil to one of the jugs, mix and set aside.

Place the flour, yeast and salt in a large bowl and mix thoroughly. Gradually pour the water and molasses mixture into the flour, mixing it with your hands. Add the other jug of water gradually until the dough is wettish but not sticky. You may have some water left over.

Knead the dough on a floured surface about a dozen times until just smooth. Divide the dough between the three tins and press down firmly.

Leave the bread to rise on the top of the cooker for 5-10 minutes or until the dough has risen almost to the top of the tins. Bake in the preheated oven for 35-40 minutes. Cool on a wire rack.

GRANARY ROLLS

Home-made rolls add the final touch to home entertaining and all family meals. If using easy blend dried yeast, add it dry to the flour in the mixing bowl.

Makes 10

INGREDIENTS
340g/12oz Granary flour
1 tsp salt
30g/1oz vegetable fat
15g/½oz fresh yeast or 2 tsps dried yeast
1 tsp brown sugar
225ml/8fl oz warm water

Place the Granary flour and salt in a mixing bowl and leave in a warm place. Melt the vegetable fat in a pan and leave to cool. Cream the yeast and sugar together with three-quarters of the warm water. Make a well in the middle of the flour and pour in the yeast mixture then add the melted fat and mix to a pliable dough, adding the remaining water as necessary. Knead lightly for a minute or two. Return the dough to the bowl, cover with a clean tea towel and leave in a warm place until the dough has doubled in size. Knead again for 3-5 minutes and shape into 10 smooth rolls. Place well apart on a floured baking tray, cover and leave in a warm place until the rolls have doubled in size.

Preheat the oven to 220°C/425°F/Gas Mark 7. Bake the rolls in the preheated oven for 15-20 minutes or until they sound hollow when tapped underneath. Cool on a wire rack.

SOFT BREAD CAKES

Soft bread cakes are mixed and baked very quickly for a bread dough. They are wickedly good when split, toasted and filled with a fried egg!

Makes 6

INGREDIENTS
340g/12oz wholewheat flour
1 tsp salt
30g/1oz fresh yeast
1 tsp brown sugar
175ml/6fl oz milk
30g/1oz vegetable fat
1 free-range egg, beaten

Preheat the oven to 220°C/425°F/Gas Mark 7. Lightly grease a baking tray. Place the flour and salt in a mixing bowl. Cream the yeast and sugar together until liquid. Warm the milk with the vegetable fat, then mix with the creamed yeast and stir in the beaten egg. Make a hollow in the flour and work the milk mixture in gradually to give a soft dough. Knead gently until smooth then form into six round cakes.

Place on the baking tray, then cover and leave to rise for 20 minutes in a warm place.

Bake for about 15 minutes. Glaze with beaten egg or milk and sugar a few minutes before removing from the oven.

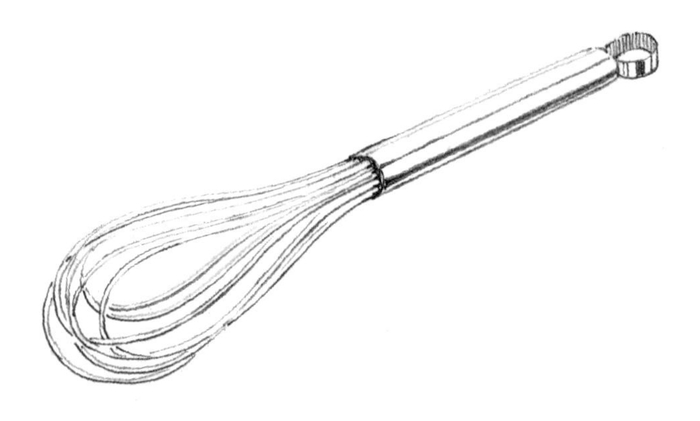

RICH STOLLEN BREAD

Stollens are a traditional European Christmas cake or bread – some people eat them buttered but I don't think this rich recipe needs the extra fat.

Makes 1 loaf

INGREDIENTS

250g/9oz strong unbleached white flour
Pinch of salt
15g/½oz fresh yeast
15g/½oz light muscovado sugar
100ml/3½fl oz milk, warmed
1 free-range egg, beaten

Filling

1 free-range egg
150g/5oz ground almonds
60g/2oz poppy seeds, plus extra for decoration
60g/2oz raisins, soaked overnight
60g/2oz currants
60g/2oz cherries, chopped
60g/2oz light muscovado sugar
30g/1oz dates, chopped
Juice of half a lemon
Almond essence

60g/2oz margarine
1 egg, beaten to glaze
60g/2oz flaked almonds

Place the flour and salt in a bowl. Cream the yeast and sugar together, add the milk and mix well. Add the beaten egg and leave for a few minutes in a warm place. Add the mixture to the flour and mix. Turn on to a floured surface and knead well for 5 minutes. Place the dough in a clean bowl, cover and leave to prove in a warm place for 40 minutes.

To make the filling, beat the egg, reserving a little, and add most of the flaked almonds and all the other filling ingredients. Mix well – the filling should be fairly moist.

Knock back or reknead the dough and roll out to a rectangle 30cm x 20cm/12 x 8 inches. Dot 30g/1oz of the margarine over the top two thirds of the dough. Fold the bottom over to one third up, then fold from top to bottom. Seal the edges firmly and make one quarter turn. Roll the dough out to a rectangle again and dot with the remaining margarine. Fold over as before but do not roll out. Place the dough in the refrigerator for about half an hour.

Preheat the oven to 200°C/400°F/Gas Mark 6. Remove the dough from the refrigerator and roll out to a rectangle as before. Cover with the filling, leaving a tiny margin around the edges. Roll up widthways to make a fat sausage shape and tuck in the ends. Brush with beaten egg.

Mark out in 2.5cm/1 inch slices, snipping either side with scissors. Cover the Stollen with the remaining flaked almonds and poppy seeds and leave to prove for a further 15 minutes.

Bake for 30 minutes. Leave to cool completely then wrap tightly in foil to store.

GRANOLA

I serve this crunchy, healthy breakfast cereal with yogurt. It also makes a good topping for baked fruit.

Makes 1.5kg/3¼lbs

Ingredients

460g/1lb organic muesli base (wheatflakes, porridge oats, rye flakes, pearl barley flakes, jumbo oat flakes)
120g/4oz sunflower seeds
60g/2oz wheatgerm
120g/4oz sesame seeds
90g/3oz soya flour
60g/2oz dried skimmed milk powder
60g/2oz desiccated coconut
120g/4oz chopped mixed nuts
175ml/6fl oz sunflower or safflower oil
175ml/6fl oz clear honey
175g/6oz sultanas

Preheat the oven to 150°C/300°F/Gas Mark 2. Place all the ingredients apart from the sultanas in a large mixing bowl. Stir with a wooden spoon until all the dry ingredients are coated with the oil and honey, then spread the mixture evenly over 2 large baking trays. Bake for about 1 hour, stirring frequently, until the mixture is golden brown. Remove from the oven and allow to cool on the trays.

Add the sultanas and mix well, then place in an airtight container and store in a cool place.

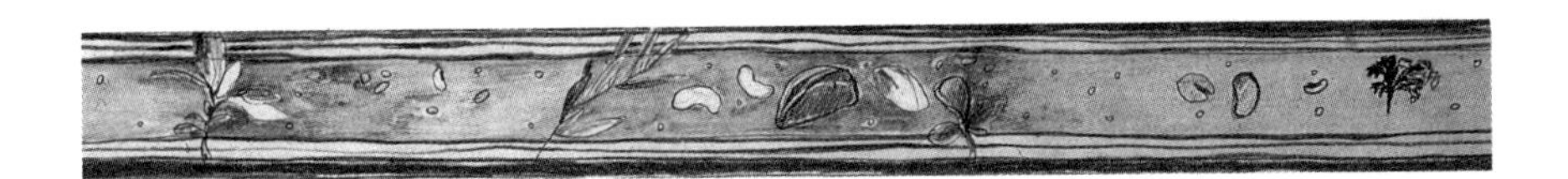

MUESLI DE-LUXE

Making your own muesli allows you to omit any ingredients that you don't like and add extra of the ones that you do!

Makes 1.6kg/3½lbs

INGREDIENTS

460g/1lb dried mixed fruit (apples, pears, apricots, prunes)
460g/1lb organic muesli base (wheatflakes, porridge oats, rye flakes, pearl barley flakes, jumbo oat flakes)
60g/2oz wheatgerm
120g/4oz sunflower seeds
175g/6oz sultanas
175g/6oz lexia raisins
120g/4oz hazel nuts
120g/4oz brazil nuts, halved

Chop the dried mixed fruit into small pieces with a pair of kitchen scissors or a sharp knife. Place in a mixing bowl with all the other ingredients, and mix well. Store in an airtight container in a cool place.

CHERRY NUT BALLS

These sweets look attractive when made with either the naturally coloured glacé cherries or the red, yellow and green dyed fruits.

Makes 16

Ingredients
120g/4oz butter or vegetable margarine
175g/6oz unrefined caster sugar
225g/8oz glacé cherries
1 free-range egg, beaten
2 tbsps evaporated milk
60g/2oz crisp rice cereal
60g/2oz walnuts, chopped
3 tbsps desiccated coconut

Melt the butter and sugar in a pan over a low heat, stirring constantly until the sugar dissolves. Chop the cherries and stir into butter mixture. Beat the egg into the milk, then gradually add to the hot cherry mixture, stirring well after each addition. Cook gently, stirring all the time, until the mixture comes together into a ball. Remove from the heat and beat in the cereal and nuts.

Divide the mixture into 16 pieces and roll into balls. Toss each cherry ball in the desiccated coconut, pressing the coconut on to the balls if necessary. Chill well before serving in individual sweet cases.

CHOCOLATE TRUFFLES

Homemade truffles are ideal for serving at the end of a meal, or for giving as a home-made gift.

Makes about 30

INGREDIENTS
175g/6oz plain chocolate
15g/½ oz butter or vegetable margarine
2 free-range egg yolks
2 tbsps brandy or black coffee
2 tsps single cream
3 tbsps cocoa powder
3 tbsps ground almonds

Break the plain chocolate into pieces, place in a bowl and melt in the top of a double boiler or over a pan of gently simmering water. Stir in the butter or margarine then remove from the heat. Lightly beat the egg yolks and add to the chocolate, beating well until evenly incorporated. Stir in the brandy or coffee and cream and chill in the refrigerator for at least 1 hour or until firm.

Divide the mixture into about 30 evenly-sized pieces and roll into small balls using your hands. Place the cocoa powder and almonds on separate plates and gently roll half the chocolates in each to coat. Place the coated truffles in paper sweet cases and chill until required.

ROCKY ROAD FUDGE

This fudge recipe is most unusual as it contains rice cereal, giving a very interesting texture.

Makes about 680g/1½lb

Ingredients

460g/1lb unrefined caster sugar
60g/2oz plain chocolate, grated
60g/2oz butter or vegetable margarine
175ml/6fl oz milk
2 tsps vanilla essence
60g/2oz walnuts, chopped
30g/1oz crisp rice cereal

Line a 20cm/8 inch square tin or dish with non-stick baking parchment. Place the sugar, chocolate, butter or margarine and milk in a saucepan and heat gently until the sugar dissolves. Stir well. Bring to the boil and continue to boil, stirring frequently, until the temperature of the mixture reaches 118°C/240°F or 'soft ball' stage on a sugar thermometer. This will take about 10 minutes.

Remove the pan from the heat and allow the fudge to cool for about 10 minutes, then beat in the vanilla essence. Continue to beat the fudge until it begins to lose its shiny appearance and starts to become thick and grainy. Quickly beat in the nuts and cereal, mixing well. Spread the fudge mixture evenly into the prepared tin and mark into squares. Refrigerate until completely cold before removing from the tin and breaking into squares.

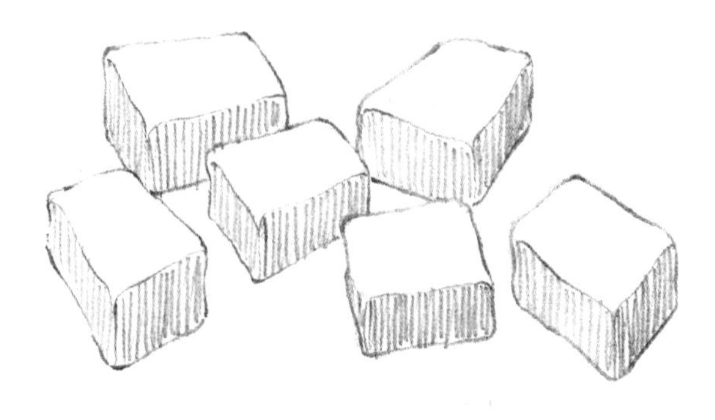

HONEYCOMB

Honeycomb is always a favourite sweet. I often spread a little melted carob or chocolate over part of the honeycomb when I make it.

Makes 460g/1lb

INGREDIENTS
225g/8oz unrefined granulated sugar
225ml/8fl oz golden syrup
1 tbsp white wine vinegar
1 tbsp bicarbonate of soda

Line a 20cm/8 inch square cake tin with well oiled aluminium foil, pressing it well into the corners of the tin and also as smoothly as possible against the sides and base. Place the sugar, syrup and vinegar in a large saucepan and heat gently until the sugar dissolves, stirring all the time. Bring to the boil and continue to boil, stirring frequently, until the temperature of the mixture reaches 146°C/295°F on a sugar thermometer.

Remove the pan from the heat. Quickly add the bicarbonate of soda to the hot sugar syrup and stir well. The mixture will foam very quickly once the soda has been added. Pour the foaming sugar syrup into the prepared dish or tin and leave in a cool place until set. Remove the honeycomb from the dish and break it up into irregular shaped pieces.

INDEX